Better Living through Reality TV

Better Living through Reality TV

Television and Post-welfare Citizenship

Laurie Ouellette and James Hay

BLACKWELL PUBLISHING
350 Main Street, Malden, MA 02148-5020, USA
9600 Garsington Road, Oxford OX4 2DQ, UK
550 Swanston Street, Carlton, Victoria 3053, Australia

First published 2008 by Blackwell Publishing Ltd

1   2008

Library of Congress Cataloging-in-Publication Data
Ouellette, Laurie.
   Better living through reality TV television and post-welfare citizenship / Laurie Ouellette and James Hay.
      p. cm.
   Includes bibliographical references and index.
   ISBN 978-1-4051-3440-8 (hardcover : alk. paper) — ISBN 978-1-4051-3441-5 (pbk. : alk. paper) 1. Reality television programs—Social aspects.   2. Reality television programs.   I. Hay, James, 1952–   II. Title.

   PN1992.8.R43084 2008
   791.45′6—dc22

                           2007014549

A catalogue record for this title is available from the British Library.

Set in 11 on 13pt Bembo
by SNP Best-set Typesetter Ltd., Hong Kong
Printed and bound in Singapore
by Utopia Press Pte Ltd

For further information on
Blackwell Publishing, visit our website at
www.blackwellpublishing.com

Contents

List of Illustrations   vi

Introduction   1

1   Charity TV: Privatizing Care, Mobilizing Compassion   32
2   TV Interventions: Personal Responsibility and Techniques
    of the Self   63
3   Makeover TV: Labors of Reinvention   99
4   TV and the Self-Defensive Citizen   134
5   TV's Constitutions of Citizenship   170
6   Playing TV's Democracy Game   203

Notes   225

Index   245

Illustrations

0.1   *Todd TV*   5
1.1   *Queen for a Day*   33
1.2   *Extreme Makeover: Home Edition*   49
1.3   *Three Wishes*   57
2.1   *Brat Camp*   69
2.2   *Honey We're Killing the Kids*   89
2.3   *Supernanny*   94
3.1   *What Not to Wear*   111
3.2   *America's Next Top Model*   128
4.1   Suze Orman   148
4.2   *It Takes a Thief*   161
5.1   *Survivor* and *The Apprentice*   189
5.2   *Wife Swap*   194
5.3   *Black/White*   198
6.1   *American Idol*   214

Introduction

In 2004, TV viewers were enlisted to help guide and shape a human subject named Todd. Under the provocative mantra "Build a Better Todd," they watched video footage of the young man's daily life and voted on the recommendations of professional experts brought in to improve his image, attitude, social life, finances, and career trajectory. After considering the suggestions and strategies for Todd's self-betterment presented during each episode's Todd Town Hall segment, viewers telephoned or texted their decision to the FX cable network. As part of his television "contract with America," the star of the reality program agreed to abide by the results of the viewer poll and transform his life accordingly. Over the course of the season, he was ordered to upgrade his wardrobe, pursue a new line of work, go on arranged dates, and undergo psychotherapy.

Todd TV adopted voting procedures to stage Todd's TV life as the outcome of a democratic process – as the government of an individual's conduct and choices by TV viewers and by Todd. Todd was required to temporarily give up his free will, bending to the wishes of the viewing public, and his lack of agency in the situations that ensued was a source of amusement. However, the point of the experiment was to cultivate Todd's ability to manage his own life, and steer his own fate by implementing the training provided by the TV program. In the parlance of political philosophy, Todd was being transformed into the sort of citizen who can be ruled through freedom, not control, and his reward for cooperating with the exercise (however humiliating it may have been) was also presented as his democratic duty to pursue happiness, self-fulfillment, and success. TV viewers were ostensibly empowered to help steer Todd's metamorphosis, but they were also invited to envision their own lives as a similar process of strategic decision-making and self-improvement. In this respect, *Todd TV* illustrates reality TV's preoccupation with "self work," and a reasoning about the nature and practice of governing in the current political epoch.

  Todd TV operates at the intersection of two phenomena – the reinvention of television and the reinvention of government – addressed by this book. The program is part of the explosion of popular reality TV that began in the mid-1990s, and continues to this day. While reality TV has existed since the earliest days of the medium, only in the past decade has it become a major force in TV culture, with a vast array of reality-based entertainment and lifestyle programming taking hold during primetime and daytime hours, on network and specialized cable channels. *Better Living Through Television* situates the surge of popular nonfiction on television within strategies of liberal governance. We examine reality TV's relationship to ideals of "governing at a distance" and consider how reality TV simultaneously diffuses and amplifies the government of everyday life, utilizing the cultural power of television (and its convergence with books, magazines, the web, and mobile media) to assess and guide the ethics, behaviors, aspirations, and routines of ordinary people. At a time when privatization, personal responsibility, and consumer choice are promoted as the best way to govern liberal capitalist democracies, reality TV shows us how to conduct and "empower" ourselves as enterprising citizens. We consider the reasons for this, and explore the possibilities for agency it opens up and closes down.

  The many subgenres of popular reality TV (dating shows, makeovers, job competitions, gamedocs, reality soaps, interventions, lifestyle demonstrations) share a preoccupation with testing, judging, advising, and rewarding the conduct of "real" people in their capacities as contestants, workers, housemates, family members, homeowners, romantic partners, patients, and consumers. In the process, reality TV circulates informal "guidelines for living" that we are all (at times) called upon to learn from and follow. These are not abstract ideologies imposed from above, but highly dispersed and practical techniques for reflecting on, managing, and improving the multiple dimensions of our personal lives with the resources available to us. Reality TV has become one of these resources. In a given week, we can learn how to succeed at work (*The Apprentice, America's Next Top Model, Project Runway*), how to win a desirable mate (*The Bachelor/Bachelorette, Joe Millionaire*), how to be stylish (*What Not to Wear*), sophisticated (*Queer Eye for the Straight Guy*) and personable (*Beauty and the Geek*), how to survive natural and manmade challenges (*Survivor, Big Brother*), how to nourish our health and psyche (*Honey We're Killing the Kids, Starting Over*), how to put our personal finances in order (Suze Orman, *Mad Money with Jim Cramer*), how to enhance an ordinary house or car (*Trading Spaces, Pimp My Ride*), how to transform our bodies (*Extreme Makeover, The Swan*, the Fitness Channel), how to maximize sexual performance and intimacy (*Sex Inspectors, Berman and Berman*), how to manage our families and domestic lives (*Supernanny, Wife Swap*, the Food Network), how to prepare for dangers and emergencies (*Storm Stories, It Takes a Thief, What Should You Do?*), and even how to restore blighted cityscapes (*Town Haul*).

Reality TV is educational in this respect – but not in the same way as formalized attempts to harness television as a cultural technology capable of disseminating the "best that has been thought and said." Conceptualized as an extension of the public university, the earliest experiments in "education by television" were abstract, didactic, unadorned, and dominated by academics, journalists, and other bona fide intellectual authorities. This is not surprising, for the citizens these programs wished to "empower" were conceived as a gullible mass that needed guidance in the liberal arts to participate in the rituals of public democracy. Today's popular reality TV addresses the viewer differently. The citizen is now conceived as an individual whose most pressing obligation to society is to empower her or himself privately. TV assists by acting as a visible component of a dispersed network of supporting technologies geared to self-help and self-actualization. Ordinary people are now welcomed on screen, providing subject matter, "case studies," points of identification, and sources of disobedience and conflict. Experts are more apt to characterize themselves as "self-made" authorities trading in applied forms of business, lifestyle, and therapeutic knowledge. While there is no solitary explanation for this, the concrete skills, interpersonal advice, problem-solving techniques, step-by-step demonstrations, intimate feedback, motivational support mechanisms, and suggestions for everyday application offered by reality TV are undoubtedly more useful to strategies of governing through self and lifestyle than educational programs of the past. Reality

TV's informal curriculum is also more profitable – not only because it combines learning with the pleasures of popular culture and the practicalities of everyday life, but because in a political climate that demands self-enterprise, the "civic" training it provides has become a desirable commodity.

Chronicling the details and challenges of lifestyles and the outcomes of ordinary people's choices and behavior, reality TV invests the minutiae of everyday life with dramatic importance. Personal advice and instruction are part of the mix, but they are infused with, and tempered by, elements of voyeurism, suspense, humor, and emotional intensity. Tellingly, many reality programs owe less to the illustrated lecture than to the converging conventions of the televised game and the staged experiment. Rarely didactic and never intentionally dull, reality games connect the process of learning and mastering "the rules" of individual and group governance to pleasures of play and suspense. Staged experiments position television as a dramatic "civic laboratory" for testing the capacities – and limits – of human subjects conceived as the agents of their uncertain destinies. Both sets of conventions informed the premise of *Todd TV*, which, like many reality shows, was billed as compelling entertainment, not as a formal tutorial in governing. We shouldn't let this prevent us from exploring reality TV's relevance to diffuse, and often profoundly contradictory mechanisms of contemporary rule. Reality TV's capacity to insert guidelines for living into the nooks and crannies of everyday life is connected in complex but important ways to what formal policymakers like to call the "reinvention of government." By aligning TV viewers with a proliferating supply of techniques for shaping and guiding themselves and their private associations with others, reality TV has become the quintessential technology of advanced or "neo" liberal citizenship.

Todd TV does not draw unequivocal conclusions about how Todd should live his life, but it does combine advice, rules, demonstrations, games, experiments, and tests to "empower" him (and his audience) through the management of conduct and behavior. This is precisely how popular reality TV governs. As the State entrusts private entities (including TV) to operate as social service providers, conflict mediators, and support networks, popular reality TV does more than entertain – it becomes a resource for inventing, managing, caring for, and protecting ourselves as citizens. Such is the case with television's high-profile efforts to actively intervene in the lives of needy individuals. It is a sign of the times that, in the absence of public welfare programs,

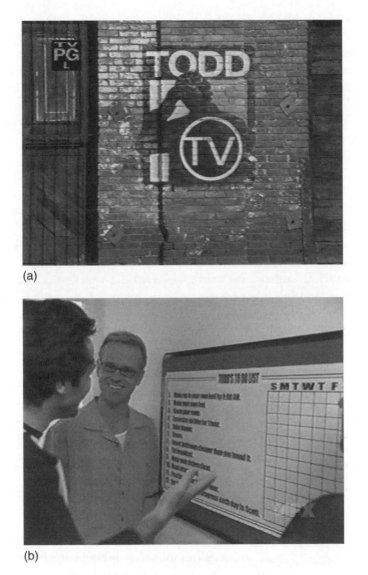

Illustration 0.1 Todd follows a "to-do" list devised by experts and viewers on *Todd TV* (Endemol Entertainment USA and Lock & Key Productions for FX, 2004)

hundreds of thousands of people now apply directly to reality TV programs for housing, affordable healthcare, and other forms of assistance. The "do-good" trend illustrated by *Extreme Makeover: Home Edition*, *Three Wishes*, *Miracle Workers*, and similar charity programs requires us to move beyond political economic and representational analysis, to consider how TV mobilizes and coordinates private resources (money, volunteerism, skills/expertise) in order to remedy personal hardships. Within the context of the reinvention of government, TV's concern with not only documenting, but with facilitating the care of needy and "at-risk" citizens through cultural commerce, philanthropy, and TV-viewer volunteerism is also a way of enacting methods of social service provision that do not involve "entitlements" and models of civic participation that do not "depend" on the Welfare State. Of course, as we will demonstrate in Chapter 1, television assists only the most "deserving" cases of need, as determined by casting departments whose assessment of hardship is informed not only by the logic of welfare reform, but by the dramatic conventions and formulas of reality TV.

The life interventions that have become a staple of reality TV also coordinate resources for diagnosing problems and transforming "needy" individuals into functioning citizens. Relying on professional coaches, motivators, and lifestyle experts, these programs advance liberal strategies of "governing at a distance" by linking social work as a residual form of public welfare to governing technologies of self-help and do-it-yourself entrepreneurialism. Some, like *Dr. Phil* and the reality soap *Starting Over*, draw from corporate management techniques, among other resources, to help women "empower" themselves through self-governed behavioral regimens. Other, more specialized, TV interventions use a combination of disciplinary and self-help strategies to enable individuals to "help themselves" overcome alcoholism and drug abuse (*Intervention*), juvenile delinquency (*Brat Camp*), shopping addictions (*Clean House*), and poor eating habits (*Honey We're Killing the Kids*), among other problems. Like professionalized social work, many TV interventions are guided by an unstated impetus to bring less educated, lower-income populations up to upper-middle-class standards. However, reality TV also brings managerial approaches to the "proper" care of the self to an array of middle-class lifestyle dilemmas, from spoiled children (*Supernanny, Nanny 911*) to household clutter (*Mission: Organization; neat*). As we will show in Chapter 2, both crisis interventions and lifestyle programs enact an entrepreneurial ethic of self-care, thus linking the TV intervention to policy trends from welfare-to-work mandates to public-sector downsizing. This is not a matter of TV programs "misrepresenting" welfare reform or having an ideological "effect" on gullible viewers. It is about television becoming more useful to a rationality of governing that emphasizes self-empowerment as a condition of citizenship. Like other strands of reality TV, interventions work by coordinating and regularizing private resources and support networks for living an enterprising life. While television has made itself integral to this project, it is still only one component of a relay of cultural technologies that may also involve related web sites, tie-in merchandise, books, self-help manuals, and podcasts.

Makeover TV is another example of contemporary television offering itself as an indispensable resource for enterprising citizenship. As the sense of social and financial security promised by an expanding educational system, "jobs for life," and guaranteed pensions comes to an end, the self becomes more important as a flexible commodity to be molded, packaged, managed, reinvented, and sold. From *Extreme Makeover* to *What Not to Wear*, the burgeoning makeover genre speaks to this shift and proposes an "empowering" solution by way of refashioning one's looks, style, and personality. This isn't offered only or even primarily to the human "targets" of television's sensational overhauls, for the applied art and science of self-presentation is something we are all increasingly expected to draw from, to various degrees. In assisting in this endeavor, television's makeover ventures build upon an existing training regime that has historically offered women techniques to bolster their value in the heterosexual dating market. They extend this rationality to other populations, including men, and other spheres of sociality, including the workplace. The assumption that we must all maximize our greatest asset – ourselves – has accelerated alongside such trends as labor outsourcing, branding, lifelong education as a substitute for job security, and corporate reinvention. In this uncertain context, we argue in Chapter 3, the makeover is offered a lifestyle game whose rules can be learned and applied. Competitions like *America's Next Top Model* and *I Want to Be a Hilton* take this a step further by bringing competition into the mix and documenting the emotional trauma and resentment of those contestants who fail to assemble themselves as flexible and enterprising commodities.

Other strands of reality TV advance a reasoning about governing by teaching individuals to take responsibility for a range of lurking risks, from bankruptcy to weather emergencies. Whether or not society has become riskier – and many would dispute this assumption – we are now offered a whole barrage of technical resources for managing our own personal, physical, household, and "homeland" security.

Reality TV is one of these resources, we argue in Chapter 4. Some ventures, like *America's Most Wanted* and *It Takes a Thief,* empower the white upper-middle class to protect itself and its property. Others, like personal finance guru Suze Orman's TV show and Bloomberg TV, offer guidelines for responsible money management, whether that means climbing out of debt in a recessive economy, or investing soundly for retirement in the age of Enron. This preoccupation with risk as an individual problem dovetails with the ethic of "personal responsibility" in that all citizens are expected to avert disaster through rational planning. The "securitization" of daily life is an important dimension of this duty, one that has only heightened with public attention to terrorism and other national security issues.

Reality TV's games of "group governance" are another site where television intersects with processes of rule. Focusing on the places – neighborhood, household, workplace – where we are expected to participate in and abide by rules and procedures of private membership, programs like *Wife Swap* and *The Real World* insert themselves into these processes of private governance. TV becomes a technology for constructing the rules or "constitutions" of everyday life. The conventions of these programs require individuals to work on themselves in the interest of the group – which can involve cooperating with others, becoming more tolerant, and adjusting behavior and expectations. Instead of assessing these shows on the basis of their representational accuracy or progressiveness, Chapters 5 and 6 consider them technical resources for enacting government in the spaces where most of us live and negotiate citizenship. TV's experiments in private governing have emerged in the context of the State's retreat from formalized affirmative action, antidiscrimination, and conflict resolution programs – and yet, they are also the place where reality TV most overlaps with democratic processes, as was the case in *Welcome to the Neighborhood,* a program that was pulled by ABC when protesters claimed it violated federal housing policy. Collectively these chapters ask what is involved (and complicated) about imagining a path to political reform through the current intersection of TV, media, and government.

Placing TV in an Analytic of Government

As government becomes more privatized and dispersed, theories of governmentality offer a useful way to conceptualize television's power.

In its simplest sense, governmentality refers to "how we think about governing others and ourselves in a wide variety of contexts."[1] Scholars who use this conceptual approach tend to focus on the proliferation of techniques through which individuals and populations reflect upon, work on, and organize their lives and themselves as a condition of citizenship. The term governmentality, particularly as it has been attributed to philosopher Michel Foucault, also refers to how power operates in modern societies.[2] Foucault used the term to elaborate his view that power emanated from expertise, or the knowledges and procedures associated with social institutions. For him, truth claims were specific not only to particular societies but also to particular institutional "rationalities." In their capacity to authorize knowledge as truthful, institutions exercised an authority over their subjects. Foucault emphasized a connection between the multiplicity of rationalities in a society (and among societies) and the dispersion of how and where power is exercised. Power operates as a network, he argued, distributed across the spheres of authority that manage social subjects and problems through specific devices, skills, techniques, regimens, and technologies. The spheres of social management set guidelines and rules (the Latin *regula* being the cognate for words such as rule, regulation, and regularity) and foster regimens through which the conduct of subjects is regulated and regularized and through which life is lived.

Foucault also emphasized the ethical dimensions of this way of exercising knowledge and power, an objective of which is the well-being and civility of the social subjects who are brought under the care of private experts and authorities. The *civility* of modern societies depends upon its guidelines, regimens, and technologies, he suggested, and in turn the State depends upon the healthiness of a "civil society." Civil society is essential to liberal capitalist societies because it guarantees a respect for rules, and in this way it helps nourish the authority and "reason" of the State. According to Foucault, it is the State's ability to encourage "freedom" as long as behavior is exercised responsibly that enables it to "govern at a distance" rather than primarily by force.

Liberalism, for Foucault and his followers, does not refer to a political ideology (as in conservative versus liberal), but instead to a "governmental rationality," or approach to governing through freedom. Liberalism as a rationality of government has long presumed that rulers should only intervene in the affairs of the "free" market and of individuals minimally, and with caution. Because of its laissez-faire sensibility, liberalism has always grappled with the nature and scope of State power, and has tried to minimize the direct "rule of the State" whenever possible. This doesn't mean that liberalism as a governing rationality is akin to anarchy, however. As the editors of *Foucault and Political Reason* point out, freedom in the liberal sense always refers to a "well-regulated and responsibilized liberty."[3] Liberalism is based on a paradox, then, in that while it advocates governing through (as opposed to against) freedom, it also expects individuals to govern themselves properly – to choose order over chaos and good behavior over deviance.

Foucault's work is especially helpful for understanding how power operates in societies whose political, economic, and cultural modernity has been inextricable from a commitment to liberal government. According to Foucault, liberalism as a governing rationality hinges on the "rational" (restrained, calculated, rule-oriented) exercise of power, and on procedures for analyzing, knowing, and calculating population and territory. Governmentality in this sense refers to a relation by the State to civil society, defined as the array of social institutions and private forms of association that comprise indispensable networks for exercising power and governing at a distance. Foucault's writing about governmentality elaborated the technical means that linked ethics (conduct and behavior) to liberalism's preoccupation with the government of the self and the State as "guardian of 'fair play' and of the rules of the game."[4] Liberalism emphasized the "wise" and judicious exercise of individual freedoms, he argued – a view that linked it not just to a general rationality in the modern world but also to specific knowledges and techniques for exercising government of oneself. For Foucault, liberalism valorizes a State that "watches over" and "looks after," measures, assesses, "reflects upon," and acts upon the most propitious technologies of government available to it. Collectively these technologies comprise (to use Foucault's clever phrase) "the reason of state," or the justifications and requirements for the State to act as it can and does.

Liberalism's emphasis upon the "reason of state" expected individuals to actively participate in their own governance. Effective government was to recognize the potential of private mechanisms of administration and management as well as *the government of the self*. To explain the State's rationalization of its role as welfare provider, Foucault often used the religious figure of the pastor, or "shepherd" who watches over his flock. This wasn't to suggest that the Church's

authority had been replaced by the State, but that the State had technologized and acted on the *pastoralism* of the existing institutions and
activity that comprised civil society – what he referred to as "pastoral
technology."[5] Lest this seem to be a parable about how modern political subjects are sheep, Foucault also elaborated how Christian techniques of "examination, confession, guidance, obedience, have an aim:
to get individuals to work at their own 'mortification' in this world."
By this he meant that the techniques of working on and watching
oneself developed through Christianity were also useful to a liberal
governing rationality. So on one hand, liberal government's rationalization of the Welfare State (or what Antonio Gramsci called "the
ethical state") has been "the tricky adjustment between political power
wielded over legal subjects and pastor power wielded over live [or
better, the life of] individuals." On the other, liberal government
authorizes and relies upon the constitutive technologies of the self, the
technical reflection and resources by which individuals watch over
themselves as "free" citizen-subjects. In this sense, as Nikolas Rose
contends, "to govern . . . is to seek an authority for one's authority."[6]
The liberal State derives its authority and reason to govern from civil
society. Citizens derive their authority and their freedoms through
various governmentalities.

Liberalism's schematization of civil society as the field of self-
governance is not only about making society civil and making government rational. It is also about making the social and the governmental
economic. "Free" market relations and liberal government developed
through one another; the modern "virtues" of laissez-faire capitalism
were articulated through liberalism's reasoning about freedoms, efficiency, and self-sufficiency as the basis for a civil society. Foucault
understood the relation between the emergence of political economy
and liberalism in two respects: First, he noted a transformation from
the "art of government" to a scientific reasoning about processes of
government, society, and populations. Second, he noted the linkage
between economy conceptualized as a "naturally" self-regulating system
and a governmental reasoning about rights and liberties. This linkage
provided the basis for envisioning government as "economical" and
"efficient." It also established a perpetual tension between the governing logic of freedoms and rights, and economic inequalities. Because
liberalism authorized a "free" market that tends to "amplify and con-
solidate" existing inequalities, it also "imagines a government whose

job it is to protect its individual subjects unequally," notes Alexandra Chasin. Simply put, those individuals who inherit wealth, and whose labor is particularly valued by the market economy, are in a better position to exercise liberal freedoms and rights that are theoretically available to all citizens.[7]

A Foucaultian view of liberal government is especially useful for understanding what some have referred to as advanced liberalism or "neoliberalism." Whether conceived as a new stage, or a deepening of liberalism's longstanding tendencies, the present stage of liberalism involves a series of initiatives and policies that have tied the "reinvention of government" to a broad rethinking and remodeling of the Welfare State. There is a greater reliance on the privatization and personalization of welfare than before as the State entrusts "pastoralism" to private entities (including media) and emphasizes that citizens be not only active, but also "enterprising" in the pursuit of their own empowerment and well-being. Most critics agree that the rationality of the "free" market is being extended much more vociferously into every sector of society, and every dimension of governing, including public programs and social services that developed in many capitalist democracies, in part to address the human consequences of liberalism's laissez-faire sensibilities.[8] The management and care of the self becomes an imperative in different, and arguably more urgent ways in such a climate, not only in the sense of replacing public services, but in terms of obliging citizens to actualize and "maximize" themselves not through "society" or collectively, but through their choices in the privatized spheres of lifestyle, domesticity, and consumption.

Better Living through Reality TV offers an analytic of government, or an examination of the reach and the limits of government, and a consideration of how it operates differently through spheres of activity and sociality. An analytic of government considers the multiple ways that individuals and populations are made and continually reinvented as active, responsible citizens. It is, in this sense, a process of *mapping* the strata and networks of government that authorize particular kinds of behavior and citizenship. Placing TV in an analytic of government emphasizes television as a resource for acquiring and coordinating the techniques for managing the various aspects of one's life. Rather than thinking about TV as a general technology, or as part of "technoculture," it seeks to identify the specific rationalities and technical applications that comprise TV and that have made it matter in particular ways.

One way is as a cultural technology that, working outside "public powers," governmentalizes by presenting individuals and populations as objects of assessment and intervention, and by soliciting their participation in the cultivation of particular habits, ethics, behaviors, and skills.

Rose's work is useful for situating television within a larger history of social and cultural technologies that have been called upon to create citizens "who do not need to be governed by others, but will govern themselves, master themselves, care for themselves."[9] This approach to governing can be traced to the nineteenth century, when industrial capitalism gave shape to working-class populations whose feared association with disease, drunkenness, squalor, criminality, and vice made elites uneasy. What Rose calls the impetus to "govern in the interests of morality and order" gained influence during this time, brushing up against the liberal desire to "restrict government in the interests of liberty and economy." The development of expertise – along with professionals to authorize and administer it – provided one way of shaping and guiding human beings toward "better" strategies of self-regulation that was not tied to official state power. Professionalized medicine, psychiatry, philanthropy, social work, and scientific charity operated as diffused technologies of "indirect government" by seeking to influence people's conduct and habits in a range of specialized arenas, including health, hygiene, morality, recreation, and domestic arrangements.[10] The emerging institutions of high culture also worked as indirect technologies of government: as Tony Bennett has shown, the political rationalities of libraries and public museums went beyond the circulation of knowledge to the installation of middle-class forms of behavior, including a propensity for self-discipline.[11] The nascent mass-culture industry also emerged as a technology for "governing at a distance" to the extent that penny newspapers, mass-circulation magazines, nickelodeons, and silent feature films circulated forms of professional advice, social rules, and procedures, and techniques for everyday living within the cultural economy of capitalist democracy. Mass media could not be counted upon to govern in the hoped for ways of rulers and elites, however. In fact, reformers worried endlessly about commercialized mass amusements precisely because they feared their capacity to instill the "wrong" habits and behaviors in the populace.

Thinking of television as a cultural technology requires us to overcome a tendency in media studies to think about media either as political economic practice or cultural practice, to think about these as fundamentally different, or to think that media can be understood only as one or both. We use the term "cultural technology" to underscore the extent to which television culture is an object of regulation, policy, and programs designed to nurture citizenship and civil society, and an instrument for educating, improving, and shaping subjects.[12] In establishing TV as a cultural technology, we offer an alternative to approaches to television culture conceived as a system of representation, meaning, and formal convention that is specific to TV, which tends to understand power as a matter of making meaning and changing minds, and understand the rules of watching and living with TV as mostly a set of stylistic and textual codes and conventions.[13]

Another implication of TV as a cultural technology concerns the arts and sciences of *cultivation*. Rather than seeing culture as art, or art as the opposite of science and administration, we consider how TV has operated as both art and science, or to invoke a premodern term, as *techne*, artfulness with certain skills and applications. The term "craft" is also a useful way of thinking about TV as *teckne* since crafting refers, more than art or science, to the everyday making and modulation that has been typical of reality TV's games, lessons, and demonstrations.[14] By thinking about TV as a cultural technology, we are emphasizing TV as a resource for acquiring and applying practical knowledges and skills. Since the late 1990s, TV has reinvented older formats such as drama and news around the expertise and authority of technicians – profilers, doctors, lawyers, police, and other emergency responders. More recently, a burgeoning regime of TV production has focused on self-help education and lifestyle instruction. Demonstrations in home decoration, car styling and upkeep, what and what not to wear, and cooking are both arts and sciences, or (put another way) they involve mastering certain techniques for beautification, health, and well-being. "Culture" in this sense refers to the *cultivation* and management of life and growth. TV as *cultivation* involves designing plans for putting things in an order to ensure maximum productivity and the achievement of goals.[15] As programs for *cultivation*, TV offers ways of tending to (of governing) the little, banal tasks of daily life and linking knowledge and skill to the *administration* of one's household, family, and self. These personal programs of cultivation also provide a way of shaping the civil society upon which liberal government depends and acts. The mastering of techniques for applying, conducting, and cultivating oneself in the best way possible is a component of improving oneself as a matter of self-governance. In this way, reality TV operates as a dimension of the private "outsourcing" and outreach through which the current stage of liberal government rationalizes public welfare and security.

Another dimension of TV as a cultural technology concerns self-cultivation as self-improvement and self-reliance. Our emphasis here is on the "care of the self" through TV programs working as technologies of governance. How has television "technologized the self," or the many selves, that are required to manage daily life? What are the possibilities for actualizing a self that is more or less engaged with television? What kinds of knowledges does "self-actualization" involve in the current epoch, and how does TV mediate these knowledges? How is learning how to accomplish certain tasks, apply oneself in particular ways, and model certain types of behavior tantamount to living a more "rewarding," "satisfying" life? Reality TV's guidelines and regimens are practical, everyday technologies of the self. They are to be applied through common exercises in which we are "put to the test" and experiment in living our lives as we do. This perspective is particularly useful in considering how TV is being reinvented to make itself more useful as a resource for expanding one's capabilities, fashioning a "better" life, and developing strategies for addressing problems or threats pertaining to one's body, household, work, property, and family. In this sense, self-cultivation is a technical achievement.

Foucault used the expression "technology of the self" to describe how an individual's freedom and agency are technical achievements that involve working on, watching over, and applying oneself in particular ways. The paradox he describes is in one's reliance upon various techniques for exercising freedom and agency. Freedom is not the opposite of control but is a matter of how one controls oneself by exercising freedom "correctly" through various technologies and rules of self-governance, including those provided by reality TV. Exercising freedom, as a matter of learning how to act and behave, makes the self a *conductor of power* in two senses: as someone empowered to take charge of one's life, and also as someone who can effectively conduct a charge (as certain metals conduct electricity), or someone who can deliver what is expected. In one's ability to practice freedom well and responsibly and in one's reliance upon the technologies of the self one becomes a good conductor of power in both senses.

TV as cultural technology of self-actualization operates as a form of citizenship training. Liberal government, particularly in the United

States, has left citizens primarily to their own devices in understanding what citizenship involves.[16] When citizenship education is privatized, television's instrumentality as a cultural technology is to link practices of self-cultivation and self-fashioning to the lessons and tests of citizenship. By demonstrating for and with viewers the techniques for taking care of oneself, reality TV supports the governmental rationalities of self-reliance that have become so pivotal to the current stage of liberal government.[17] Conceptualizing television in this way takes us beyond the concerns of political economy and cultural studies to a consideration of the technical resources through which we reflect and act upon ourselves as citizen-subjects. It moves us beyond an understanding of governing that is limited to formal institutions, processes, and rituals such as voting to a broader consideration of how we come (partly through media) to govern ourselves and our lives in ordinary, dispersed, and highly personalized ways. Analyzing television as a cultural technology that both enables *and* directs the government of the self also requires us to think outside analytical binaries such as resistance/domination and freedom/control.

While we introduce these terms in order to think about reality TV as a set of demonstrations in civic virtues and good citizenship through self-fashioning, we want to stress that these lessons do not necessarily affirm the *settledness* of rules and laws, nor do they have predictable results or "effects." Their political mattering needs to be understood in terms of how they are taken up, applied, and acted upon by institutions, associations, and citizens in the making. To emphasize the unsettledness of reality TV's guidelines for living, we reiterate that its lessons often take the form of *experiments* or "civic laboratories,"[18] in which human subjects are tested on their ability to master certain technologies of citizenship, and to fashion themselves in relation to particular civic virtues. As is evident in *Todd TV*, the successes are as important as the failures, and the experimentalism matters as much as the game of competition. Collectively and cumulatively, the experiments point to television's effort to try out, refine, reinvent, and act upon available technologies of citizenship as solutions to perceived problems of government. In this respect, *Better Living through Reality TV* seeks to understand the conditions for testing and demonstrating the government of the self in relation to current political rationalities. We are less focused on how reality TV validates or subverts liberalism as an ideology than in how it catalyzes and *acts upon* techniques and rationalities of governing. Analyzing how television is being instrumentalized as part of programs of social service, social welfare, and social management does not begin with the assumption that TV always has authority, or that it produces predictable or uniform political effects. TV's political effectivity must be understood in terms of the complex, varied, and interlocking resources through which TV is authorized to operate in certain ways, and to authorize the particular forms of behavior upon which a *civil* society is achieved, secured, and mobilized.

Placing TV in an analytic of government has led us to rethink some of the terminology that defines television. One has to do with an object of our analysis – the TV program. While the term most commonly is used to refer to any kind of production on television, our inflection focuses on the regularity and regulating quality of television as a framework for taking small steps in living life that may be promised or imagined to have enormous (and not just monetary) rewards. In this framework, the program involves taking these steps through a series of small tests, each requiring a correct response and a small reward or pleasure, before proceeding. In this way, the TV program is being reinvented as an instructional template for taking care of oneself and becoming self-enterprising as a path to (among other things) "empowered" citizenship. This way of conceptualizing the TV program allows for the customization and personalization of regimens for managing the different spheres of everyday life.[19] It also leads us beyond TV to other media, materials, and technologies (magazines, books, the Web, MP3 kits) that constitute larger, interdependent cultural networks or relays of resources and support. To consider TV programs as resources for personal regimens we need to understand how television is instrumentalized as one component of these interdependent networks. Yet, it is also the case that TV programs are different from other media in their serialization and daily regularization. So, although the TV program may direct viewers to other resources for becoming active custodians of their lives, television provides the framework for starting and maintaining a regimen for better living. Unlike other media that require users to search out and to pick resources, TV's programmatic serialization supports in its provision of a *framework* for better living.

Placing TV in an analytic of government is also useful for understanding the heightened attention to the "care of the self" in a political rationality that values private over public, self-sufficiency over "dependency," and personal responsibility over collective or "socialistic" conceptions of society. Without dismissing the individual rewards of self-actualization, it is important to recognize how the present stage of liberal governing undercuts earlier promises of equality, prosperity, and security. In certain respects, reality and lifestyle TV represents nothing short of the current conception of social welfare, or the means through which all citizens – whatever their resources and histories of disenfranchisement – are expected to "take responsibility" for their fate. Understanding how TV operates as a new form of neoliberalized social service, social welfare, and social management involves turning attention to the formation of *specific* networks between TV, the State, and private (volunteer and corporate) entities, which act upon each other and which citizens must rely upon and navigate. Focusing on TV involves recognizing that neoliberalism cannot be understood as a paradigm without attending to the everyday practices of living through and within the governmental rationalities that comprise and reproduce it.

Reinventing Government

Better Living through Reality TV focuses on how reality TV has materialized within the current stage of liberal government. While the comprehensive histories of liberalism and television are well beyond our scope, it is helpful to begin by sketching out some of the ways that government and television have been reinvented through one another. The discourse about something called "reinventing government" emerged in the United States in the 1980s, and intensified in the 1990s. It would be simplistic to suggest that this discourse was entirely new, however. As Foucault's work demonstrates, liberal government has always been inclined to survey and act upon the programs and associations that comprise civil society, and to rationalize itself through improving, "advancing," and modernizing the technologies of government in this way. Liberalism "inaugurates a *continual* dissatisfaction with government, a *perpetual* questioning of whether the desired effects are being produced, of the mistakes of thought or policy that hamper the efficacy of government, a *recurrent diagnosis* of failure coupled with a *recurrent demand* to govern better," explains Rose.[20] The paradox, as Rose suggests, is that government becomes a mechanism for diagnosing, correcting, and curing the ailments of government. This informs the discourse of government's "reinventing" itself, a broad political effort to overcome or overturn what were increasingly viewed as perversions of liberalism by the policies of social welfare enacted from the 1930s through the 1960s. The intensification of the concern with making over government, and of designing a government that "frees" citizens of cycles of dependency on government set into motion by these "perversions," is a dimension of what Rose and other political observers describe as the advanced or "neo" stage of liberalism.[21]

By neoliberalism, we refer to the historical formation that has emerged from the renewal of liberalism as an "improvement" over the past.[22] The early stage of the discourse of reinventing government emphasized the value of public–private partnerships and outsourcing the activities of government to businesses. This discourse developed through an emerging group of think tanks, political action groups, and private associations dedicated to correcting what they considered to be the ineffectiveness of "big government." One prominent buzzword concerned the "privatization" of government, a phrase associated particularly with Peter Drucker's influential 1968 book *The Age of Discontinuity*.[23] Drucker, like the economist Friedrich von Hayek (whose theories were also beginning to gain prominence and influence in the United States during the 1960s), cited Nazi Germany and the Soviet Union as evidence of a malaise resulting from government of the social, caused by the diminishment of individual freedoms at the hands of government interventionism.[24] Drucker argued that government ailed from decades of expanding bureaucracies and the swelling size of public welfare programs administered by the federal government. The remedy he proposed was "reprivatization," whereby corporate management would become the model, and in certain cases the administrative arm, of state government.[25]

By the 1980s, Hayek's provocation to imagine a new liberalism, and Drucker's rationale for public–private partnerships to reform state government, had developed into reform initiatives.[26] The discourse about reinventing government gained traction through campaigns to describe Ronald Reagan's administration policy as the Reagan Revolution, and his 1984 reelection promise of a "new morning in America." Over the late 1980s, Republican and Democratic candidates for city and state government extolled the virtues of "restructuring," "right-sizing," and "catalyzing" private agencies to take over public administration, and promoted slogans like "decentralization" "entre-preneurial government," and "results not rules."[27] In October, 1989, the cover of *Time* magazine asked "Is Government Dead?," while the story inside reflected on one of Reagan's favored aphorisms, "Govern-ment isn't the solution; it's the problem."

"Reinventing government" subsequently became the key term in the Clinton administration's explanation of its policy objectives. During his campaign in 1992, Bill Clinton endorsed David Osborne and Ted Gaebler's influential 1992 book *Reinventing Government: How the Entrepreneurial Spirit is Transforming the Public Sector*, claiming it "should be read by every elected official in America. Those of us who want to revitalize government . . . have to reinvent it. This book gives us a blueprint." Early in his presidency, Clinton established the National Partnership for Reinventing Government (NPRG), with Vice Presi-dent Al Gore as its point person. Its aim was to "make the entire federal government less expensive and more efficient, and to change the culture of our national bureaucracy away from complacency and entitlement toward initiative and empowerment." Perpetuating the terminology of the 1980s critique of "big government" as bureaucratic, the Clinton administration cast its plan for reinventing government as a public–private "partnership" to be achieved by "changing govern-ment to be more results and performance oriented," "serving people [as customers] better," "changing the way that government works with business and community," and "transforming access to government through [information/communication] technology." While coming this time from Democrats, the initiative acted upon an array of city and state initiatives that predated the Clinton administration – such as the Empower American initiative for "public–private partnership" launched in 1993 by the Republican former Housing and Urban Development Secretary Jack Kemp – that were already making the work of government coextensive with the operations and management of private programs.

While the NPRG might have been partly a political strategy to coopt a trend that had gained momentum during the Reagan and Bush eras, it codified both a model for administering welfare in sync with deregulatory policies, and the energetic "makeover" of public agencies built through and associated with the Democratic party.[28] The NPRG also justified the Clinton–Gore administration's role in the passage of welfare reform legislation, including welfare-to-work policies and the

Personal Responsibility Act of 1996, that promised to break cycles of dependency by "empowering" recipients to "help themselves" by demonstrating their "personal responsibility" as citizens to the State and to themselves. In addition to welfare reform, the Clinton administration encouraged volunteerism, creating both the Corporation for National and Community Service and Americorp, a federally funded organization that rearticulated Kennedy-era Peace Corps and Vista Volunteer programs. Contrary to those 1960s programs, however, the civic responsibilization associated with mobilizing a network of volunteers and nonprofit groups was bound to a logic of citizenship that emphasized personal responsibility.

The expansion of public–private partnerships, welfare reform, and volunteerism during the Clinton era helped rationalize yet another reinvention of government proposed by the Bush administration, a "compassionate conservatism" whose primary cure for publicly administered welfare was a Faith-Based and Community Initiative (FBCI).[29] As a network for privatizing forms of social welfare through church and civic associations, the FBCI claimed to offer "a fresh start and bold new approach to government's role in helping those in need." Too often, explained its web site, "the government has ignored and impeded the efforts of faith-based and community organizations. Their compassionate efforts to improve their communities have been needlessly and improperly inhibited by bureaucratic red-tape and restrictions." As of 2003, no fewer than seven government agencies were called upon to assist in correcting this problem, coordinated by an Office of Faith-Based and Community Initiatives and supported by the Compassion Capital Fund. The FBCI became the "umbrella" for the USA Freedom Corps Volunteer Network, the Volunteers for Prosperity (a volunteer-arm of the USAID), and the Citizen Corps, which quickly became a branch of volunteerism associated with Homeland Security. Through these volunteer service networks, the Bush administration boasted that 64.5 million US citizens had participated in volunteer services – a number that increased by 5 million during his presidency. The FBCI, as a rationality for welfare administration and reform, was able to mobilize both an expanding array of private programs for administering welfare, and a prevailing reasoning about "taking care of oneself" as a means to self-empowerment and active citizenship. Yet in the Bush administration, acting upon private, religious, and community agencies became a framework not only for reinventing government but also for

improvement (for *finally* getting things *right*) by administering government programs through moral and religious agency and authority. As
yet another experiment in liberal government and a deepening of the
trend toward neoliberal public policy, the FBCI has made social welfare
moral by redefining its "virtues" as a new relationship between government, the church, and communitarianism. For example, whereas
the Clinton era Hope VI program was about nurturing "public–private
partnership" and "restoring" community activism in the reinvention
of public housing (and by example social welfare), the Housing and
Urban Development arm of the Bush administration's FBCI had a new
mission of linking homeownership to good citizenship and assuring
that the US Department of Housing and Development (HUD)'s
rehabilitation programs were accomplished less directly through
"government intervention" and more through Community Development Corporations.

The FBCI was the initial experiment for demonstrating a "new"
authority *and* responsibility on the part of government, private institutions, religious and community programs, and citizens. Although the
experiment has continued, the FBCI became subordinated to the Bush
administration's "war on terror" and the accompanying rationale for a
Homeland Defense. In Bush's address to the US Senate commending
them for support of his "faith-based" legislation in 2001, he stated that
the initiative would "encourage more charitable giving and rally the
armies of compassion that exist in communities all across America"
(emphasis added). The contradiction of a FBCI in a "war on terror"
has been that only certain religious and communitarian programs –
those that have "proper" religious and political authority – are considered legitimate by this agency.

If a primary objective of public–private partnerships and volunteer
service networks during the 1990s was achieving greater *efficiency* by
privatizing welfare, casting government in a supportive role, helping
citizens take care of themselves, then the institution of a Homeland
Security after September 11, 2001 emphasizes *security* through "public–
private partnership," with "Homeland Security" as the ridgepole and
primary rationalization for all other forms of social welfare. The Bush
administration has rationalized a strategy for Homeland Defense through
policies and experiments that have made waging a "war on terror"
tantamount to the purposes of social welfare and security – not only
a matter of diminishing programs of social welfare and security that

had been instituted since the 1930s, but of redirecting their usefulness through a different model of security and of state/civilian responsibility.[30] The Citizen Corps and other programs of citizen "empowerment" have been recent examples of the new regime of public–private partnerships and volunteer networks. Within this governmental rationality about welfare citizenship and civic responsibility, Homeland Security is nothing short of a new "social security."[31]

The relation between FBCI and Homeland Security is a significant development for thinking about the most recent strategies for "reinventing government," because the former's effort to act upon private networks (as religious and moral providers of welfare) shaped the latter as the largest department created by the federal government since the presidency of Harry Truman. Although the Bush administration has been criticized by libertarians in his own party for "reinventing government" *as* "big government," Homeland Security is profoundly a department that operates in a "supportive" posture – educating citizens about how they can look after themselves by locating private resources, as evidenced by its response to Hurricane Katrina, which demonstrated just how deeply this "state of the art" bureaucracy is about offloading responsibility rather than providing assistance.

As Paul du Gay argues in *In Praise of Bureaucracy*, the rationale for the "entrepreneurial government" which has developed since the 1980s requires that government be reinvented to cure a moral and ethical defectiveness attributed to the modern bureaucracy perceived as endemic to public planning, welfare, and administration.[32] While bureaucracy has been a feature of corporate management as well as of public administration since the late nineteenth century, the aversion to bureaucracy has been most fervently and commonly directed over the last three decades at public administrative bureaucracy. According to this rationale, state bureaucracy is a moral danger that breeds dependency, limits growth, and suppresses freedom. The proponents of entrepreneurial government promise to solve this problem by making government operate more like a corporate enterprise, and by replacing the bureaucrat with the manager (and the citizen with the consumer). The rationalization of entrepreneurial government, as represented particularly by "compassionate conservatism" and the FBCI's sponsorship of civic volunteer networks, is also, however, profoundly moralistic. As du Gay explains, "the defining feature of entrepreneurial government is its generalization of an 'enterprise form' to all forms of conduct

– 'to the conduct of organizations hitherto seen as being non-economic, to the conduct of government, and to the conduct of individuals themselves.'" To correct the malaise of public administration involves not only making private agencies more responsible for public assistance – as in the moral crusade of Bush's effort to mobilize "armies of compassion" and the "outreach" programs of TV discussed above – but also transforming individuals into more responsible, accountable, and enterprising managers of themselves. An economy that requires workers to undergo lifelong retraining to make themselves relevant within a "flexible" workforce and to compensate for the deterioration of both corporate-sponsored and state-sponsored pension systems also requires endless training about how to manage the various aspects of one's everyday life where one is increasingly at risk and exposed.

Reinventing Television

How does television, and particularly reality TV, fit into the reinvention of government? Considering (albeit schematically) three *historical conjunctures* allows us to clarify how television operates within the current stage of liberal government, with its strategies of privatization, volunteerism, entrepreneurialism, and responsibilization. The first conjuncture is the emergence of broadcasting in the United States as a technology for conjoining the public and private interest. This is a complicated history, already addressed by several scholars,[33] but some points are worth emphasizing. Since the 1920s, US broadcast policy has attempted to solve certain tensions, contradictions, and problems about what commercial broadcasting as a "public service" entails. These include how to make broadcasting compatible with reasoned and principled oversight, how to oversee the "rational" balance of programming and distribution of programmers in the name of the public good, and how best to represent the freedoms and responsibilities of *private* broadcasting companies. Early US policy was not unique in regulating broadcasting as a public service, but in the United States this quickly became a very specific set of problems and solutions, for the provision of broadcasting as public service has been inseparable from the provision of safeguarding "free TV." This involved not only broadcasting's relation to private ownership by what had become major broadcasting and cinema corporations following World War II, but also to a governmental rationality in which radio and television mattered as technologies of territorial/global expansion, mass suburbanization, market growth, and mobility. Unlike broadcasting in the rest of the world, broadcasting in the United States was not produced or distributed through publicly administered agencies (e.g., the British Broadcasting Corporation, or BBC), and so a distinct governmental problem about its relation to education/welfare/service developed. As a Cold War model of "economic government," the State *supported* and, through a supportive role, policed the freedom of broadcast industries to operate and to form national and regional networks as long as they represented something called "the public interest." This rationale presumed that the public interest was best served by the growth and self-regulative capacities of the private sector, even as government and industry continually sought propitious arrangements for accomplishing "oversight." During the period following World War II, this arrangement was rationalized partly in terms of "propaganda" in Nazi Germany and the Soviet Union (and to a lesser extent, the paternalistic or autocratic example of British broadcasting) and partly in terms of the grave responsibility of the United States, and its commercial television system, to be a good model for liberal democracy to the rest of the world.

Television developed in the United States after two decades of reflection about how best to regulate private broadcasting.[34] In this sense, TV emerged as a problem of government – specifically, how to advance a self-regulating, for-profit, private industry that provided a "public service."[35] Since the foundation of commercial broadcasting had already been rationalized, this became mainly a matter of ensuring program quality and diversity, which (especially during the Cold War era) were considered tantamount to citizenship, civil society, democracy, and the health of the nation. In 1946, on the cusp of the emergence of broadcast TV, the federal government outlined the kinds of services it was supposed to provide – "entertainment, religious, commercial, educational, agricultural, fraternal" – even as it clearly laid the responsibility for doing this with private companies, stating that the responsibilities for improving broadcast services rested with "forces" other than the federal government.[36] The "other forces" included, first and foremost, "self-regulation by the industry itself," but also professional journalistic critics, citizen councils, colleges and universities, and workshops – in short, a range of private associations and agents comprising a civil society mediated through radio and television. The regulatory role of the Federal Communication Association (FCC) during TV's emergence during this period had mostly to do with granting and reviewing broadcast licenses, as a way of rationalizing – i.e., making orderly, fair, and responsive – the idea of commercial television as a public service.

Within this conjuncture, TV's orientation as an educational medium came less from broadcasting companies than from philanthropic and academic sources. The Ford Foundation, university educators, and social scientists like Wilbur Schramm provided the impetus for early experiments in educational programming and the creation of a limited Educational Television Network (ETV). Their demands for "better" television were influential in reinforcing the fundamental distinction between education and entertainment through which broadcasting emerged as a problem of government.[37] The liberal ideal of maximizing private profit in the name of the public good was unrealizable to the extent that "public service" was closely tied to unprofitable high cultural and informational programming. This had been demonstrated by the 1920s, in the case of radio. The emergence of deeply marginalized educational (and later public) TV channels partly managed this problem, but posed other worries and recurring controversies. If educational TV smacked to some of experiments in state-sponsored broadcasting, commercial TV's contribution to "mass culture" continued to undermine, as Dwight MacDonald had famously argued, the distinction between the gullibility of citizens in "totalitarian" states and the rationality of liberal government in democratic nations such as the United States.[38]

This is not to say that commercial TV in the 1950s completely lacked programs of civic, educational, and cultural uplift. NBC and CBS programmed short-lived adaptations of literary and theatrical works, all carrying the brand of single sponsors (e.g., *Goodyear Playhouse*, *Kraft Television Theater*, *Philco Television Playhouse*). The Ford Foundation's *Omnibus* (1952–9) is the most dramatic example of programming whose cultural import was tantamount to viewer improvement through liberal arts instruction, and therefore to the shaping of citizenship through television. While these programs became increasingly anomalous to the objectives of commercial broadcasting during the 1950s, television was replete with forms of technical instruction that operated as a cultural technology in a different way. Popular TV genres of the 1950s provided ethical demonstrations and moral exercises about the micro-mechanisms of civil society, and guided citizenship in that way. A popular domestic comedy like *The Adventures of Ozzie and Harriett* represented problems and solutions in domestic and family governance that were not entirely disconnected from mental hygiene classroom films shown during those years.[39] From its earliest foray into TV production in 1954, The Walt Disney Corporation developed instructional entertainment for children, from science documentaries to lessons in good conduct produced for *Walt Disney Presents* (ABC and NBC) to the activities of the Mickey Mouse Club, which provided both an extension of and alternative to the institutions of public schooling.[40] Through its entertainment, in other words, commercial programming demonstrated the viability of the private institutions comprising a "civil society."

The discourse of *diversity* in programming became a key objective of the 1960s, the second conjuncture of TV as public service. This was the theme of FCC Chairman Newton Minow's 1961 address to the National Association of Broadcasters, in which he famously deemed US commercial television a "vast wasteland." Minow criticized the mediocrity of television, attributing the problem to the absence of "educational, religious, instructive, or other public service programming."[41] Minow was concerned with the same problem as earlier reformers – that is, broadcasters' favoring of "shallow" and formulaic entertainment over unprofitable high cultural and informational formats. However, unlike previous FCC officials, his plea for "more choices" presumed that greater government involvement could maximize "free enterprise" as a path to better television. "I urge you," he stated to broadcasters, "to put the people's airwaves to the service of the people *and* the cause of freedom" (emphasis added). Minow's formula for achieving these goals involved a paradox: On the one hand, the regulator wanted to avoid sacrificing the public interest to an industry driven purely by commercial interests (permitting "yourselves [the media industry] to become so absorbed in the chase for ratings, sales, and profits that you lose the wider view"). On the other hand, he wanted to avoid turning the FCC into a state bureaucracy (not allowing "ourselves to become so bogged down in the mountain of papers, hearings, memoranda, orders, and the daily routines that we close our eyes to the wider view of public interest"). Minow's rationalization of the TV problem gestured toward the creation of a state-supported Corporation for Public Broadcasting, yet remained committed to public–private partnership in which "excellence" in TV was to be an objective both of corporate management (as a purveyor of ratings and sales) and of education (as a purveyor of quality TV, cultural uplift, and good citizenship).

A similar commitment to the advancement of TV as a public service through a self-managing private media industry was apparent in President Lyndon Johnson's rationale for the 1967 Public Broadcasting Act. In the United States, federal funding for public broadcasting hinged on intersecting goals: uplifting the mass citizenry while helping to deliver an underclass out of poverty through televised liberal arts education, and serving the cultural needs of "opinion leaders" ill-served by commercial television's amusements.[42] Public TV was also a programmatic experiment in achieving, representing, and safeguarding diversity as enhanced program choice. In all of these ways, public TV's formation became a prong of a new stage of liberal government which John F. Kennedy had christened the New Frontier, and Johnson had just as ambitiously extolled as the Great Society. Public TV, as a form of state welfare and as public service, was rationalized in terms of its potential to educate. As Johnson stated, "I am convinced that a vital and self-sufficient non-commercial television system will not only instruct, but inspire and uplift our people."[43] The problem was how to fashion a public service that, in Johnson's words, was "absolutely free from any Federal Government interference in programming." The Corporation for Public Broadcasting was safeguarded from "state control" not only through its private nonprofit status, but through its reliance on monetary contributions from corporations and private donors (here, public TV mirrored other public-service programs, including Housing and Urban Development and NASA, that were advancing liberal government as public–private partnerships). The connection between public TV and these other fledgling, partly privatized programs of public welfare and services was, in some instances, quite direct – as when Johnson directed the relatively young NASA and the Department of Health, Education, and Welfare (HEW) "to conduct experiments on the requirements for such a ["public-broadcast"] system, and for instructional TV, in cooperation with other interested agencies of the Government and the private sector."[44]

The third conjuncture of television began in the late 1970s and continued into the 1980s, as TV was reorganized through the proliferation of cable and satellite channels. At this stage, the problem of how to manage program diversity was "solved" through a deregulated media economy that emphasized viewing flexibility and greater "consumer choice." Ideals of liberal education and uplift through mass broadcasting gave way to the *empowerment* of cultural collectivities conceptualized as taste and lifestyle clusters and to shaping citizens through these technologies. For example, the mantra of early MTV broadcasts was "We want our MTV!" – a rallying cry for mobilizing youth through television as never before, except at the fringes of programming. The identity politics of the 1960s, which had in part informed the Great Society experiments in governing, became a basis for *liberalizing* broadcasting through private cable and satellite technologies.[45] Since commercial TV was no longer dominated by the three broadcast networks, and lack of program choice was no longer the unresolvable dilemma it had been perceived to be during the 1950s and 1960s, public TV's mission as a dignified alternative to mass entertainment also began to matter differently from before. The earlier idea of public TV was difficult to maintain amid the proliferation of cable channels, each representing not only a segment of the public as lifestyle cluster, but their own forms of television as pedagogy.

To speak of TV's *reinvention*, and to understand this process in terms of the initiatives to reinvent government over the 1980s and 1990s, is to recognize how the "TV program" was changing through the proliferation of cable networks. TV programs were no longer simply broadcasts, but were constitutive of a network's brand and the basis for viewers' investment in specific forms of televisual association and membership. They became part of the *network as program*, integral to its representation of a particular lifestyle. The serialization of TV made it suited to operate as part of a daily regimen, and the programmatic potential of *cable* networks meant that the TV program (as regimen) could become a technology for self-actualization (i.e., for being young, or a woman, or black). The network made TV integral to living, shaping, and often improving one's life through a set of resources that could be oriented to the requirements of particular lifestyles and lifestyle problems. So, for example, MTV converted from nonstop music videos during the 1980s to a network comprised of multiple genres representing different aspects of a youthful lifestyle during the 1990s. Collectively, the proliferation of new channels also required more refined technologies of consumer choice and self-enterprise, such as the remote control, the time-shifting VCR, and more recently the

DVR, to make the TV program more useful within one's particular lifestyle. In this sense, the TV program became about the civic virtues and tools of specific forms of televisual membership as cultural citizenship. Or, put another way, televisual citizenship became tied to techniques of participation and membership, and to the investments of economic and cultural capital by viewers and channels comprising the cable network paradigm.

The capacity of cable networks in the United States to have developed as technologies of self-actualization became particularly evident in the 1990s, with the emergence of entire networks devoted to popular lifestyle instruction. Some of the most successful of these networks have included the Home and Garden Network, the Food Network, the Fine Living Channel, Fit TV, the Learning Channel, and the Do-it-Yourself Network. As the decade progressed, cable networks not specifically devoted to lifestyle instruction began to integrate more pedagogic elements into their schedules. This did more than deepen the role of the cable network as helping "program"; it also linked the discourse of self-actualization to practical technologies of self-management and the care of the self. While television prior to this stage presented some of the material to make this connection, it lacked the rationales for doing so. Only in the current stage of liberalism, with its specific requirements of entrepreneurialism and self-responsibilization, do the techniques of everyday self-management become so central to television's governing role. This explains why makeover productions, which have existed since the origins of broadcasting, have only fairly recently begun to proliferate across a wide range of TV networks.

The convergence of media has also contributed to television's role in disseminating technical strategies of self-management and care. The reinvention of the TV program has enabled television to become more instrumental within existing cultures of self-help, which have been valued since the 1980s and which are now considered an integral component of post-welfare government. The strategy of embedding the TV program within lifestyle clusters inserted television within an economy for delivering viewers to the commercial providers of resources required to maintain those lifestyles. In so doing, it provided a mechanism for delivering customers from one medium (TV) to another, a point that Andrew Goodwin has made about the formation of MTV.[46] Political-economic analyses have shown how reality TV facilitates a similar means of capitalizing upon "tie-ins" amongst media.[47]

We wish to underscore how TV's salience to a governmental regime of self-help has brought it into a vital relation with other technologies of self-actualization and self-management. This includes older media such as magazines, books, and manuals that are being repurposed through other media or as packages, such as holistic healer Deepak Chopra's combination of book and MP3 player. However, television's instrumentality as a technology of contemporary citizenship particularly relies on Web-based resources. The Web has become a resource through which enterprising individuals can help themselves, and many TV programs since the late 1990s have mobilized it as a way to personalize and customize televisual instruction. In some respects, TV's convergence with other forms of media has revitalized the ideal of home-based education as citizenship training. At the same time, the portability of these media has extended the potential scope of televisual education to multiple locations and spheres of activity.[48] TV's lasting value may have to do with its rootedness in daily life, as a serialized framework for personal regimens. One may need to work to seek out advice on the Web or in a magazine, but TV *delivers* pupils punctually at predictable times of the day. TV's programmed features – what Raymond Williams famously described as its structured "flow" – make it less a medium that one "picks up" than a medium one synchronizes one's life with. Sticking with a regimen sometimes requires the means of regularizing lifestyle and choices in this way. Such is TV's "helping" culture.

While we have considered the relation between reinventing government and TV in three conjunctures, our project seeks to describe an emergent one. TV's insertion into an economy for delivering viewers/consumers from one medium to another is central to our account of the current stage of liberal government in two respects. The first is that the "TV network" is not simply a relay within various communication networks or a generalized "network society." It has become an integral relay within the entrepreneurial networks of welfare provision and private social support. The second is that citizenship is less an objective or outcome of TV's ideological work on subjects than an achievement that depends upon the TV programs through which one actively enters into these networks. The following chapters provide an analysis of this emerging conjuncture by tracing some of these entry points and showing how they connect citizens, government, and television.

Chapter 1

Charity TV:
Privatizing Care, Mobilizing Compassion

On January 16, 2006, *The New York Times* announced a positive trend in reality TV: "do-good" programs had emerged to provide housing, healthcare, and general help to the needy. The article focused on *Miracle Workers*, an ABC series that intervenes in the lives of "seriously ill people who lack the contacts or the money for treatment." A team of doctors and nurses provided by the TV network steers people to the "latest medical breakthroughs" while TV cameras "capture the drama of patient-hood, from consultations to surgery to recovery." ABC pays for medical treatments not covered by private health insurance, as was the case in an episode featuring the Gibbs family of Florida, whose father and son underwent surgical procedures to remove brain tumors that cost the commercial TV network more than $100,000. Besides footing the bill for the surgeries, ABC's medical team "asked the questions they did not know to ask, held their hands, made the arrangements," reported *The Times*. According to Mr. Gibbs, who described his family as "average people," it was television's close involvement that got them through the ordeal.[1] At a juncture when reality TV is being offered as a solution to the plight of people like the Gibbs and, implicitly, to the lingering social problems of a post-welfare society as well, the management of "neediness" presents a useful place to begin our examination of contemporary television as a technology of governance.

This chapter considers TV's efforts to intervene in the lives of "real" people cast as unable (or unwilling) to care for themselves adequately in the current epoch of privatization and self-responsibilization. It is a sign of the times that hundreds of thousands of individuals now apply directly to reality TV programs not only for medical needs, but also for decent housing (*Extreme Makeover: Home Edition, Town Haul, Mobile Home Disasters*), tuition, and income assistance (*The Scholar, Three Wishes*), transportation (*Pimp My Ride*), disaster relief (*Three Wishes, Home Edition*), food, clothing, and other basic material needs (*Random One, Renovate My Family*). This is not an entirely new phenomenon: In the 1950s, game shows such as *Queen for a Day* and *Strike it Rich* showered needy contestants with cash prizes, goods, and services donated by sponsors. However, today's charitable interventions are much more extravagant and prolific, appearing on network and cable channels during daytime and primetime hours. They have also become more specialized, as programs differentiate themselves by focusing on specific populations and needs. The interventions are now more likely to take place outside the TV studio, with professional helpers going "on location" and portable cameras documenting the results. Most importantly, TV's foray into the helping culture is now more intensely aligned with the rationalities of deregulation and welfare reform. Within the context of the search for new ways to deliver social services, its interventions can be sanctioned as providing a public service in ways that *Queen for a Day* and other precursors were not.

Illustration 1.1   *Queen for a Day* brought charity to TV in the 1950s, but was panned by critics as tasteless and exploitative (ABC, 1956–60; NBC, 1960–4; creator and producer Edward Kranyak)

Television, especially in the United States, is not required to do much more than maximize profit. The notion that it must serve something called the public interest has been more or less obliterated by deregulatory policies. As Michael Eisner, former CEO of the Disney Corporation, which owns ABC Television, stated bluntly in 1998, "We have no obligation to make history; we have no obligation to make art; we have no obligation to make a statement; to make money is our only objective." Nonetheless, Stephen McPherson, president of ABC's entertainment division, now contends that television is more than a "toaster with pictures," as famously claimed by Mark Fowler, chairman of the Federal Communications Commission (FCC) under Ronald Reagan. Although *Miracle Workers* was being packaged and sold as entertainment, McPherson played up its charitable and educational contributions to *The Times*, insisting that "whatever the rating," ABC had done a good thing by providing "knowledge and access" to unfortunate people who lack the "wherewithal to get the best treatment" on their own.

McPherson did not dwell on how quickly ABC would pull the plug in the event of a less-than-desired rating or other business factors: such is the fate of all television produced within the operating logic of the market. Instead, he emphasized the ethical possibilities of cultural commerce, particularly TV's capacity to mobilize private resources (money, volunteerism, expertise) in order to help needy individuals overcome hurdles and hardships. When joined to the conventions of reality entertainment, this enterprising and personalized approach to social problem solving allows television to do good without providing unprofitable "serious" news and public affairs programming.[2] However, critics who fault TV for failing to provide substantial journalistic attention to health-care policy, poverty, homelessness, public-sector downsizing, and similar issues also fail to fully grasp the significance of charity programs built around the "empowerment" of people whose everyday lives are clearly impacted by these issues. TV's relationship to the "public interest" has been severed from the ideal of preparing the masses for the formalized rituals (deliberation, voting) of democracy and linked to a "can-do" model of citizenship that values private enterprise, personal responsibility, and self-empowerment – the basic principles of George W. Bush's Ownership Society. Instead of rejecting any allegiance to the public good, as many predicted would occur with broadcast deregulation, TV has quite aggressively pursued a form of civic engagement that enacts the reinvention of government. As we will demonstrate, for-profit TV programs like *Miracle Workers* have proliferated alongside the proposition that State involvement in the care of citizens is inefficient, paternalistic, and "dependency-breeding" and the related imperative that citizens take their care into their own hands. McPherson's self-congratulatory praise for television's recent efforts to tap the resources of the private sector and help individuals navigate a plethora of consumer choices and make sound decisions about their well-being speaks to the affinity between deregulated public interest activity and contemporary welfare reform.

From "Welfare State to Opportunity, Inc."

To understand the political rationality of reality-based charity TV, a brief detour through the conceptual history of welfare will be helpful. We take our bearings partly from political theorist Nikolas Rose, who situates the changing "mentalities" of government leading up to welfare reform within stages of liberalism.[3] According to Rose's account, the liberal state was called upon to become more directly involved in the care of citizens in the late nineteenth and early twentieth centuries, a period of time that happens to correspond with the development and progression of industrial capitalism. As relations among elites and workers became increasingly antagonistic, rulers were "urged to accept the obligation to tame and govern the undesirable consequences of industrial life, wage labor and urban existence in the name of society."[4] What Rose calls a "state of welfare" emerged to provide basic forms of social insurance, child welfare, health, mental hygiene, universal education, and similar services that both "civilized" the working class and joined citizens to the State and to each other through formalized "solidarities and dependencies." Through this new "social contract" between the State and the population, Rose contends, the autonomous political subject of liberal rule was reconstituted as a "citizen with rights to social protection and social education in return for duties of social obligation and social responsibility."[5]

In the United States, where faith in the market's ability to regulate society is especially strong, the 1930s and the 1960s stand out as key moments in the "state of welfare." The depression of the 1930s spawned a crisis of capitalism that required federal intervention to buffer. New Deal reforms signaled a new way of conceptualizing the State's responsibility to "protect citizens from the vicissitudes of life."[6] Two types of federal welfare programs were created: national insurance programs to manage the collective risks of unemployment, old age, disability, and catastrophic illness, and need-based public assistance programs. In the 1960s, these programs were expanded in the name of the War on Poverty and the Great Society, extending the promise of "social protection and social education" while also bringing socially and economically oppressed populations further into the disciplinary arena of the public agencies responsible for overseeing their welfare.

As Rose and others have shown, the revised social contract inherent to a "state of welfare" has been contested since its inception. In the 1970s, however, the critique began to escalate, as critics across the political spectrum charged the Welfare State with fiscal waste and limiting "individual freedom, personal choice, self-fulfillment, and initiative."[7] In the United States, need-based programs were especially vilified, but more recently even those popular social insurance programs (such as social security) that escape stigma have been targeted for privatization in the name of efficiency, choice, and empowerment. As this rationale suggests, "undoing" welfare involves more than rolling back the Welfare State – it also entails enacting market-based strategies of governing and reconstituting citizenship as the "free exercise" of choice and responsibility.[8] This occurred in the 1990s. As Lisa Duggan argues, the push to "de-statize" welfare was disarticulated to some extent at this point from punitive, and overtly racist and sexist characterization of welfare "cheats" and "freeloaders" that had gained currency in the Reagan era. Instead, the basis for welfare reform was tied to a promise of empowerment through self-help.[9] The justification for imposing strict time limits on welfare benefits and implementing welfare-to-work policies was to enable people caught in a state of dependency to "help themselves," claimed politicians. As this was occurring, social service provision in general was also being outsourced and privatized: "In one policy domain after another – pensions, education, transportation, criminal justice, and environmental protection to name a few examples – we are moving away from having governmental agencies actually delivering services toward service delivery by private firms," observed one analyst of the move from "Welfare State to Opportunity, Inc.":[10]

The American Welfare State is not dead yet, but it is fading away. Its replacement, Opportunity, Inc., seems to be growing brighter by the day. These two forms of governance, Welfare State and Opportunity Inc., differ in their methods, goals, and not the least, rhetoric. The Welfare State delivers benefits to recipients in order to cushion them from the harshness of markets. Opportunity, Inc., in contrast, seeks to assist clients in becoming independent actors within markets. The Welfare State is not inherently provided by the government, nor is Opportunity, Inc., provided by the private sector. As part of the Welfare State, private firms can simply deliver benefits. Opportunity, Inc., does not intrinsically consist of private forms. Government agencies, too, can act to empower citizens to become economically independent. However, the transition from Welfare State to Opportunity, Inc. often does, in fact, involve the transfer of responsibility for social service delivery from governmental agencies to private firms. Federal, state, and local governments are all creating public-private partnerships (most often, through contracts) to operate social welfare functions; as measured by the numbers of partnerships, services and dollars, these efforts are growing.[11]

Since taking office in 2000, George W. Bush has further cut federal funding for public housing, food stamps, energy assistance, and most other need-based welfare programs. He reauthorized welfare reform law of 1996 (which ended welfare as a federal "entitlement") and increased the time restrictions and work requirements imposed by the original legislation so as to "empower" people by moving them "off welfare rolls." Bush has also promoted marriage as a component of welfare reform, arguing that "stable families should be the central goal of American welfare policy," and allocating a significant portion of his welfare budget to programs (outsourced to private firms) that encourage marriage between low-income couples. He has promoted private and personal responsibility as the twin bedrocks of post-welfare society, telling TV viewers during his inaugural address: "What you do is as important as anything government does." Bush has promoted the further privatization of public services and has sought to develop "armies of compassion" to address lingering social needs. He established the USA Freedom Corps to promote volunteerism as a solution to problems ranging from illiteracy to poverty, and a President's Council on National and Community Service comprising leaders from business, entertainment, sports, nonprofit agencies, education, and the media to cultivate a private ethic of "service and responsibility."

The White House's reliance on "partnerships" with the private sector, including the culture industries, to accomplish welfare reform also speaks to the advancement of liberalism. Thomas Streeter has shown how the corporate sector has always played a high-profile role in government in the United States (including broadcast policy), to the point where "corporate liberalism" is a more accurate description of liberalism as it developed in the country.[12] However, we are seeing a new twist on this, in that government is increasingly expected not only to embrace corporatism, but to be itself revenue-generating. Advanced or "neo" liberalism entrusts the market to improve upon the Welfare State by "relocating" its focus on governing through social service within the realms of commerce and consumption. Such is the reasoning, we contend, that currently informs reality TV's do-good trend.

While enterprising helping ventures like *Miracle Workers* warrant critique, the leftist tendency to dismiss them as manipulative – for creating a sense of "false consciousness that things are being taken care of" in the absence of the Welfare State, in the words of one critic – doesn't take us very far. We can't understand TV as a technology of governing by comparing representation to "reality" or evaluating the political effectivity of texts. Charity TV is ultimately about a thoroughly commercial medium's move into new social roles and relationships than it is about ideological positioning in any simple sense. To create *Miracle Workers*, for example, TV producers formed alliances with patient-support groups, hospitals, and health-care professionals, and through these private associations became involved in the social work (screening, evaluating, outreach, testing, counseling) of the medical establishment. In determining eligibility of need and administering the flow of care to "deserving" cases, television took over the role of institutionalized charity and, later, public welfare office. By distributing the surplus of capitalism in the manner of its choosing, it advanced a corporate liberal governing strategy that can be traced to the tax-sheltered philanthropies of robber-baron industrial capitalists. The difference between the charity work underwritten by the Carnegie Corporation and other industrial giants and today's TV interventionism is that television has situated the power to shape social life through philanthropy entirely within the logic of the commercial market: There's no distinction – and no presumed need for one – between do-good activity and the manufacture and sale of cultural product. Finally, television facilitated solutions to needs that might once have been addressed by the State with "efficiency" and cost-cutting zeal, implementing extreme versions of risk-management strategies practiced by HMOs and private insurance carriers (only those surgeries with at least a 90 percent success rate were considered for funding by the TV program).

Our aim here is not to mythologize the state of welfare, but to show how TV is working to produce substitutes for it that require analysis on their own terms. It is not a stretch to suggest that reality TV now offers what passes as welfare, and if this is the case we must come to terms with its productive strategies as well as its limitations. While we situate this development within the move to reinvent government, we don't wish to overstate the break from the past, for residual and emerging techniques of governing converge and sometimes collide in TV's charity productions. As John Clarke reminds us, welfare states have historically been deeply contradictory, involved in the "management and regulation" of subordinated populations as well as the provision of services. Moreover, as Rose argues, their success in "implanting in citizens the aspiration to pursue their own civility, well-being and advancement" is what makes newer market-based strategies of governing possible.[13] Reality TV's foray into privatized forms of social service demonstrates this complexity.

Programs like *Miracle Workers* enact templates for self-empowerment as well as commercial alternatives to the provision of social services, but they also draw in part from public welfare's relationship with needy subjects. Because the recipients of TV's concerns are not conceived of as entirely self-sufficient citizens, their capacity to govern themselves through their freedom is subject to question. This uncertainty manifests itself in numerous ways, from the rules and instructions circulated to applicants to a programmatic reliance on surveillance and close supervisory relationships. Reality TV does not acknowledge inequalities of class, gender, and race and cannot explain neediness in such terms. While much is made of the tragic circumstances that lead individuals to television for help, it therefore cannot completely escape the lineage of disciplinary techniques long deployed by charity workers, social workers, and welfare case managers in their bureaucratic relations with needy subjects.

Reality TV modifies these residual techniques, however, by bringing social service into the market and linking its execution to consumer choices, from what TV show to watch and what products to consume, to what volunteer opportunity to pursue and what cause to support. In this sense, it enacts a governing strategy that, as Wendy Brown contends in her critique of neoliberalism, "involves extending and disseminating market values to all institutions and social action."[14] We might even say that reality TV "neoliberalizes" social welfare by managing all conceivable human problems and needs from the vantage point of cultural commerce. Rather than merely lamenting this as evidence of capitalism's further encroachment, we now turn our attention to exactly *how* television manages neediness. As we will show, do-good TV does not hide the "truth" about the changing state of welfare as much as it literally reconstitutes it as a new and improved product of private initiative.

ABC TV: Governing "Better" Communities

Two strands of reality TV have been institutionally positioned as performing a public service in addition to entertaining audiences and making money for shareholders: charity programs and life interventions. Charity programs focus on helping needy people turn their lives around by providing material necessities such as housing (*Extreme Makeover: Home Edition, Mobile Home Disasters*), transportation (*Pimp My Ride*), food (*Random One*), and medical care (*Miracle Workers, Three Wishes*). Life interventions focus on helping the needy by teaching them how to manage and care for themselves and their families properly. The distinction can be blurry, since TV's offers of material help are almost always accompanied by some type of life coaching, therapy, or professional advice, and life-changing ventures often involve cash prizes, giveaways, product placements, and other commercial rewards in addition to the provision of counseling, training, and expertise. We will examine life interventions in the next chapter, while focusing here on charity TV's contribution to the privatization of care and the mobilization of compassion.

The ABC network has played a pivotal role in revitalizing and updating charity TV, and has established the basic cultural template for addressing material needs within the intersecting logics of cultural commerce and welfare reform. The template works like this: TV aims to fix a specific problem or hardship on behalf of an individual or family. It does not do this alone, but works with an alliance of corporate sponsors, donors, experts, skilled laborers, nonprofit agencies, and TV viewers. TV plays the pivotal administrative and "outreach" roles, determining instances of need, orchestrating the interventions, tapping into existing resources for accomplishing them, and documenting the progression of needy subjects from "before" to "after."

Behind the scenes, the Disney Corporation, ABC's parent company, is a member of the intersecting public–private partnerships and alliances that are working to accomplish the "reinvention of government." Disney was a corporate sponsor of the 2005 meeting of the National Conference on Volunteering and Service, which was organized by the Corporation for National Community Service, the Points of Light Foundation, and the USA Freedom Corps, a national volunteer network established by George W. Bush. At the conference, leaders from the public and corporate sectors met to strategize how to develop "volunteer service" (a term used to describe everything from corporate giving to bake sales) to meet America's "pressing social needs." The role of corporate and personal responsibility was made clear by the keynote speeches: US Department of Health and Human Services Secretary Mike Leavitt lectured on the importance of "economic goodness" (a term for compassionate capitalism) and the closing remarks were delivered by Mark Victor Hansen, bestselling author of the self-help book *Chicken Soup for the Soul*. It is telling, but not surprising that popular media figured so prominently, for as Rose and others point out, cultural technologies (such as self-help books) that promise to "empower" individuals become more relevant to practices of citizenship as the State reconfigures its governing capacities and caring responsibilities.

ABC's Better Community Outreach Program is an example. Developed in 2005 under the direction of ABC's McPherson, the Better Community program has a mission of using television to cultivate compassion, volunteerism, and learning in American life – terminology similar to the rhetoric used by Bush and other reformers. The venture is entirely voluntary on the part of ABC, which is no longer required to serve something called the "public interest" as defined and overseen by formal regulators. Rejecting the historical connection between television that serves the public and serious news/information, the Better Community program approaches its outreach goals through popular entertainment, including soap operas, sitcoms and, especially, reality programs. Through its programming and web activities, ABC also aims to bring "pro-social messages" to TV viewers in the service of "empowering" them to learn about the causes that ABC supports. Viewers are asked to participate in an ethical agenda that ABC has determined for them, and to fulfill their civic responsibilities by serving as volunteers in related causes. The public interest is more or less identical to ABC/Disney's corporate aims, as explained on the Disney web site:

> ABC Corporate Initiatives oversees community outreach for the ABC Television Network. Through programming, events and promotions, it identifies and facilitates opportunities that serve ABC's corporate objectives and responsibilities as a corporate citizen. Branded under ABC's A Better Community, all efforts follow a mission to utilize the reach and influence of the media to establish effective community outreach initiatives that serve the public interest, inform and inspire.[15]

The purpose of the Better Community "brand" in relation to the aims of charity TV as a whole is to publicize ABC's role in the mobilization of resources to look after the needy through organizations the TV network did not establish, but that it aligns itself with and acts upon. ABC refers to its relationship with these organizations, which include Habitat for Humanity, Points of Light Foundation, National Center for Healthy Housing, and the Better Business Bureau, as "partnerships." In 2005, ABC situated *Extreme Makeover: Home Edition*, which debuted the previous year, as its most visible cultural contribution to "community outreach" and began referring to Sears and other *Home Edition* sponsors as full-fledged "partners" of the Better Community brand. ABC emphasizes the charitable dimensions of *Home Edition* on air and on the Better Community web site, and uses the program to direct TV viewers to resources (including Sears stores, the Sears American Dream charity, partner organizations, and the Better Community web site) for actualizing their own compassion/personal responsibility. So integrated are television programming, commerce, charity, and volunteerism that ABC does not even refer to *Home Edition* as a TV program in the old sense of broadcast media. On the Better Community web site, the series is also called a "partner" of the ABC Better Community brand, a term that refers not only to its institutional connections but to *Home Edition*'s mission of networking to build a "better community, one family, one house, one donation at a time."

Because *Home Edition* set important precedents for the current wave of charity TV it is worth examining its charitable logic in some detail. According to ABC, *Home Edition* currently receives over 15,000 applications each week from families seeking to improve their housing situations in some way or another. Each season, approximately one dozen are offered home makeovers that are completed in seven days. TV viewers are informed of the chosen family's special needs and attributes as the Home Edition bus wheels into their town to surprise the winning candidates. Their run–down houses are transformed on camera in a "race against time" carried out by a cast of technical experts (architects, stylists, and designers) and a revolving crew of local contractors and construction workers. The narrative suspense hinges on whether or not the team can complete the renovation in time. They always do, proving time and again the program's ability to "transform lives" with a degree of efficiency and speed only the private sector can provide. According to ABC, the transformation of the houses is ultimately a mere catalyst for improving the tragic lives of the residents who live in them. This emotional payoff occurs during the "reveal," when the displaced residents return from a complimentary vacation to Disney World to witness the "unbelievable transformation of the house" and viewers come to understand how the TV crew has "impacted the lives of the deserving families."

The goodwill gesture doesn't cost ABC anything. With high ratings, *Home Edition* is a proven moneymaker. Local businesses and builders are solicited to donate services and materials while corporate sponsors such as Sears and Ford provide household appliances, vehicles, and decorative touches. In a recent essay, John McMurria takes issue with *Home Edition*'s integrated corporate sponsorship deals, noting that the program is essentially an hour-long product placement for Sears and other companies. McMurria contends that commerce has compromised *Home Edition*'s "good Samaritanism" and suggests that in non-commercial hands it would be a better, more authentic example of public service. McMurria is suggesting that the hero of the program be changed from the corporate sector to the public sector, so that the emotional high associated with *Home Edition* can be mobilized for socialism.[16] While we sympathize with these concerns, the traditional leftist perspective orienting McMurria's analysis is ultimately limited in its capacity to grapple with the complexities of governmental power. Replacing corporate sponsors with public agencies may indeed produce a different TV show – but that show would be linked to another history of governmental relations, as Rose and Clarke remind us in their caution against romanticizing the complicated history of the Welfare State. *Home Edition*'s ability to fold the legacy of charity as a pre-welfare strategy of managing neediness into cultural enterprise is what makes it an actualized example of the "political rationality" that presently shapes welfare reform. Besides calling upon the private sector to resolve needs, *Home Edition* promotes the particular behaviors and forms of conduct that emerge from this political rationality, including homeownership, self-sufficiency, entrepreneurialism, and volunteerism. The program does not simply "encode" these activities ideologically; it demonstrates them, enacts them, and directs TV viewers to a range of resources for accomplishing them on their own. This "can-do" approach to the privatization of public service is not without contradictions, but it does require a different conceptual focus than has typically guided television studies.

TV Outreach and the Ownership Society

The premise of *Home Edition* hinges on the unavailability of welfare as an entitlement. However, the program's credibility rests on the idea that the alternative to the Welfare State – private do-goodism – is reasonable and fair. This can be tricky, given the tension between the extent to which many people in the United States apparently feel unable to care for themselves (hence the large volume of applications received) and the fact that ABC will ultimately turn most of them away. One way the tension is minimized from the outset is through a focus on homeowners and an exclusion of apartment dwellers, including residents of public housing and Section Eight facilities. The houses may be small, run-down, sparsely furnished, and/or on the brink of foreclosure, but they nonetheless exist as symbols of the so-called Ownership Society. By establishing this basic program rule, *Home Edition* does not have to deal with the factors that prevent many Americans from achieving homeownership.

The programmatic focus on homeowners serves another role as well, in that it provides the basis for promoting home ownership as a foundation for executing personal responsibility and therefore good citizenship. *Home Edition* is not explicitly positioned in relation to housing policy reforms such as reduced federal spending on public housing and shakeups (including a greater role for faith-based charities) at the Department of Housing and Urban Development (HUD). Nor does it directly promote George Bush's American Dream program, which siphons funding away from public housing services to promote homeownership in low-income populations through (limited) forms of down-payment assistance as well as homeownership education and training programs. *Home Edition* does, however, present homeownership as an appropriate accomplishment that distinguishes the worthy poor from welfare recipients still caught in a cycle of dependency on the State. In the following episode summary from the ABC web site, we can see how *Home Edition* simultaneously makes extreme socioeconomic hardship visible and erases the public sector as a viable or desirable resource for the needy. At the same time, it finds human agency and hope in a woman's personal responsibility as a mother, which is evident from her heroic efforts and sacrifices to provide her children with a privately owned home (however small and broken-down). The fact that she has obtained this symbol of the Ownership Society through her own work and ambition is precisely what qualifies this woman for *Home Edition*'s attention. She is classified as worthy of help because she exemplifies the path to freedom and self-empowerment emphasized by neoliberal policies and discourses:

> Veronica and her family have had a life of adversity and struggle. Having bought the first and only home she could afford, Veronica raises her eight children – including two sets of twins – in a home that would be cramped for a family of four, let alone nine. A strong woman, she is determined to raise her children in a safe and loving home, keeping them off the streets and away from violence for good. But the house isn't much of a safe haven. The extremely hazardous Ginyard home has exposed live wires sticking out of the drywall, mold from constant flooding in their basement and holes in the walls and ceilings. The kids have to sleep in makeshift bedrooms in the basement and the attic. Veronica works two jobs just to make ends meet and uses public transportation to travel to and from work, as her run-down car sits in the driveway. The house, the struggle to pay the bills and the years of stress has taken a toll on her, but despite everything, this hard-working single mom is determined to provide the best life for her family.[17]

The aim of instilling the practice of homeownership is taken up more explicitly by the Sears American Dream Campaign, *Home Edition*'s principal do-good partner. Both the TV program and the ABC Better Community web site direct TV viewers to this campaign, which is described as a "community commitment" to help people "maintain and outfit their homes and families" by providing financial assistance as well as educational programs. According to Sears, homeownership is not only about having a place to live or even achieving a desirable lifestyle. Along with organized religion and the family, it is also a mechanism for minimizing social and material problems, from criminality to financial stress. In this sense, homeownership is positioned as a technique for performing one's civic obligations within what Rose calls the "new regime of the actively responsible self." Rose argues individuals are now expected to fulfill their duties as citizens by taking care of and actualizing themselves, first and foremost. The American Dream campaign situates owning a home as one way of doing this:

> Did you know that in communities where home ownership is common, children excel in school and adults are more likely to be involved in their communities by voting, volunteering and attending religious services? Additionally, where home ownership increases, crime declines and businesses thrive. That's why the Sears American Dream Campaign is not only helping American families achieve and preserve their American Dreams, it is helping to strengthen the fabric of our communities . . . Homes are the foundation of our families, neighborhoods and nation. Home equity creates wealth for low- and middle-income families. It's easy to see that increasing home ownership and maintenance may be the single most effective way to fortify the foundation of our country.[18]

The Sears American Dream campaign web site links the governing rationalities of privatization and personal responsibility to consumer training and the sale of Sears home merchandise. Through a partnership with NeighborWorks, a nonprofit agency created by the US Congress to "revitalize communities through affordable housing opportunities, training and technical assistance," the Sears American Dream web site offers practical tips for affording a home and taking care of it properly once that goal has been accomplished. The section "Get in Shape with Financial Fitness" educates low-income people on how to obtain a home, focusing on personal behaviors such as "create a financial goal with a timeline," "establish a budget and stick to it," "control your wants and focus on your needs," and "find a trusted financial advisor." Having evoked irresponsible choices and irrational consumption as the cause of financial difficulties, the web site then teaches people how to become responsible consumers of the home-related products sold in Sears stores. This consumer training is presented, alongside the "financial fitness" advice on homeownership, as another dimension of "community outreach": "Now that you've got your house, you need to transform it into a home, which means making lots of decisions about appliances and décor," explains the section on "Home Maintenance," which directs users to printable checklists to help them "get into the habit" of taking care of houses (including lawns), as well as specific techniques for "choosing" appliances and other accoutrements. As the web site explains:

> It takes a lot of work to outfit and maintain a home and family. For homeowners, especially for those struggling to make ends meet, an ounce of prevention is definitely worth a pound of cure. That's why the Sears American Dream Campaign is educating low- and moderate-income families nationwide about the importance of home maintenance. It's just one way the Sears American Dream Campaign is strengthening communities one home at a time.

Casting Needy Individuals

Another way that *Home Edition* narrows the pool of applicants is by choosing families with "unique and extraordinary" situations. Public welfare programs rely on measurable and verifiable data (i.e., income, hours worked, marital status, number of children, time on welfare) to determine eligibility of need; all applicants who meet these "objective" requirements are entitled to benefits (presuming such benefits exist). *Home Edition,* on the other hand, helps only a small number of families: "We can't help everyone, even though we wish that we could," explains the program of its limited capacity to manage unmet housing needs. The lucky few are selected by the casting department, which raises the important question: What does it mean when a process that has historically been carried out by social service professionals is turned over to commercial entertainment agents? The ABC web site solicits applications to *Home Edition* on the basis of two criteria – having a home that "desperately needs attention" and having a "compelling story to tell." However, the program's much more narrow focus on personal "tragedies and traumas" was confirmed by an internal 2005

ABC memo obtained by the Smoking Gun, an investigative web site. Sent to local ABC affiliates, it described a list of the specific "tragedies" it hoped to feature on upcoming episodes of *Home Edition*, from a child killed by a drunk driver to muscular dystrophy, and urged local station personnel to look for such cases in their areas. This is not surprising, since previous seasons of *Home Edition* have also emphasized families coping with childhood illnesses and chronic diseases. The debut episode set the stage by renovating the home of a working-class family whose small daughter was recovering from leukemia. This search for personal trauma is rooted in the economic interests of ABC in that its casting professionals search for stories with the emotional impact to produce high ratings and therefore profitability. However, it also works as a device for determining eligibility of need and classifying the "worthy" poor.

Attempted self-sufficiency and an ethic of volunteerism also determine which families are selected, maintains executive producer Tom Forman:

> We look for people who deserve it. It's tough to judge. It's people who have given their whole lives and suddenly find themselves in a situation where they need a little help. Most of the families we end up doing are nominations. The kinds of families we're looking for don't say, "Gee, I need help." They're quietly trying to solve their problems themselves and it's a neighbor or a coworker who submits an application on their behalf.

By rewarding those who struggle without expecting or asking for help, *Home Edition* discourages what reformers call "dependency." At the same time, it positively singles out people who demonstrate personal responsibility to others. Low-paid public employees who protect the United States from external and internal threats – including military personnel, police officers, and firefighters – appear often. Usually, such recipients have fallen into financial insecurity because of an illness or other unforeseen circumstance. In one episode, a national guardsman whose family suffered greatly financially when he was called up for active duty in Iraq was presented with a home renovation. Typifying how official government (in this case the military) not only cooperates with but also facilitates the privatization of care through TV, the soldier was flown home for an unscheduled visit to view the final

(a)

(b)

Illustration 1.2   Families must sell themselves as worthy and needy in their application videos. In this episode of *Extreme Makeover: Home Edition*, a minister "devoted to community service," his wife, and his three daughters request the program's help with a crumbling pavement and other problems they cannot afford to fix (Endemol Entertainment USA and Lock & Key Productions for ABC, 2005)

reveal, and various military agencies promoted the episode on their web sites.

Individuals who take up duties of the Welfare State within the context of their personal lives are often rewarded for doing so by *Home Edition*. Social workers who adopt large numbers of homeless and/or chronically ill children and struggle financially to care for them on their own modest salaries have appeared on several episodes as personifications of the "compassionate citizenship" promoted by the Bush administration. In a related episode, a poverty-stricken woman who had "turned her own life around" was operating a small nonprofit charity out of her home. The mission of Sadie Holmes Help Services, Inc. was to help other poor people in the woman's low-income community by providing them with donated food, clothing, and furniture. When the donations overtook the woman's small house, according to ABC, she moved her family into a rented apartment. When the house was badly damaged by a hurricane and a subsequent fire, her homeowner's insurance was cancelled, and she was unable to afford the needed repairs. She nonetheless managed to continue operating the charity out of the now dilapidated home, while her family made do in the small apartment. The woman was rewarded by *Home Edition* with a brand new home, not only because her own house was beyond repair but because she exemplified the political value placed on individuals who, despite their own disadvantages, are devoted to an individualized ethic of compassion and responsibility. Taking welfare quite literally into her own hands, this woman not only overcame her own dependency but channeled her own limited resources (her unpaid labor, the house) into services the public sector no longer wishes to provide.

While the needy families who appear on *Home Edition* are revered as decent citizens whose pitiable circumstances are mainly due to extraordinary bad luck, their neediness nonetheless prevents them from playing an active role in the transformation of their home. There is a contradiction between the claim of using the market to empower people and the fact that they are not really allowed to exercise their "freedom of choice," to use the terminology of neoliberal reformers. *Home Edition*'s professional experts decide what physical and cosmetic changes to make to the house without consulting the family members and, in the process, assume paternalistic authority over them. Although this paternalistic relationship is cloaked in kindness it constitutes a hierarchy of freedom and authority nonetheless. Behind the scenes, *Home Edition*'s address to potential candidates is much more authoritarian. The application process incorporates a history of regulating, monitoring, and controlling welfare recipients, as documented by Linda Gordon, John Gilliom, and other historians.[19] To be considered, individuals must answer questions about household income, education level, existing debt and involvement in lawsuits, and prior conviction of a crime, whether as "simple as a driving violation or as serious as armed robbery." They are not trusted to tell the truth about this last question in particular, and so are warned: "Be honest: We will find out sooner or later through our comprehensive background checks." The applicants must also agree to provide three years' worth of official tax records to prove their answers to the above questions if they are selected. While enacted as a private alternative to welfare, *Home Edition* collects, evaluates, and stores the same information gathered by public welfare offices (even if it does not guarantee "benefits" as a result). It presumes that people who ask for help are more prone than middle-class people to criminality and dishonesty and that they have no inherent right to privacy. Because of this, they can be governed in much harsher ways (i.e., subjected to background checks and verification technologies) than the liberal ideal of "governing through freedom" would suggest. *Home Edition*'s purpose is not only to govern needy people but also to ensure its own profitability. The impetus to weed out individuals who might be discovered to be amoral or unworthy is also about protecting the *Home Edition* brand.

There is another way that *Home Edition* resonates with welfare reform discourse, and that is by illustrating and rewarding enterprising activity among the needy. An example here is an episode featuring the African-American Kirkwood family of Port Orchard, Washington. The family applied to *Home Edition* when they found themselves living with exposed wiring, open walls, and poor ventilation caused by a failed home-remodeling project. Their main concern was a toxic black mold creeping over their floors and walls, which eventually forced the parents and their five children to move into a crowded motel room. The case fit the criteria for *Home Edition* in that the Kirkwoods' story was not only dramatic but also life-threatening: "Their house was making them sick . . . their dream – to get back in." The family documented the situation (including the oozing mold) using home-video equipment and concluded their tape with the plea: "ABC: please do something." However, more than a year passed and nothing was heard from the TV network. According to the *Home Edition* application, this non-response is typical: "Due to the volume of applications received," families are never contacted unless they are chosen to appear on the program. Eventually, *Home Edition* did take up the Kirkwoods' case in a two-hour episode that addressed the family's struggle to get onto the TV program, and thus offers some insights into the selection process. In the explanation for the "special" nature of this episode, viewers are introduced to 11-year-old Jael Kirkwood, who not only filed the application but also used her ingenuity to get the family on the air. While Jael admits to having been devastated when she didn't hear back, much is made of the fact that she didn't take no for an answer. The girl began telephoning *Home Edition*'s casting department on a daily basis and contacted families from past episodes for their advice on getting the attention of producers. She also visited the mayor of Port Orchard, who contacted *Home Edition* on her behalf, and who was praised on camera as the right sort of public official who goes the extra mile for her constituents, not by directing them to local care resources but by getting their case accepted by national television. However, Jael's "sheer determination" is said to be the deciding factor. While the arguments for welfare reform are never explicitly stated in the episode, Jael's precocious drive to take responsibility for her needy family by mobilizing every resource at her disposal is rewarded against an implied counter-image of the stereotypical welfare recipient who must learn not to passively cling to government "entitlements." This image is historically coded in racial and gender terms, despite the move away from explicit stereotyping in neoliberal discourse.

Welfare recipients, as Martin Gilens and others have shown, have long been conceptualized within political and popular discourse as lazy, dishonest, helpless, and unmotivated.[20] While neoliberal policies officially minimize these stereotypical associations, they lurk within the rationalities of welfare reform and reappear in television's attempt to manage neediness. Black Americans are even more likely to be constructed this way, given the intersection of economic and racial disenfranchisement in the United States. The role of the mother in the reproduction of welfare "dependency" comes into play in this discourse as well, in that the figure of the black, unmarried welfare mother has come to stand for the negative connotations of need-based welfare programs, particularly their cyclical nature. Jael's turn to *Home Edition* for help is differentiated from this representational legacy and situated within the proactive, self-enterprising activities that make up "good citizenship" according to neoliberal regimes. As *Home Edition* explained, it was "the tenacity of one girl" (and implicitly not a formalized system of rights and responsibilities) that got the family the "home they deserve." At the end of the episode, the camera lingers on a group of neighbors gathered outside the Kirkwood house, mingling with the family members, the masses of anonymous workers and volunteers, and the *Home Edition* cast, while the musical theme "We'll Make it Through" plays in the background. The scenario draws from a nostalgic image of community cooperation (agrarian barn-raising rituals come to mind), but the long list of sponsors/partners that follow affirms that without television's involvement the Kirkwoods would be nowhere: It was TV that recognized and rewarded Jael's enterprising skills, and it was TV that mustered the private resources for the intervention and administered the flow of care.

Self-enterprise is required of people who wish to appear on *Home Edition* as needy families. While applicants are addressed as potential criminals, they are also advised to be enterprising, to work hard to "sell themselves" to the producers and potential audiences on camera. Because the individuals who apply for help are not presumed to possess the know-how to sell themselves on their own, detailed instructions are provided. In addition to answering socioeconomic questions and signing legal documents, would-be families are required to produce a video narrative (borrow a camera if you don't have one, instructs *Home Edition*). They are guided in this process by a complete shot list, tips for handling the camera properly (no zooms allowed), and a sample script. The videos must follow certain conventions established by *Home Edition* to solicit viewer empathy, including having children give the guided tour of their own rooms (if they have one) and filming the entire family outside the home for an introduction that incorporates the scripted line "Hi, ABC, We're the _____ Family (big waves and smiles and lots of energy.)" Successful applicants must follow these guidelines, a requirement that puts ABC in a position of cultural power while also making the production of *Home Edition* more cost-efficient (the free home videos are used to introduce the families). All members of the household are required not only to appear in the video but to sell their stories to a potential TV audience of millions: "We understand that talking about your situation can be difficult but please do not hold back and PLEASE don't turn off the camera if you feel emotional." They are also instructed to make themselves "camera ready" and are presented with tips on personal grooming and wardrobe choices: "Please know that IF you are selected for the show this tape could be used on television so make sure appearances are fit for TV! Ladies, please take the time to put on light makeup and do your hair. You should dress as if you were going out for a family dinner or nice lunch," advises the application.

Privatizing Care, Mobilizing Compassion

Home Edition's affinity to the neoliberalization of welfare and the privatization of social services was clarified by a number of "After the Storm" episodes devoted to helping communities affected by Hurricane Katrina. Because the devastation of an entire geographic region was at stake and thousands of families qualified as "exceptionally needy and deserving," the program could not rely on its usual strategies of selection. The new aim was to undertake relief efforts that "would benefit more than one family." This did not mean channeling resources into state and municipal governments: any role of the public sector in both preventing and resolving the crisis was eradicated by these episodes. Instead, the *Home Edition* team channeled energy and resources into assisting local nongovernmental private relief efforts such as a privately funded low-income health clinic that was displaced by the storm and was operating out of a double-wide trailer, and a hard-hit New Orleans church that doubled as a local charity for homeless people.

Other strategies for helping Katrina victims were tied to cultural commerce, such as sending busloads of displaced families who lost everything in the disaster on a complimentary $250 shopping spree at Sears. Besides demonstrating the urgency of restoring private, nongovernmental, and faith-based charities to their full operating capacities, storylines stressed the role of both corporate goodwill (Sears and its American Dream campaign played a prominent role in all of the revitalization efforts) and individual consumption to the restoration of normalcy. When Laura Bush agreed to appear in a cameo on one of the special Katrina episodes, *Home Edition*'s relationship to welfare was made explicit: On the White House's official web site, Bush said she went to the filming to discuss the importance of "partnerships," from the Sears truck filled with donated goods to volunteer medical workers to the Army Corps of Engineers. "This is what it's going to take . . . partnerships between governments, between corporations, between individuals, faith-based groups to make sure all of these people will really be able to rebuild their lives." The *Los Angeles Times* put it more bluntly, explaining that "Mrs. Bush's spokeswoman saw a conservative message in the show's usual story line: the private sector doing good work, rather than waiting around for the federal government to do it. That, she said, was what the First Lady wanted to endorse."

The private sector enlisted by *Home Edition* to manage the lingering needs of a post-welfare society is not limited to corporations and businesses: it also includes "armies" of individuals who are called upon to voluntarily donate their time and personal resources to the care of the less fortunate. At the end of each episode, *Home Edition* host Ty Pennington also encourages the audience to log onto the ABC Better Community web site, where ABC talent quote Martin Luther King, Ralph Waldo Emerson, Walt Disney, and other well-known figures in streaming public service announcements that extol volunteerism as civic obligation (the announcements are also broadcast on television). TV viewers are encouraged to take steps toward fulfilling this obligation by seeking out the organizations and charities featured on the web site – including nongovernmental housing agencies such as Habitat for Humanity and Home Aid and the Sears American Dream Campaign – and by researching volunteer opportunities through ABC's partnerships with the Points of Light Foundation, Volunteer.org, and other agencies. In this effort to transform TV viewers into civically engaged citizens, ABC encourages allegiance not to the State or the body politic, but to an ethical "community" filtered through the Better Community Brand. In this sense, it constructs a template for citizenship that is not unlike the participatory charities (such as Race for the Cure) analyzed by Samantha King. Drawing from Rose, King's research shows that in "the contemporary organization of political responsibility, subjects are addressed and understood as individuals who are responsible for themselves and others in their 'community.'" This responsibility is not to be demonstrated by "the paying of taxes to support social welfare programs, or by the expression of dissent and the making of political demands on behalf of one's community, but through participation in practices of volunteerism and philanthropy." Do-good reality television works in similar ways, by aligning TV viewers with an individualistic ethic of compassion and the technical means through which it can be harnessed for the good of the "community."[21]

Volunteerism is promoted, not just as a personal and community responsibility but also as a venue for middle-class consumer choice and lifestyle maximization. Tips on volunteering provided courtesy of the Corporation for National and Community Service, a public-private agency devoted to "supporting the American culture of citizenship, service and responsibility," situate the importance of finding the "right" volunteer position as a choice that will lead not only to service but to self-fulfillment. "Sometimes the hardest part of volunteering can be finding an opportunity that fits your personality," explains the site, which recommends customizing the experience to one's personal interests, beliefs, and experiences so that it is "enjoyable and reward-ing." Not only are volunteers elevated to a position of civic power over the "needy" in their capacity to determine which causes are interesting and worthwhile, they are also encouraged to see the prac-tice of compassion as a variation of other consumer-related activities. Unlike the restrictive guidance imposed on people who apply to appear on *Home Edition* and the paternalistic requirement that the chosen families leave the renovations entirely up to the experts, TV viewers are offered the "freedom" to tailor their own volunteer experi-ence from a list of possibilities, not unlike the shoppers who, with just one click, are invited to customize the look of home-décor merchan-dise using the Sears Virtual Makeover Program. For TV viewers who are not inclined to volunteer, compassionate consumption presents another sanctioned (though less customizable) way to participate in the mobilization of private helping resources through television. In the Katrina episodes, people moved by the human toll of the disaster were asked to contribute money to Winds of Change, a fundraising drive organized through the integrated partnership between *Home Edition* and Sears. And on the Better Community web site, they are asked to help by purchasing *Home Edition* DVDs, with the promise that $1 per unit sold will be donated to charity.

The Proliferation of Charity TV

Home Edition's ratings success did not go by unnoticed by the televi-sion industry. In 2005, NBC announced that it also was "granting wishes for deserving individuals" for a prime-time television show entitled *Three Wishes*. Hosted by Christian recording artist Amy Grant, the program offers help to individuals with a range of needs that are not limited to housing. Each week, the program travels to a small or mid-sized town, typically in the Southern and Midwestern Bible Belts. A huge outdoor tent bearing the corporate logo of Home Depot and other program sponsors is set up in the "town square" (Home Depot was also a sponsor of the 2005 National Volunteer Conference in Washington). Thousands of local people wait in line to enter the tent so they can plead their cases to the *Three Wishes* casting agents in person. The viewer sees only a tightly compressed version of this fusion of the updated breadline and the small-town faith revival. The implications of the mass rejections that ultimately ensue are greatly minimized by a narrative focus on the three individuals who are helped on each episode. In interweaving stories, Grant and her on-camera assistants work tirelessly on behalf of these individuals to solve their immediate material problems and make their wishes come true.

The criteria for determining who deserves help are not made explicit but, as with *Home Edition*, some key themes are apparent. Beneficiaries of the interventions often have tragic circumstances that are evoked to

Illustration 1.3   *Three Wishes* host Amy Grant greets the residents of Brookings, South Dakota as they wait in line to present their "cases." Only three will have their wishes granted by NBC (NBC Universal TV for NBC, 2005)

rank their needs above those of others who also spent hours in line hoping to appear on the program. Seriously ill and disabled people (particularly children and teenagers) who need costly medical treatments they cannot afford are often chosen, and here *Three Wishes* anticipated ABC's *Miracle Workers*. By facilitating access to these services *Three Wishes* enacts a high-profile private alternative to publicly funded health and insurance programs (such as Medicaid and medical disability) that is limited in its capacity to help only a handful of the millions of Americans who require some form of assistance with medical care. Unlike the familiar image of the impersonal, slow-moving bureaucracy and surly personnel associated with state welfare programs, the *Three Wishes* team provide swift, energetic, empathetic, and personalized attention to the people who appear on the show. As TV "caseworkers" the hosts are able to focus entirely on coming up with solutions to the special needs of individuals whose stories they have heard personally and who they come to know intimately. However, the caseworkers have another crucial job besides attending to needy subjects. Their role is also entrepreneurial in that they must personally mobilize and coordinate the private resources required to make their wishes come true.

Like *Home Edition*, *Three Wishes* classifies and rewards certain modes of conduct, including personal responsibility and compassion for others. This code of ethics and conduct is differentiated from the system of state-sanctioned rights and responsibilities emphasized during the welfare stage of capitalism. As the *Three Wishes* casting call explains, "We are looking for emotional stories of people in need. We want to help deserving people. People who always help others, but never think of themselves." In the debut episode, a sick high-school teacher was characterized this way when the program agreed to grant her request for a new football field. From her hospital bed, the teacher explained that her students needed a place to play competitive football. The public school where she worked did not have the resources to purchase new turf for the field; nor did the town where the high school was located. *Three Wishes* did not dwell on the reasons for this funding shortage, but instead asked a private manufacturer to donate the needed materials. The host handling the case flew across the country to meet personally with the CEO of the company on camera. While the executive initially stammered that he was "not in the business of philanthropy," he did agree to make the donation, probably because television was involved. In this episode, *Three Wishes* demonstrated "compassionate" capitalism as well as specific techniques of enlisting the corporate support of nonprofit causes.

By granting the teacher's wish, *Three Wishes* demonstrated a private solution to a particular (and seemingly isolated) local problem that is actually part of a larger pattern – inadequate and profoundly unequal funding for public schools, particularly those located in low-income areas. Other episodes also gloss over the shrinking public sector by granting individual wishes that compensate for shortages of municipal and state resources. In one, *Three Wishes* secured private funding to build a town library to fulfill the dream of a sick teenager who loved to read books. According to the American Library Association, "America's libraries are now facing the deepest budget cuts in history. Across the country libraries are reducing their hours, cutting staff or closing their doors – drastic measures that were not taken even during the Great Depression." To overcome this problem, some supporters of libraries have advocated the pursuit of "diversified" private resources to insulate the public library system from a "dependency" on tax-based government funding. Although *Three Wishes* did not reference this trend, it did enact the new method of library funding within the highly emotional context of one girl's chronic health problems. In a similar vein, *Three Wishes* agreed to help a young woman burdened with many thousands of dollars in student loan debt. Many recent college graduates are in this situation because federal grant and tuition assistance programs created during the Great Society era have been drastically downsized. Even low-interest student loans – which, unlike grants, must be repaid when the student graduates – are becoming harder to obtain: This episode of *Three Wishes* appeared around the time the House Education and the Workforce Committee approved $14.5 billion in cuts to spending on student loans – a move that critics said would cost the average student borrower $5,800 more to attend college. It was in this broader but unstated context that *Three Wishes* staff personally contacted Iowa Student Loan, the nonprofit lending institution to which the student was indebted. According to a Des Moines newspaper, the president/CEO of Iowa Student Loan was "happy to help" the Iowa State University graduate's wish come true, but he also emphasized that his decision to waive her loans was an exception, not the rule. "Many young people begin their post-college career already in debt," said the official, who placed responsibility for the situation squarely on parents and the young and advised, "it's never too early to start financially planning for college."[22]

Three Wishes also demonstrates personal responsibility and self-enter-prise in storylines that often overlap with contemporary welfare reform discourse. The program has helped several low-income single mothers with a wish to become better providers for their children by making it possible for them to pursue higher education and/or start their own small businesses. The women who are helped by NBC have, impor-tantly, already "chosen" the path toward self-empowerment. The program is very clear to differentiate them from an implied image of single mothers who "wait around for" or "depend on" Welfare State entitlements. It is worth noting that when the public sector explicitly appears on *Three Wishes*, it is shown to be a rigid bureaucracy that is more hindrance than help to those who seek to empower themselves and their families. The program does call attention to elaborate systems of rules and paternalistic forms of address found in public bureaucra-cies, but these are dismissed as unavoidable annoyances rather than power dynamics worth addressing. In one episode, a boy wished for a new pickup truck for his stepfather. According to the narrative, the boy was grateful to the man for taking care of his family when his father died, and here the intervention overlapped with the current promotion of marriage and stable two-parent families as a way to overcome the need for welfare programs for low-income women and children. Upon discovering that the boy had not been adopted by his stepfather owing to the maze of official paperwork involved, host Amy Grant used the power of television to push the documents through a stalled bureaucratic process. After taking TV cameras into the county courthouse, she eventually tracked down the appointed judge during his off hours (he was at the airport, flying his personal plane) to obtain the necessary signature.

Three Wishes circulates discourses, or ways of thinking about welfare, the public sector, the family, and corporate America. However, like other charity programs it goes beyond this discursive role to also present applications, demonstrations, and techniques that are governmental in the sense of shaping and guiding human behavior toward specific ends. The *Three Wishes* Dollars program is an example of how charity TV incorporates behavioral action on the part of participants as well as viewers. According to NBC publicity, this "community outreach" program (which doubles as publicity for *Three Wishes*) works through the marriage of commerce and individual actions. The network kick-started the *Three Wishes* Dollars venture by traveling to 15 "markets" to grant a wish to a local charity and "surprise shoppers and restaurant patrons by picking up the tab at select retailers, including grocery stores and restaurants." NBC pays the retailers with $1 bills carrying *Three Wishes* stickers, which "cashiers will then distribute to customers with their change." The corporate goal is to "drive recipients" to the NBC/ *Three Wishes* web site by "encouraging consumers to use the marked dollars to fulfill another person's wish to coincide with the show's theme." According to Barbara Blangiardi, vice-president of marketing and special projects at NBC, "It's about touching people individually and creating and weaving a magical web of support and community around these individual wishes . . . We thought this grassroots program that . . . demonstrated and exemplified the [purpose] of the show was the kind of thing we wanted to do." NBC also stated an intention to track and publicize the ways in which consumers used their special *Three Wishes* dollars. In the trade press, NBC executives predicted that the dollars would continue to generate good deeds. Summing up how commerce and compassion intersect in the network's approach to community outreach, Blangiardi explained: "We are using the stickered dollar bills so the currency will get into the marketplace. And [we want to] encourage people to use that money to do something for someone else. This is a unique execution for us."[23]

Cable networks from Arts & Entertainment to MTV have also moved into charity TV programming, recognizing that reality-based do-good ventures are not only good for the network's image but can also be a successful venue for high ratings. As one A&E executive put it, "Television used to have a public-service factor. Now the cable industry is finding a way to embrace those roots and offer entertainment programming that might also do some good. That's the magic bullet if you can get both." While the charity programs developed by cable tend to be aimed at specialized audiences and focus on a single need, such MTV's car-makeover show *Pimp My Ride*, they incorporate many of the conventions and techniques discussed so far. The A&E network, which is owned by the Disney Corporation, has developed a broader approach with *Random One*, a grittier version of charity TV that overlaps with the domestic/lifestyle intervention discussed in the next section. The official aim of this program is to "breathe life" into the parable of the Good Samaritan by "scouting the streets of America looking for people who need help solving everyday problems." According to the *Random One* web site, the program also demonstrates the "power of grassroots philanthropy, defined as people helping people one at a time." Toward that end, it advocates for "individuals who are ready to better themselves," asking the question: "What can we do to help you help yourself?" Episodes have helped homeless people find shelter and unemployed people find jobs, among other good deeds. Even more than network charity programs, *Random One* emphasizes the need for personal responsibility. It does not claim to make people's dreams come true, nor does it present television as a safety net. In fact, it does not even accept applications, but instead selects people who need help on a "random" basis. What the program claims to offer is a "nudge, helpful push in a life-changing direction," one that will presumably fold into the larger society via the tips for making a difference, from donating old clothes to the Salvation Army to "cleaning up a local park or playground," promoted on the *Random One* web site. Sometimes it works and sometimes it doesn't, says A&E. The impetus to rise above the needs of the post-welfare society is on the individual.

Charity TV is mainly a United States-based production (although some of the shows, including *Home Edition*, do circulate internationally). This is undoubtedly related to both the economic dominance of US culture and advertising industries and the minimized state of welfare in the United States compared to other parts of the world. However, the format has begun to spread internationally, particularly to locations that, for complex reasons, lack a state infrastructure for providing social services. One example is Iraq, where *Labor and Materials*, a variation of *Extreme Makeover: Home Edition*, debuted in 2004 to address the unmet needs of Iraqi families whose homes had been destroyed during the ongoing US intervention. According to a description of the program, "In 15-minute episodes, broken windows are made whole again. Blasted walls slowly rise again. Fancy furniture and luxurious carpets appear without warning in the living rooms of poor families. Over six weeks, houses blasted by U.S. bombs regenerate in a home-improvement show for a war-torn country."[24] Corporate sponsors do not figure in this example of public service; instead, each episode of *Labor and Materials* encourages Iraqi TV viewers to donate the goods and services needed for future interventions. What links the program to the US version of charity TV, and to the interventions we will examine in the next chapter, is the enactment of private care through television as a foundation of "good" government.

Chapter 2

TV Interventions:
Personal Responsibility and Techniques of the Self

In fall 2005, television's Dr. Phil went on location to communities devastated by Hurricane Katrina. In addition to encouraging volunteerism and raising relief funds through his nonprofit Dr. Phil Foundation, the PhD-holding talk-show host visited makeshift shelters where he counseled victims how to overcome anger and fear, and "rebuild their lives" in the aftermath of the worst natural disaster in national memory. His gallant attempt to mobilize nongovernmental resources to deal with the emergency is another example of TV's proactive role in the privatization of social services. However, Dr. Phil's even more pressing concern with storm-related psychological issues and hurdles moved beyond the handling of material needs to the management and care of the "self" as a way of overcoming hardship. When Dr. Phil brought his bestselling brand of self-help to the Houston Metrodome and invited displaced individuals who were "upset with FEMA" or had been "drinking since the hurricane" to appear on his therapeutic TV program, he also brought the governing capacities of another strand of reality TV – the life intervention – into focus.

Since its cultural explosion in the late 1990s, popular reality TV has presented an array of techniques for diagnosing personal problems and transforming so-called needy and "at-risk" individuals into successful managers of their lives and futures. "Life intervention" is the term we use to describe these programs, which mobilize professional motivators and lifestyle experts, from financial advisors to life coaches, to help people overcome hurdles in their personal, professional, and domestic lives. The intervention can focus on transforming a person's entire relationship with her/himself, or it can attempt to resolve specific problems related to raising children (*Supernanny, Nanny 911, Brat Camp*), work (*Starting Over*), marriage and dating (*Dr. Phil, Shalom for the Home, Judge Judy*), household management (*Clean House, Mission: Organization*), personal finances (Suze Orman), hygiene (*How Clean is Your House*), health and fitness (*The Biggest Loser, Honey We're Killing the Kids*), or addiction (*Intervention*). Makeover programs (*The Swan, Queer Eye for the Straight Guy, Extreme Makeover*), which will be analyzed in the following chapter, can also work secondarily as life interventions, in that they often provide some form of therapy, life coaching, or motivational guidance to help people overcome their inner "problems" and link the desired "outcome" of physical transformation to future personal and professional achievements.

Since the late 1990s, life interventions have become an expected staple of reality TV programming, on major network as well as specialized cable channels. With their steady supply of therapeutic experts and lifestyle managers, these programs have brought about what might be called the neoliberalization of social work through reality TV, a phenomenon that is connected in complex, and sometimes contradictory, ways to the political rationalities of welfare reform outlined in the previous chapter. In the early twentieth century, social workers sought to disseminate the science of "right living" to working-class and immigrant populations, believing that positive changes of habit and conduct would improve the quality of life for these groups, and consequently stabilize society as a whole.[1] Social workers (and before them, charity workers) were integral to the dispersion of liberal strategies of governing through "freedom," in that they offered new forms of expertise that would make it possible for people to regulate and manage their everyday lives without direct supervision or coercion. Social workers cast their gaze on a wide range of "problems" related to health, sanitation, nutrition, delinquency, child welfare, household management, recreation, and social and mental hygiene. Eventually, many of their concerns and techniques for "watching over" needy and "at-risk" populations were folded into public programs and services overseen by the expanding Welfare State. Reality TV draws from social work's twin legacy as a professionalized helping intervention and as an indirect and diffused mode of behavioral guidance and social control. However, reality TV also reprivatizes social work by conceptualizing and conducting life interventions within the neoliberal logic of self-entrepreneurialism and commerce. There is still an emphasis on instilling the right way of doing things as a matter of an individual's "free choice," but the training involved is now more explicitly tied to the governing authority of the market.

During the Progressive Era, social workers were part of a class of reformers who, in addition to improving individuals, also fought to temper and regulate the power of industrial capitalism through federal policy interventions, from child labor laws to food safety legislation. In the 1960s, social work became a home for politically conscious professionals who sometimes aligned themselves with movements for social change, including civil rights, economic justice, and feminism. The advocacy potential of social work's turn was also illustrated by a crop of progressive dramas that appeared on television during that period. As Mary Ann Watson and Aniko Bodroghkozy have shown, these programs played out contradictions of liberal government through professionals who attempted to insert themselves into struggles and policy debates over racial discrimination, abortion, and fair housing, among other issues. One of the most provocative of these dramas, *East Side/West Side*, featured a social worker who recognized the impact of structural inequalities on the "needy," and on his own (mostly unsuccessful) efforts to intervene in their lives in meaningful ways.[2]

While dramas like CBS's *East Side/West Side* (1963) enacted the contradictions of radicalized social work, today's reality TV focuses on instilling self-management techniques in individuals. TV's current foray into social work combines the technical knowledge of lifestyle experts with entrepreneurial discourses to provide detailed instructions for helping oneself overcome personal hardships and difficulties. The programs hinge on a paradox, in that they often resort to authoritarian governing techniques such as "home visits," hidden camera surveillance, pedantic lecturing, and close supervisory relationships in an effort to produce self-sufficient citizens who are "free" because they do not rely on the State or any other institution for discipline, care, or sustenance. The human subjects addressed by the interventions are typically presented as less knowledgeable and less personally motivated than the imagined TV audience, which makes it possible for the viewer to maintain some distance from "at-risk" individuals who struggle (sometimes unsuccessfully) to overcome personal hurdles by mastering the practical lessons on offer. However, the TV viewer is also invited, and even expected, to be part of an empowering mission that spills beyond the TV program into interactive web sites and tie-in merchandise, including books, DVDs, and workbook exercises. In this way, reality TV draws from the disciplinary capacities of social work to diagnose and classify the needy as "other" people who require (if only temporarily) harsh modes of supervision, and offers itself as a rather more benign resource of self-care to the general population.

Empowering "Unruly" Individuals

Life interventions operate within the cultural economy of commercial television. Their governing rationalities are realized within a market logic that values private ownership, profit accumulation, and post-Fordist principles of flexibility and mass customization. Like charity TV, the format relies on strategic "partners" (including corporate sponsors, advertisers, clinics, professional associations, and nonprofit agencies) to enact its helping missions. TV as social service operates within networks of support, offering serialized entertainment/ instruction tailored to lifestyle clusters (women, youth). While television carries out its work independently of the State, the State plays an indirect role by activating and mobilizing the spirit of public–private cooperation in which the life intervention has thrived. It does the work that the State no longer has to do, through the rationalization of social service as a network of government in which TV is integral. TV is not only part of a privatized network of social service, it is also enterprise, and therefore life interventions fuse the aims of cultural commerce (ratings, advertising, and product-placement revenue, licensing, and merchandising tie-ins) with claims of public service. Within this framework, the programs deploy a continuum of governing strategies, from detainment in a private facility to self-help strategies that liken running one's life to managing a business. Their governing aims run the gamut from instilling good behavior in children to improving one's health and longevity to avoiding toxic relationships to achieving self-esteem as a path to professional growth. What unites the TV programs that we are calling life interventions is a concern with producing citizens who are not merely capable, but ultimately grateful to learn how to govern themselves to their full capacities. No matter how strict and controlling some of the techniques used can appear, the impetus is not really to display cruelty and punishment as a means of deterring "misbehavior," as Michel Foucault hypothesized of the pre-modern spectacle of torture in public. The rationality or point of the life intervention is to enact the idea that people who are floundering must be taught (by any means possible) to maximize their capacities for normalcy, happiness, material stability, and success.

As Wendy Brown points out, the capitalist state relies on a combination of overt and indirect strategies to produce idealized citizens who are self-sufficient as well as self-governing.[3] Harsh penal policies ("Three Strikes You're Out") and welfare-to-work schemes exemplify the former, whereas the pedagogical aims of George Bush's "Compassion Agenda," which advocates such things as character education in schools, and the circulation of information to ensure personally "responsible" nutrition as a cure to national health crises, exemplify the latter. However, given that the long-standing liberal ideal of "governing at a distance" has reached its zenith in a climate of privatization and welfare reform, cultural technologies (including television) are arguably more important than official government in the production of "good" (i.e., hard working, law-abiding, healthy-eating) citizens. As Nikolas Rose explains, cultural technologies are integral to modern approaches to governing precisely because they can translate the particular goals of rulers and authorities into diffuse guidelines for living with no obvious connection to official government, formal laws or regulatory procedures. This isn't a conspiratorial process, nor is it predictable or seamless.[4] What Rose and others call "governmentalities" come together from a nexus of sites including human and social sciences, the corporate sector, culture industries, the public sector, and politics. Our goal here is to show how these loosely aligned governing agendas are played out – and toward what ends – through reality TV. Life interventions are an obvious place to begin this work, as their transformative aims are so clearly stated most of the time.

The most authoritarian interventions focus on real people cast as incorrigible, self-destructive and/or out-of-control. Here, television intervenes by dealing with so-called troubled populations who have chosen to exist "outside" society's rules and norms. Due to an apparent inability to regulate themselves through their freedom, these individuals must be controlled by altogether harsher means. In 2005, ABC's *Brat Camp*, modeled after the BBC series of the same name, followed a cast of young people who had been sent to an expensive private "boot camp" for disobedient teenagers. SageWalk, a "therapeutic wilderness" school, bills itself as an "intense intervention program for troubled teens between the ages of 13 and 17 who may be experiencing emotional, academic, and/or behavioral problems." Overseen by a CEO, and staffed by professional therapists (many with social work credentials), the school immerses teenage customers with "issues" ranging from ADHD to drugs, promiscuity, and fighting in individual and group therapy, while also teaching them wilderness survival skills intended to cultivate personal responsibility and a "better understanding" of behavioral consequences and outcomes. According to news reports, ABC contacted psychologists, educational consultants, and similar professionals to locate troubled teens for the series, which was sold to SageWalk as a "documentary." The network picked up the bill for tuition (up to $425 per day) for the right to record and broadcast what occurred at the "brat camp." Since the participants were minors, their individual right to "choose" was trumped by those of their parents, who authorized the camp visits as well as ABC's involvement in the program. While it is very unlikely that any of the teenagers were literally forced to appear on the TV show (news reports suggest that many welcomed a chance to "be on TV"), the idea of detainment was built into the governmental logic of *Brat Camp* through editing, narration, and publicity, and in this way it became part of the program's "truth" about troubled teenagers. The implied comparison of the "brat camp" to juvenile halls, boys' homes, detention centers, and other places where young delinquents have been sequestered historically situated the program within a history of dreaded confinement and punishment.

However, the "brat camp" was also situated as an efficient and empowering alternative to bureaucratic disciplinary facilities. The point of voluntarily confining one's children to the pricey wilderness "school" was not to drill obedience into them as a matter of force, but to teach them how to manage and empower themselves through choice. While in the remote wilderness environment, the teenagers are forced to endure physical "challenges" including long nature hikes with heavy backpacks, surviving the elements on their own for days at a time, and camping in tents without material comforts. The idea is that Mother Nature provides an ideal context for learning self-discipline, care of the self, and the need to accept personal "responsibility for actions and

If convicted, Isaiah could face a maximum
of 2 years in jail and a $15,000 fine

Illustration 2.1 TV interventions don't always deliver behavioral "outcomes," as ABC's *Brat Camp* acknowledged when a teenager was arrested for vandalism following his release from the program (Shapiro/Grodner Productions, distributed by E4 to ABC, 2005)

consequences." The brutality of the outdoors is played up on the TV show, and so too is the severity of the psychological retraining. Staff members are tough, authoritarian, and unrelenting, and the cameras often "catch" the teens in escalating states of physical and emotional distress. However, the spectacle of punishment (getting sent to the "brat camp") is tempered by the discourse of personal empowerment. Not unlike welfare recipients who must be forced to work "for their own good," the teens are immersed in a disciplinary regime so that they can learn to succeed in life. While this is partly tied to the prevention of lawbreaking and other "dangerous" habits, it is also linked to entrepreneurialism and what Rose calls "lifestyle maximization." Sounding as much like a Dale Carnegie seminar as a delinquency center, SageWalk publicity describes a mission to "facilitate the success and emotional growth of every student, while helping them to identify and reach their fullest potential." Toward that end, the techniques and exercises are designed to instill "confidence, self-reliance, leadership, a strong work ethic, honesty, positive behavior, anger management and healthy coping skills.[5]

The bold premise of *Brat Camp* – that "troubled" teens can be swiftly transformed into functioning citizens through an intensive outdoors regime while TV cameras look on – sets up "outcomes" expectations not unlike neoliberal reforms that hold welfare case-workers accountable to the number of employed individuals they produce. When news reports revealed that several "graduated" campers had been arrested for crimes and misdemeanors, including spraying graffiti and driving a boat recklessly, *Brat Camp* was blamed for failing to rehabilitate the young people as promised. The "relapse" of unruli-ness on the part of the teens speaks to an important distinction between neoliberal governing rationalities and the actual experience of complex, flesh-and-blood individuals. We can't assume that programs such as this one are so powerful as to mold participants (or TV viewers) in directions of their choosing. However, we do need to pay attention to the interventionist aims of *Brat Camp* and similar ventures, for they play an important role in translating the preferences of government "on high" into guidelines for succeeding in a "fend-for-yourself" post-welfare society that in some ways is not so unlike the brutal wilderness camp. Finally, we need to call attention to the broader rationalities that inform the programs, so as to shift the terms of their critique away from the extent to which they are – or are not – "effec-tive." Some professional therapists and social workers were disap-pointed with the program, for example, because it obscured the "long-term follow-up care" required to maximize the benefits of wil-derness therapy and led viewers to a false impression that the teens had been dramatically transformed "for good" in the space of a few weeks. We need to move beyond this sort of functionalist analysis and its equivalent in cultural studies – the "resistive" viewer – to unravel why life interventions have proliferated on TV, how they attempt to transform people, and how these governmental agendas speak to broader social and political currents.

While *Brat Camp* intervenes in the lives of incorrigible minors who are committed to transformation by their parents, some TV interven-tions sidestep the liberal ideal of "governing through freedom" for the greater good of helping individuals who are "self-destructive" and unable to recognize their handicap. *Intervention,* an Arts & Entertain-ment program, is built on the assumption that such "addicts" are unable to behave rationally and therefore rely on friends and family to perform this role. In each episode, A&E works with friends, family members, and professionals to facilitate an "intervention" on behalf of two individuals who do not realize what is happening until the "confrontation" occurs. The show is packaged and sold as reality entertainment, and its primary goal is therefore to make money by selling advertising. However, it is also positioned as a public service, albeit in an applied form. Television does not merely educate TV viewers about the "problem" of addiction, as a traditional news report or documentary might do. Rather, it actively intervenes to solve particular manifestations of the problem, which involves taking up duties normally carried out by trained social work professionals. TV performs the business of social work by identifying addiction as a problem, screening and evaluating cases, documenting their severity, interviewing witnesses, consulting doctors and other professionals, coordinating a "confrontation" about the problem and providing access to a residential treatment facility that it chooses and pays for. People who are unable to self-regulate their consumption of drugs and alcohol are usually the focus, yet those suffering from eating disorders, shopping compulsions, gambling habits and other addictive behaviors are also the subjects of interventions.

Intervention is very graphic in its portrayal of drug-induced compulsions and other "abnormal" behaviors. In a particularly vivid episode, a bulimic woman demonstrated to the camera how she vomited into disposable plastic bags in order to conceal her problem from loved ones (she was apparently told she was participating in a documentary about eating disorders, not an intervention). Without dismissing the concerns of people who participate in the programs, it is important to recognize the extent to which "out-of-control" behaviors are documented in order to justify repressive governing techniques that, even as they are carried out by individuals and the private sector rather than state institutions, contradict the idea that we are all rational consumers/actors capable of looking out for our own interests in a market-driven society. Similarly, it is also worth noting the extent to which "excessive" consumer behaviors and desires with many interpretations and social determinants are construed as horrible individual tics that – if caught in time – can be brought under control by professionals. The rhetoric of free "choice" in relation to the care of the self looms large as well, in that while the addicts are nearly forced into treatment programs by those who "watch over" them through everyday surveillance, the rationale is framed in terms of their future empowerment. Again, the question to be answered is not whether TV can bring about behavioral modification, but how the interventions work – in conjunction with other programs, discourses, and forms of media culture – as technologies of citizenship that can translate particular governing aims into everyday terms with practical applications.

Brat Camp and *Intervention* are exceptional in their use of bullying, cajoling, trickery, and force. Most TV interventions unfold through a voluntary engagement with counselors, motivators, and life coaches. Governing in the name of freedom, these ventures emphasize rules and regulations only as a means of maximizing life, liberty, and happiness. However, even in the absence of force, life interventions still seek to guide and shape human beings toward particular ends that uphold the goals of the authorities, however beneficial or "freely chosen" they may be. Of all the popular reality formats, they come closest to resolving the paradox of liberalism, defined by Rose as finding a "means by which individuals may be made responsible through their individual choices for themselves and those to whom they owe allegiance, through the shaping of a lifestyle according to grammars of living that are widely disseminated, yet do not depend on political calculations and strategies for their rationalities or for their techniques."[6] Escaping association with official government of any kind, the "popular pedagogies" performed by reality TV seek to transform individuals into empowered actors who can learn to overcome their problems with the nudging of experts. While the proliferation of ever more specialized programs of self-help has surely contributed to the increased "governmentalization" of everyday life, this doesn't require a centralized state or even formal authorities to administer. On the dispersion and privatization of social work in the era of the "actively responsible self," for example, Rose writes:

> Social work, as a means of civilization under tutelage, gives way to the private counselor, the self-help manual and the telephone helpline, as practices whereby each individual binds themselves to expert advice as a matter of their own freedom. The regulation of conduct becomes a matter of each individual's desire to govern their own conduct freely in the service of the maximization of a version of their happiness and fulfillment that they take to be their own, but such lifestyle maximization entails a relation to authority in the very moment as it pronounces itself the outcome of free choice.[7]

There is nothing new about popular media performing as everyday cultural technologies. Commercial magazines have promoted health, wealth, nuclear families, and other agendas shared by rulers and policymakers for many decades, and have circulated techniques of the self (including shopping) for achieving these ideals. What is new, we contend, is the intensity with which popular reality TV has taken up and regularized post-welfare grammars of choice, personal responsibility, and self-empowerment and applied them to a whole range of "problems" that encompass everything from obesity to housecleaning to ineffective parenting. Because television is serialized and easily accessible without much planning within the private space of the home, and because it has established such a central place within the rhythms of everyday life, its capacity to govern informally is also potentially greater than other media, including magazines and books, which require a different type of engagement on the part of the individual who must seek them out on their own. Reality TV's techniques for achieving "happiness and fulfillment" via the management and care of the self overlap with the contemporary reasoning of welfare reform, not least because it is television's commercialism – its allegiance and accountability to the "free" market – that authorizes its ability to intervene socially. Despite funding cuts to virtually every need-based public welfare program, Congress voted in 2005 to fund the pending transition to digital television to make sure that households without digital sets, or who don't subscribe to digital cable or satellite "will be able to keep their television sets working after broadcasters switch from analog to digital signals."[8] If reality TV is what currently passes as social welfare, as we argued in the previous chapter, the State has staged its own intervention to ensure that television (unlike the high-tech cultural products of the digital divide) will continue to be available to one and all.

Self-Empowerment on Daytime TV

In recent years, life interventions have appeared on primetime television as part of the general makeover/lifestyle trend in reality entertainment. On any given evening, TV viewers might encounter nannies teaching parents how to manage unruly children, organizers teaching homeowners how to empower themselves by decluttering, financial advisors teaching people how to get out of debt by tackling their emotional problems, housecleaners teaching working mothers how to improve their quality of life through sanitation, and nutritionists teaching families how to achieve good health by exercising and eating better. TV viewers' interest in such topics may speak to a growing preoccupation with middle-class "lifestyling" practices, as Charlotte Brundson argues.[9] However, all of these programming examples draw (however implicitly) from the governing legacy of social work and tap into the discourse of privatization, personal responsibility, and self-empowerment that gave shape to welfare reform. In that sense, they enact strategies of governing within specialized and often problematized lifestyle domains. To understand how primetime's life interventions can work as technologies of everyday government, it will be helpful to chart the transformation of daytime television that predated them.

In the late 1990s, as national welfare reform policies were being discussed and implemented, reality-based self-help formats took over daytime television. One was the syndicated courtroom program, which mushroomed after the success of *Judge Judy* to become the fastest growing format on daytime for several years. While not an intervention format per se, the courtroom program promoted a logic of personal responsibility and self-help that anticipated many of the overtly interventionist reality formats, and is therefore worth discussing in some detail. Since the life lessons offered by the programs were explicitly aimed at lower-income women said to be the principal "at-risk" population for welfare dependency, their alignment with changing strategies of governing was also particularly clear. Ostensibly about resolving micro-disputes within the privatized space of the simulated small-claims courtroom, the format quickly established itself as a resource for the government of the self. Particularly in the hands of Judith Sheindlin, the bestselling self-help author and former New York City judge who rules on *Judge Judy*, it became a pedagogical device for turning people caught in the drama of everyday hardship into self-reliant and "empowered" citizens.

Sheindlin aims to cultivate self-empowerment and "rational" decision-making skills in her role as a television mediator/motivator. She is not a therapist or social worker, but she often performs these roles on her programs. In addition to probing the habits and conduct of the lower-income individuals who mainly appear in her private courtroom, she lectures on the need to "take responsibility" for one's actions to avoid "wasting the court's time" in the first place. Much of the guidance is aimed at women, who are advised to avoid risky men, be "smart" about relationships, develop self-esteem, earn their own living, understand the consequences of their actions, and quit depending on others – including the State – for handouts. *Judge Judy* fuses postfeminist discourse to "techniques of the self," a term Foucault used to describe methods of working on and caring for the self as a matter of one's obligation to the self. All "women have the power to make decisions, to call it as they see it, to take no guff,"[10] she professes on the TV show and in her books – they just need to realize it. Conversely, women who do not thrive and prosper create their own misfortunes by failing to "empower" themselves: "'If you're a victim, it's your fault.' 'Stop being a victim. Get a grip! You're the one who's supposed to make a direction in your life.' All those messages I tried in Family Court to instill in people – primarily women. [The TV show] sounded like something that would not only be fun, but worthwhile as well."[11]

Judge Judy did not emerge in a vacuum: Feminist scholars have shown how the march toward welfare reform has occurred in tandem with the acceleration of self-help programs aimed mainly at women. From advice books on intimate relationships to self-esteem-building initiatives required of welfare mothers, self-help regimens promise to "solve social problems from crime and poverty to gender inequality by waging a social revolution, not against capitalism, racism and inequality, but against the order of the self and the way we govern the self," argues Barbara Cruikshank.[12] The solution to women's problems is construed as having the right attitude, learning to make good decisions, and taking responsibility for one's fate in the name of self-empowerment.[13] In this sense, self-help is a technology of citizenship that teaches women how to "evaluate and act" upon themselves so that the social workers, medical establishment, and police "do not have to," says Cruikshank.[14] It works not through force but through the promise of self-fulfillment and the circulation of practical techniques for realizing these goals. Self-esteem is to be accomplished for the individual's own benefit, but also for the benefit of a society that will no longer have to carry the "burden" of the needy citizen:

> Personal fulfillment becomes a social obligation in the discourses of self-esteem, an innovation that transforms the relationship of self-to-self into a relationship that is governable. Self-fulfillment is no longer a

personal or private goal. According to advocates, taking up the goal of self-esteem is something we owe society, something that will defray the costs of social problems, something that will create a "true" democracy.[15]

Judge Judy uses the power of television to bring a self-help regimen to women who are living out what feminist philosopher Nancy Fraser has called the "post-socialist" condition.[16] It offers up television as the most efficient way to resolve tensions steeped in the unacknowledged dynamics of gender, class, and race, but it also classifies those who come to rely on television as needy individuals who must learn to care for themselves and solve their own problems. In presenting personal responsibility for the care of the self as an ethical duty, *Judge Judy* and other courtroom programs exemplify Brown's argument that the "ideal" neoliberal citizen is an "entrepreneurial actor" whose moral autonomy is measured by their capacity for "self-care – the ability to provide for their own needs and service their own ambitions." As Brown argues, if the "rationally calculating individual bears full responsibility for the consequences of his or her action no matter how severe the constraints on this action, e.g. lack of skills, education and childcare in a period of high unemployment and limited welfare benefits," the problem of the "mismanaged" life can become a way of "depoliticizing social and economic powers."[17]

The courtroom format was also one of the first examples of popular reality TV to be institutionally positioned as a form of "public service." The television industry was quick to insist that it "educates" as well as entertains by acting as a "moral compass" for people seeking guidance and insight as well as resolution, in the words of one TV station. However, "morality" was also being redefined by the programs in relation to the neoliberal project of caring for the self in as efficient and strategic a way possible. For example, many of the accompanying life lessons enacted on *Judge Judy* are aimed at people who have foregone marriage and/or the nuclear family, with couples who choose to live together "outside of wedlock" of particular concern. However, the issue isn't whether living together is wrong, but that such arrangements are much too risky for the individuals involved. In this sense, *Judge Judy* translates official governing strategies such as mandating marriage education and welfare-to-work schemes as mechanisms for preventing women's dependency on the State, even as it operates entirely independently of those policies. While Sheindlin does not present the failure to marry as a moral problem in the same way that certain religious discourses might, she promotes marriage as a "smart" behavior and specific techniques for navigating intimate relationships in the meantime, including getting personal loans in writing, not "living together for more than one year without a wedding band," and not "purchasing homes, cars, boats or animals with romantic partners outside of wedlock."[18] Individuals are moreover told that they must learn to impose these "rules" upon themselves, for their personal protection and because there is "no court of people living together. It's up to you to be smart. Plan for the eventualities before you set up housekeeping."

If the citizen idealized by *Judge Judy* is self-esteemed and calculating, she is also self-sufficient. The work ethic is the linchpin of Sheindlin's template for self-empowerment. Women who "depend" on welfare benefits are very harshly cast as unmotivated and irresponsible rather than disadvantaged, evoking Nancy Fraser and Linda Gordon's observation that the stigmatizing discourse of "dependency" that surrounds welfare presumes gender, class, and racial parity. Women (including single mothers) are held personally accountable to a "white, middle-class male" work ethic, even as they lack the material advantages and resources to perform as traditional breadwinners.[19] While this expectation marks a shift away from the patronizing assumption that all women are helpless and therefore "naturally" dependent on men (or in their absence, the State), it offers no venue to acknowledge or address social inequalities. On *Judge Judy*, all women are fully capable of supporting, caring for, and empowering themselves and their children provided they follow Sheindlin's guidelines. They can be the mistresses of their own fate, if they choose to be.

Not long after *Judge Judy* debuted, a motivational therapist named "Dr. Phil" became a semi-regular feature on *The Oprah Winfrey Show*; in 2002, he began hosting his own self-help-oriented alternative to the increasingly sensationalized and "unruly" talk shows that dominated daytime TV during the 1990s. Dr. Phillip McGraw, a PhD-holding psychologist, quickly established himself as a sterner, more sober version of other ratings-chasing hosts by canning the spectacle, enforcing order, and using television to deliver what he called empowering "life strategies." While other talk shows had presented therapists and other experts who psychoanalyzed the ever more "outrageous" guests who appeared, McGraw built his program around techniques for overcoming ordinary hurdles and problems, and invited TV viewers at home to actively participate in this brand of self-empowerment through an interactive web site and a growing empire of bestselling self-help books, workbooks, DVDs, and other merchandise. One of McGraw's recurring life lessons across all of these venues is "Take Care of Yourself" – not because there's no real alternative, but because "people who consistently win are consciously committed to self-management. They are the most important resource they have in achieving their goals. They actively manage their mental, physical, emotional and spiritual health." And, all of McGraw's teachings offer "techniques of the self" as the means of achieving this goal.

In his later work, Foucault traced an ethic he called the "care of the self" to ancient Greece, showing how techniques of working on, taking care of, crafting, and testing the self that flourished during that time formed the basis of a "government of the self."[20] For Foucault, techniques of the self are the practical "procedures, which no doubt exist in every civilization, suggested or prescribed to individuals in order to determine their identity, maintain it, or transform it in terms of a certain number of ends, through relations of self-mastery and self-knowledge." Foucault was not referring to the "hidden meanings" and unconscious drives that concern psychoanalytic conceptions of the self. He was interested in the practical application of knowledge to one's self, which led to questions such as "What should one do with oneself? What work should be carried out on the self? How should one 'govern oneself' by performing actions in which oneself is the objective of those actions, the domain in which they are brought to bear, the instrument they employ, and the subject that acts?"[21] Building on Foucault's questions, Graham Burchell suggests that we conceptualize techniques of the self as being made up of theoretically distinct but inseparable components: the "suggested" techniques that seek to shape our actions, and the actual ways in which we work on ourselves. Because these components are always in dialogue with each other, the "government of the self" involves a constant interplay of power and agency that isn't predictable. Foucault agreed on this point, arguing that government is a "contact point where technologies of domination of individuals over one another have recourse to processes by which the individual acts upon himself and, conversely . . . where techniques of the self are integrated into the structures of coercion."[22] For Foucault and Burchell alike, techniques of the self must always be contextualized, for they are not "essential" qualities of human nature but rather specific knowledges and self-shaping practices that can and do change historically. At the present juncture, the techniques of the self circulating on and through popular reality TV often have something to do with the cultivation of self-empowerment through personal responsibility and choice.

To analyze reality TV's relationship to the interplay that Burchell describes, we would need to consider more closely the ways in which actual people incorporate Dr. Phil's techniques into their self-shaping strategies and practices. Such research is beyond the scope of this book, which focuses on charting a changing rationality of liberal governing as well as television's role in demonstrating and enacting it. Our task is to trace the techniques of the self that have proliferated in relation to the reality TV boom, while always keeping in mind the complexity of their application. Dr. Phil is important because he was one of the first TV motivators to apply a neoliberal reasoning of governing to a wide range of everyday and altogether ordinary "problems," from marital difficulties to weight issues. And, although the doctor's educational credentials and past experience as a professional therapist lend a stamp of authority to his helping strategies, it was his ability to fuse techniques of the self to practices of "personal accountability" that made him such a powerful translator of neoliberal currents. One of McGraw's principal techniques for self-empowerment is to "acknowledge and accept accountability for your life" and "understand your role in creating results." As in welfare reform discourse, the individual is responsible for managing her own fate through acts of choice:

> You cannot dodge responsibility for how and why your life is the way it is. If you don't like your job, you are accountable. If you are overweight, you are accountable. If you are not happy, you are accountable. You are creating the situations you are in and the emotions that flow from those situations . . . Every choice you make – including the thoughts you think – has consequences. When you choose the behavior or thought, you choose the consequences . . . When you start choosing the right behavior and thoughts – which will take a lot of discipline – you'll get the right consequences.[23]

Dr. Phil promises to empower people in need by showing them how to empower themselves. The paradox is that in order to achieve empowerment, the individual must perpetually follow a system of "Life Laws" established by Dr. Phil. These laws underscore the self-work that is performed on the TV program and are offered to TV viewers in a more elaborate form via McGraw's self-help books, workbooks, and web site (which features links to lessons, quizzes, and "self-tests," and interactive self-shaping activities such as keeping an online journal). This system of self-regulation draws entrepreneurial techniques as well as authority from the business sector. As suggested by Life Law #7, "Life is Managed, Not Cured," the individual is to become an effective (and perpetual) manager of her/himself. This involves identifying strengths and weaknesses, learning techniques of self-discipline and self-motivation, and adapting the "rules" to each new thought, situation, or challenge that occurs across the various facets of everyday life. The move from "passive and dependent" to "active and empowered" hinges not only on perpetual work on the self, but turning the self into a commodity or managerial "resource" for securing "payoffs" such as satisfaction and success. The philosophy of working on the self, for the self, is stated on the *Dr. Phil* web site:

> You are a life manager, and your objective is to actively manage your life in a way that generates high-quality results. You are your own most important resource for making your life work. Success is a moving target that must be tracked and continually pursued. Effective life management means you need to require more of yourself in your grooming, self-control, emotional management, interaction with others, work performance, dealing with fear, and in every other category you can think of. You must approach this task with the most intense commitment, direction and urgency you can muster. The key to managing your life is to have a strategy. If you have a clear-cut plan, and the courage, commitment and energy to execute that strategy, you can flourish.[24]

Dr. Phil conveys the idea that it us up to the individual to empower her/himself in episodes with names like "Self Matters," "How to Make Millions," and "Creating Happiness." However, the TV program does not completely trust people's capacity to accomplish this on their own and therefore offers step-by-step "Formulas for Success" to guide and assist them. The extent to which freedom and agency are to remain perpetually contingent on generic templates for maximizing one's current and future success speaks to the contradictions of neoliberalism's presentation of self-sufficiency as an essential freedom. One way this contradiction is managed by Dr. Phil is through techniques of "personal accountability," an aspect of managing the self that is to be called upon at junctures when things are not going well. The principal technique for measuring personal accountability is the "lifestyle audit." As this business term would suggest, the lifestyle audit is a practical strategy for determining the individual's contribution to failed goals and undesired life "outcomes." Auditing has gained currency in the downsized public sector as a way of keeping government accountable to the rationalities of the marketplace. Dr. Phil applies the technique to everyday life with exercises that include writing down everything that "you are doing" to contribute to personal failures.

The "sample audit" provided on the *Dr. Phil* web site leads the individual into a detailed assessment of the technical minutiae of her personal behavior and conduct. In the theoretical situation, a woman is unhappy in her marriage. Since heterosexual marriage is an unquestioned ideal on *Dr. Phil*, the audit focuses on what the woman has done (or is doing) to bring about her misery. Leaving is not an option, for a "bad marriage doesn't exist without a lifestyle to support it." The wife's specific problem – she doesn't like being left at home while her husband goes out to socialize – is to be traced to the "elements in her lifestyle" that support his undesirable behavior, which in the sample audit include gaining too much weight, neglecting her appearance, not having appropriate clothing to wear on social occasions, and developing health problems that make her "too tired" to socialize. The idea is that the individual can change an undesired life "outcome" by delving into the details of the situation and honing in on the undesired "results" of their own behaviors and actions. By writing down, reflecting on, and working to change her lifestyle habits, the woman in the sample audit can eventually achieve personal happiness within her existing marriage.

In 2004, another life-intervention format appeared on daytime TV, claiming to help women "reinvent" themselves with the help of life coaches, psychologists, corporate sponsors (called "partners"), and non-profit agencies. *Starting Over* fuses the popular conventions of the reality-based soap opera ("docu-soap") with a total immersion in the sort of self-empowerment training offered by *Judge Judy* and *Dr. Phil*. Created by Bunim–Murray Productions, the production company responsible for MTV's *The Real World*, it sequesters six women in a private-group home facility, where they work with professionals and each other to achieve particular life goals while cameras document the process. When the women have learned sufficient techniques for pursuing their goals independently, they formally "graduate" from the *Starting Over* house, and another individual who requires help moves in. Women come to the program with a range of specifically designated "problems," including addiction, weight issues, dating difficulties, unwed pregnancy, and unemployment. To overcome them, the women participate in group therapy as well as results–oriented coaching sessions, customized self-tests, and professional workshops, while the cameras observe and record. There is also some unstructured interaction among the women caught on tape, in which problems and goals are further discussed, friendships are formed, and interpersonal tensions emerge.

Starting Over teaches many of the "techniques of the self" discussed so far, including calculated decision-making, personal accountability, and self-esteem. While these strategies for working on and governing the self are informed to various degrees by the governing rationalities of welfare reform, they are expressed as the hopes and desires of the women themselves. During the first season, the *Starting Over* program intersected with the aims of welfare reform as codified by the Personal Responsibility and Work Opportunity Reconciliation Act of 1996 by casting a young single mother who was African-American with a goal of breaking the "cycle of welfare dependency." The biography created for Rain exemplifies what Rose calls the governmental impetus to reconstruct the "will" of welfare subjects through a "model of enterprise, self-esteem, and self-actualization.[25] According to the *Starting Over* web site, Rain's "dependency" can be overcome by her strong "will" to change herself – a will that the TV program's life management professionals can develop and shape:

> Rain has been scraping by on government assistance, but she wants to be more than just another statistic on the welfare. She began a lucrative career in long-haul trucking, to help improve her situation, but it didn't last long due to sexual harassment and separation from her children. Rain has a willingness to achieve and just needs some help breaking free from the system, so she can begin to build a new life for herself and her daughters.[26]

Entrepreneurialism is both a resource and a technique of self-help on *Starting Over*. Corporate "partners" provide some material assistance to the women, including graduation gifts and modest "startup" funds to obtain apartments, start small businesses, and pursue other life goals. The program's therapeutic approach is also drawn from enterprise. The resident counselors are called "life coaches," a term that originated in the corporate sector and has now made its way into the helping professions, where it refers to personal motivators who are less concerned with the so-called "talking cure" than with helping customers achieve specific goals and outcomes. The governing authority of the life coaches stems not only from their ability to "get results" with self-help strategies but from the market, where they are said to be very much in demand, as evidenced by their *Starting Over* biographies, which call attention to their speaking gigs, self-help books, DVDs, and other products, including personalized online guidance. The main coach on *Starting Over* is Rhonda Britten, a "life strategist" who also appears as the "Life Doctor" on the BBC's *Help Me Rhonda*, a reality-based TV show that "transforms people's lives" and has been featured in seminars on US public television. Drawing from the discourse of self-help, she explains her approach as guiding "the women of *Starting Over* back to their personal power" and giving them "the skills and confidence to fulfill their personal vision." Britten is joined by Iyanla Vanzant, a "spiritual" counselor who, in addition to appearing on *Starting Over*, operates a prison ministry and is CEO of her company, Inner Visions Worldwide, Inc., which operates a "Spiritual Life Maintenance Center" and a certification program in Spiritual Counseling and Life Coaching. Bringing faith into the neoliberalization of social work more directly than other daytime programs, she takes a "spiritual" approach to self-help that "teaches people how to move beyond whatever has happened in their lives in order to do and be what we came to life to do and be." On the *Starting Over* web site, the life coaches market themselves, their products, and their services to TV viewers who are always constituted as potential customers. The commodity they are selling is self-esteem, or at least the ability to develop self-esteem swiftly, for a price, through proprietary, results-oriented techniques only they can provide.

This "can-do" entrepreneurial ethos informs the helping strategies practiced on *Starting Over*, as well as their value to client-customers. One of the program's star pupils, a woman named Andy, established a helping enterprise of her own after graduating from the *Starting Over* house. Her business, Dollars and Cents, claims to empower women by teaching them how to dress for success on a budget. She now has her own web site, where she promotes her makeover services, and she also appears on *Starting Over* as a lifestyle expert. The enormous value placed on self-entrepreneurialism, coupled with the program's focus on specific (and therefore measurable) outcomes, creates a context in which "failure" is highly visible as well. For example, the *Starting Over* web site also features a link to Rain's personal web page, where she candidly describes a hard spell after graduation and several unsuccessful entrepreneurial ventures (including a stint selling Mary Kay cosmetics). Rain is able to use her entrepreneurial skills as what Foucault called a counter-strategy, in order to publicize her difficult experience after leaving the *Starting Over* house and to document her inability to achieve an outcome of financial self-sufficiency. However, the logic of self-help offers Rain no way to explain her situation, other than to express disappointment in herself and resolve to try harder.

Starting Over presents a glimpse – however mediated by television through technologies of casting, direction, camera, and editing – into the complex interplay between "suggested" techniques of the self, and work that people do on themselves. We witness the women's some-times ambivalent and resentful response to the life coaching they receive, as well as their attempt to process and apply the lessons they have learned to their past experience and future conduct. However, this interplay occurs within the self-empowering agenda of the program, which mandates the women to cooperate with the professionals to their full capacities or else to accept personal responsibility for "failures," such as not "graduating" from the house as scheduled or being asked to leave the facilities altogether. A similar constraint is at work in the support system the women develop among themselves. The residents of the house often form intensely supportive relation-ships, acting as empathetic listeners, constant encouragers, sounding boards, and surrogate coaches. In these relationships, "techniques of the self" that are not bound to the professional regimens can and do emerge, to the extent that the women share their personal experiences, insights, strategies, and suggestions with each other informally. In some ways, this supportive female bonding simulates the feminist conscious-ness-raising group with an important difference: there is no impetus within the "can-do" political rationality of the *Starting Over* program to move beyond individualized work on the self to strategize about structural and institutionalized experiences of sexism, racism, and eco-nomic exploitation.

The interplay between *Starting Over* and TV viewers occurs within similar types of constraints. Like *Dr. Phil*, *Starting Over* is a regularized form of self-help that enters the home as serialized entertainment. The TV viewer is not required to seek out a self-help regimen to informally engage with these programs, which is what distinguishes reality TV from other cultural technologies, including self-help books. However, both programs also enlist old and new media technologies to create a multilayered viewing experience that extends well beyond the television "text," and that enables the TV viewer to engage more directly with the techniques of the self that are demonstrated on camera. The *Starting Over* viewer is invited to actively participate in the self-empowerment ethos of the program by discussing episodes in online chat rooms; subscribing to the *Starting Over* newsletter; making use of "Life Resources" and "Life Coaching Tips" featured on the web site; reading the biographies, diaries, and updates of cast members; and possibly purchasing merchandise peddled by the program's branded experts for their own projects of reinvention. "Interactivity" is not limited to a richer engagement with practices of meaning-making as theorized by scholars of television fandom, nor is it purely a marketing scheme that exploits participation for commercial purposes. Like other reality-TV life interventions, *Starting Over* encourages a form of "interactivity" that is about the practice of self-shaping, and in this sense it has much in common with women's magazines, which have long engaged female readers in techniques of self-improvement. The program televises "real" women who are deeply immersed in a professional regimen of self-help, but it also mobilizes the TV viewer to work on herself using the resources it provides. This dynamic process of self-work can never be fully directed by *Starting Over* or any cultural technology, but it is steered toward the entrepreneurial governing logic of goals and outcomes. For example, *Starting Over* offers a "support system" for TV viewers who wish to "start over" in their own lives. The woman defines a specific ("keep it simple") goal, and the program sends an email announcement to a list of family and friends. The *Starting Over* staff promises to help her stay "motivated as you make progress towards your goal" through a "series of regular email check-ins and updates." The circle of friends is invited to become a "personal support system – almost like your *Starting Over* housemates. They'll send you an encouraging email and help you stay committed to your goal. Who knows, they might even set a *Starting Over* goal of their own." If the woman accomplishes her designated goal, *Starting Over* sends a celebratory announcement to the email circle. The woman also qualifies for the chance to be featured in the "Tell Your Friends You're Starting Over" section of the *Starting Over* web site or on a special TV broadcast. Similar to women who appear on the TV program, she is rewarded for working on herself for herself, within a governing rationality that offers self-empowerment as the only solution to women's problems.

Primetime Interventions: Governing through Lifestyle

While daytime TV enlists the female viewer in entrepreneurial forms of social work on the self, primetime interventions often focus on problems that materialize in the realm of family and lifestyle. Since the late 1990s, a cadre of reality programs have emerged to teach individuals and families how to diagnose problems of everyday life so as to better manage their children, households, health, and leisure time. While this programming is not as obviously synchronous with welfare-reform policies as are ventures like *Starting Over*, it does circulate techniques for a "government of the self" that complement the current political value placed on individual choice, personal accountability, and self-empowerment. In an era when the State has given the job of looking after the welfare of citizens to individuals and the private sector, reality TV's efforts to help real people improve their "quality of life" plays another governing role as well. As Brown points out, the "withdrawal of the state from certain domains, and privatization of certain state functions does not amount to a dismantling of government, but is a technique of governing – rational economic action suffused throughout society replaces express state rule or provision."[27] What happens is that neoliberal regimes shift the "regulatory competence of the state onto responsible, rational individuals," with the aim of encouraging them to "give their lives a specific entrepreneurial form." As "lifestyle" becomes one of the principal domains through which citizens are expected to look after themselves in the name of their own interests, their capacity to make "rational" choices in matters of health, consumption, family, and household takes on more urgency. Entrepreneurialized guidance in "lifestyle maximization" and the care of the self replaces the watch of the State as the mechanisms through which "free" individuals are governed across daily life, and through which they come to govern themselves in the name of self-fulfillment and improved quality of living.

The explosion of reality-based health- and nutrition-related programming is one example of TV's enlistment to resolve the dilemma of citizens who do not make the "right" choices when assigned the rational responsibility of their own governance and self-care. Such fare abounds on the Discovery Channel, The Learning Channel, and other cable venues, including Fit TV, a network entirely devoted to teaching consumers how to develop a lifestyle based on home exercise, rational grocery shopping, and healthy eating. Network television has also taken up these concerns: In 2005, ABC debuted *The Biggest Loser*, a primetime weight-loss program with a focus on the health benefits of keeping trim. The network provides the services of nutritionists and personal trainers to people who agree to slim down on television, and offers a cash prize to the person who sheds the most body fat. The program's rationale isn't tied exclusively to appearance. The benefits of achieving a healthy lifestyle, including longevity, being accountable to one's children, and improving one's job performance, are emphasized as the truly important reasons for losing weight. The team of professionals advises and motivates the contestants as they carry out intense physical exercise regimes, learn about nutrition, and develop balanced and "disciplined" eating habits. Evoking Foucault's discussion of the care of the self in ancient Greece, where the feast was one of many rituals for testing one's capacity for self-control, the cast was regularly tempted with vast displays of decadent foods to test their determination and willpower.[28] At the end of each episode, the "outcome" of these physical and mental activities is measured live on television in a dramatic weighing ceremony.

TV viewers are invited to stage their own life intervention by slimming down and "getting healthy," using the resources provided by the program and its multimedia components. The "text," in the old sense of broadcast media, is only one element in a network of cultural technologies that coalesced around the *Biggest Loser* concept. Viewers are invited to take part in its interventionist ethos by applying an array of technical suggestions and motivational strategies to their own weight-loss regimes. ABC has constructed an interactive web site complete with nutritional guides, dieting tips, sample recipes and menus, customizable exercise regimes, and weight-loss tools, including a body mass index calculator. Tie-in merchandise – including workbooks and the *Biggest Loser* exercise DVD – is available for purchase, and participants are also urged to join the *Biggest Loser* email club and sign up for informative podcasts. Finally, for people on the go there is also the much-promoted *Biggest Loser* wireless service. For only $2.99 per month, anyone with a cell phone can sign up to receive a daily health tip, an exercise pointer, or inspirational message. In extending these body- and health-management resources and techniques to individuals, ABC fuses popular entertainment (weight loss as a competitive game) and self-shaping activities with current requirements of governing, including the need for citizens to accept personal accountability for the consequences of their lifestyle choices. And in this sense, *The Biggest Loser* intervenes in the "micro-moral domains" of everyday life in ways that are quite similar to the self-help programs found on daytime television.

The logic of personal accountability is rendered even more explicit on *Honey We're Killing the Kids*, a series that originated on the BBC and now appears in the United States on The Learning Channel. Each week, a stern nutritionist named Dr. Lisa Hark sets out to demonstrate how "everyday choices can have long-term impacts on children, and offers both the motivation and the know-how to help turn families' lives around." The program intersects with the "reinvention of government" in its emphasis on outcomes: Armed with the latest scientific research and a team of advisors from Harvard and Johns Hopkins universities, Hark aims to change the "bad habits" of an actual family in a period of just three weeks. However, as the urgency of this time-compressed mission cannot be fully contained by rational discourse, the episodes lean toward the hyperbolic. The parents, who are openly chastised for smoking and overeating, are shocked into a household-regime change by Hark's bold accusation they're "killing their kids" by letting them eat too much junk food and play video games and watch television instead of exercising. Digitally-aged images of the children at age 40 created with "state-of-the-art" technology and "certified assessments based on measurements and statistics" are profoundly exaggerated. As if the sallow skin, stained teeth, heavy jowls, stringy hair, and dour facial expressions weren't enough, Dr. Hark tells the parents their children are "at risk" for developing obesity, diabetes, heart disease, cancer, and other life-shortening diseases. In teaching care of the self, the program literally objectifies the child-subject,

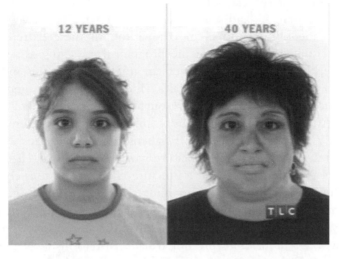

Illustration 2.2   Honey We're Killing the Kids uses computer imaging and scare tactics to encourage proper nutrition and family exercise regimens (Entrant Co.: BBC, UK for The Learning Channel, 2006)

turning him/her into an undesirable stranger. Not surprisingly, the parents generally gasp out loud, and swiftly agree to cooperate with the doctor's "rules, guidelines and techniques" for transforming the children's health and lifestyle.

The televised crash course that ensues follows the template of many primetime lifestyle interventions. The doctor arrives at the home, observes the family in their natural habitat, diagnoses their problems, locks up all the junk food, introduces a set of rules, and sums up their new and improved lifestyle with a list of easy-to-memorize slogans (e.g., "Sack the Sugar," "Exercise Together"). Cameras capture initial resentments, mid-episode slip-ups and the eventual mastering of the "healthy" lifestyle they have come to desire as their own. At the end of each episode, the "outcome" of the regimen is demonstrated by new digitally-aged photographs that show the children looking youthful and healthy. The parents are greatly relieved and dutifully promise to enforce the new diet and exercise regimen once the doctor has moved on to assist other needy families.

While the episodes are redundant, this doesn't diminish the importance of *Honey We're Killing the Kids* as an example of the neoliberalization of social work through television. This program teaches personal responsibility for the care of the self by diagnosing and rehabilitating cases of "ignorance" and self-neglect, and allowing the TV viewer at home to identify as normal in comparison to these extreme cases. However, this doesn't prevent the program from acting as a resource to the health-conscious: TV viewers are invited to seek out and master the skills required to create a healthy lifestyle on the program's web site, which includes interactive resources, games, and merchandising tie-ins. And, while there's no direct link between the diffuse aims of reality TV and the policies of official rulers and politicians, there are some similarities of reasoning that are worth considering. *Honey We're Killing the Kids* has appeared at a juncture when the State is concerned about health and fitness but unwilling to do anything about it that would compromise the "hands-off" approach to government regulation favored by neoliberal regimes. Unlike the Progressive Era, when social workers of all kinds promoted national reforms as well as individual compliance, today's helping culture is mainly focused on the self. When public-interest organizations do push for policy action, they are cast as controlling and paternalistic institutions who wish to regulate freedom of choice. During the 2004 House Government Reform Committee's hearings on "The Supersizing of America," Marshall Manson of the rightwing Center for Individual Freedom criticized the Center for Science in the Public Interest for pushing "extreme" measures such as regulating the food sold in schools and "mandated labeling of restaurants with detailed nutrition information." Linking the regulation of culinary commerce to the erosion of free choice, Manson told the committee:

> Our democracy is founded on the idea that individuals have basic freedoms. Among these, certainly, is the right to choose what we put on our plates and in our goblets . . . anti-food extremists like CSPI would gladly take away that freedom and mandate our diet in order to save us from ourselves. It is time for these zealous advocates to understand that it is not the federal government's job to save us from ourselves by making our choices for us.[29]

As Manson stated, the only legitimate option for the State within this reasoning is to encourage "responsible decision-making" in consumers who are not only "free" to manage their own health but are expected to do so. Toward this end, George W. Bush launched a program called Steps to a Healthier US to encourage "simple improvements in physical activity, diet and behavior" as a means to controlling chronic disease. The program is sponsored by the Presidential Program on Physical Fitness and Sport (www. Fitness.gov), a State program that dates back to the Kennedy administration and is now administered through more than 600 "partnerships" with corporations, nonprofit agencies, and local governments. This is in turn linked to the President's Challenge, a privately-based network of corporate, nonprofit, and regional/municipal partners, including major sports and athletic businesses, food companies (Burger King, Coca-Cola, General Mills), and a number of television networks (including ESPN and the Cartoon Network). These networks of partnerships between government, corporations, and non-profit agencies speak to the State's role in facilitating the privatization of welfare through public–private educational initiatives and the relegation of care to the corporate sector.

This approach to welfare relies on cultural technologies to govern at a distance by shaping and guiding behavior toward "rational" choices and outcomes. *Honey We're Killing the Kids* works as such a technology, and within these networks of support it attempts to help solve the "crisis" of obesity by locating its causes in bad habits and issuing a "critical wake-up call for parents." Promoting personal accountability through rational shopping and eating, it presents resources for choosing a healthy lifestyle as a matter of one's freedom and empowerment. Reformers like Manson have no problem with commercial TV shows taking up this persuasive role, because their authority to govern is sanctioned not by the State, but by the commercial logic of "supply and demand." *Honey We're Killing the Kids* exemplifies television's role in the entrepreneurialization of social work, in that the market − not the State − is responsible for ensuring the health outcomes of the population. It illustrates Rose's argument that while healthy bodies are still a "public value and political objective," we no longer need state bureaucracies to "enjoin healthy habits of eating . . . with compulsory inspection, subsidized incentives to eat or drink correctly and so forth." In the new domain of consumption, "individuals will want to be healthy, experts will instruct them on how to be so, and entrepreneurs will exploit and enhance this market for health. Health will be ensured through a combination of the market, expertise, and a regulated autonomy."[30]

Like other TV life interventions, *Honey We're Killing the Kids* puts the impetus to succeed in health and in life on self-governing individuals. It brings a lucrative new version of social work into the home via reality entertainment, and ignores big-picture issues such as the high cost of organic food, substandard health care for low-income populations, reduced funding for food stamps and other welfare programs, and a class system that makes fast food a more viable lifestyle option than the lean protein, vegetables, and wholegrains promoted by nutritional experts. The irony of commercial television preaching nutritional fitness as an individual solution to national health problems is not lost on those of us who remember Ronald Reagan insisting (in the midst of debates over funding cuts to school lunch programs) that "ketchup is a vegetable." What *Honey We're Killing the Kids* is also telling the masses signified by excess flesh, cigarette habits, and addiction to television is that their pleasures in food are irrational and must be rehabilitated by experts. Hidden camera footage of resentful children (and sometimes their parents as well) breaking into the forbidden junk food stashes is replayed to condemn those who are unable to self-police their forbidden cravings (though the break-ins can also be interpreted as resistance to this power play). *Honey We're Killing the Kids* blames the health crisis on people's uninformed habits and ungoverned desires, and promotes the idea that our social, economic, and physical fate in life is determined only by the little choices we make, not the social structures we inhabit.

Primetime TV interventions focus on diagnosing and solving lifestyle problems within the family and the domestic sphere. This concern emerged in tandem with official government's promotion of the two-parent heterosexual family as a strategy for empowering low-income populations, particularly mothers and children. According to George W. Bush, "Stable families should be the central goal of American welfare policy." Reality TV promotes stable, functioning families by circulating regimens, skills, and rules related to household organization, cleanliness, time management, and parenting. A cadre of instructional-entertainment programs from *Wife Swap* (ABC) to *Decorating on a Dime* (Home and Garden Network) cater to women's presumed role in carrying out strategies of government within the domestic economy of the home. *How Clean is Your House* (Lifetime), which originated on the BBC before arriving in the United States, exemplifies how television helps women who are now expected to be self-sufficient workers as well as homemakers by teaching them the "forgotten" skills of domestic management, in this case sweeping, dusting, scrubbing, and scouring. The program draws from, but also entrepreneurializes and tempers, through humor, a long history of experts (charity workers, social workers, domestic scientists) seeking to instill habits of cleanliness in the masses. In each episode, experts in hygiene and sanitation arrive at an untidy home, conduct a thorough inspection, diagnose sanitation problems, and demonstrate proper housekeeping techniques using brand-name products (the product placements are also pitched on the *How Clean is Your House* web site, where TV viewers can discuss housecleaning tips and play interactive cleaning games like Wipe-down). Extending the concept to problems of personal hygiene, the BBC has developed a spin-off of *How Clean is Your House* called *Too Posh to Wash*. Other programs bring lifestyle experts into the home to deal with the problem of clutter, on the grounds that decluttering the home can facilitate personal empowerment as well as better functioning families. "Think of it as "residential rehab, an interior intervention," says *Clean House*; "Organization is hard work, but in the end you will feel as if a huge burden has been lifted off your shoulders," claims *Mission: Organization* (Home and Garden Network).

While the focus is on empowering individuals (mainly women) to achieve domestic proficiency, the shows also intervene in social and psychological hurdles, from poor self-esteem to "compulsive shopping," a recurring diagnosis across the intervention format that exists in perpetual tension with reality TV's commercialism. For example, on an episode of *Clean House*, a single mother who turned to shopping to "fill a void in her life" was encouraged to recognize her "problem" and learn a rational and controlled approach to consumption at the same time she was acquiring new products to transform her over-crowded and chaotic home into a functioning environment for herself and her child.

Reality TV's high-profile nanny programs bring together many of the techniques of the self we have discussed so far. *Supernanny* (ABC) was also spun off from a series of the same name on the BBC; Fox developed a virtual clone called *Nanny 911*. Both programs enlist very stern but compassionate British nannies to teach parenting skills and overall household management to frazzled parents, particularly mothers. The programs are positioned as resources for "saving" the modern family, and in this way are tied to the Bush administration's moralization of governing through the promotion of traditional family values and faith-based social authorities. The emergence of the nanny as a

STEP 5: Explain the bad behavior

Illustration 2.3   Mothers are taught how to manage their homes and discipline their children more effectively on *Supernanny* (Ricochet Productions for ABC, 2006)

figure for mobilizing "real-life" behavioral change in the home has occurred alongside criticism of the "nanny state," especially in the United Kingdom. While the term "nanny state" implies that official government intervention in social life is paternalistic and therefore wrong, the TV nanny governs within the private context of commercial television, which makes her interventionist approach to reforming family life not only tolerable, but in sync with rationalities of welfare privatization and personal responsibility. ABC has situated *Supernanny* within its Build a Better Community outreach project which, as we saw in Chapter 1, represents a "do–good" trend in neoliberal television policy. Fox has also played up the public-service dimensions of *Nanny 911,* though not as explicitly. However, both programs "instruct" within a commercial rationality of maximizing profits by earning high ratings. The fusion of commerce, expertise, morality and entrepreneurial techniques of the self make these programs another example of how reality TV has reinvented social work.

Supernanny promises to relieve the stress of family life with promotions that ask "Are your kids a handful?" "Are you exhausted?" "Is your house a 'zoo'?" But if the show makes ordinary household difficulties more visible, it ignores their material context, including long work hours, inadequate daycare, the "double shift" of paid work and housework for women, and the lack of flextime policies and other reforms that truly would make life easier to manage for many people, including parents. The program also focuses almost exclusively on "helping" heterosexual nuclear families, so that techniques for managing the family and the home are situated within this sanctioned ideal. Like *Nanny 911*, *Supernanny* promotes obedience and responsibility in children, and attempts to instill rational ways of developing these attributes. While there is no formal link between the nanny programs and official policy, their focus on "old-fashioned" household dynamics echoes the philosophy of "compassionate conservatism." George W. Bush has promoted welfare reform on the grounds that the "feel-good, permissive values of the 1960s undermined the strength of families and helped create dependency on government," which ultimately harmed low-income populations.[31] Besides giving rise to student rebellions and countercultures, the 1960s were also an era when so-called lenient parenting techniques gained currency. Nanny TV reverses this image by guiding and regularizing government inside the home. While the shows "help" middle-class families, as opposed to welfare citizens, the impetus to undo the permissive family value system responsible for "dependency" in policy rhetoric can be seen in the techniques and skills offered to parents (especially mothers) who are enlisted to govern their children in the name of domestic harmony.

The program opens with Jo Frost in a posh English cab, watching video footage of the week's needy family on her laptop computer. With her British accent, authoritative demeanor, and nostalgic Mary Poppins-like appearance (matronly dress suit, tight bun, umbrella), she's marked as "different" from the masses of female childcare workers, devalued as they are in the United States as well as Britain. That's important, because after observing "family dynamics" and taking mental notes for a brief period, Frost diagnoses flawed parenting habits and implements a new system of strategies and rules. After explaining where the adults have gone wrong, she offers a solution that is part social work, part parenting education, and part domestic science. No matter how large the problem, it can be overcome with a household routine, a list of household rules, and a methodical approach to handling the children's misbehavior. However, achieving domestic order does take considerable effort: "It's a tough lesson for a parent to retrain themselves," explains one frazzled mother.

The episodes are all very similar, with a revolving cast of exhausted mothers, peripheral fathers, and preschool children who bicker with siblings, talk back to parents, snack between meals, and throw temper tantrums. Since the double shift is still deeply gendered, Frost pitches lessons in domestic time-management mainly to the mothers, who often work full-time while also managing the children and the household. In one episode, Mom manages the family plumbing business from home, while also doing the housework and caring for two preschoolers. She's wiped out to the point of tears, but the program promises to "fix her broken spirit" in less than two weeks. Toward that end, Frost systematizes the mother's workday with a color-coded, wall-sized schedule, allowing several hours "off" from the business to focus exclusively on the misbehavior-prone children (the time is made up in the evening when they are in bed). On another episode, Mom works full-time as a telemarketer, while also keeping house and caring for preschool twins and a 9-year old. She thought working from home would give her more "mommy time" (and reduce childcare costs), but her "flexible" job has become a living nightmare. We see her perched at the living-room computer taking calls on a headset while the children run amok; when the inevitable squabbles and mishaps force her to abandon her work station, she worries out loud that her boss will fire her. At the end of the day, she's so tired she falls asleep with the children, leaving her husband feeling abandoned and single ("unacceptable," according to Frost, who fails to suggest that he help out more). While it remains unclear exactly how an improved household routine can help this woman, there's no mention of hiring a babysitter, let alone government or corporate reforms such as subsidized daycare. Like other life interventions performed by television, *Supernanny* values self-reliance over "dependency" and social upheaval.

While household routines are important, a properly self-governing family also requires that children know and follow rules. At least one child per episode is branded as a chronic misbehaver, and the problem is attributed to faulty parenting. Occasionally parents are lectured for shouting and/or using force, most of the time they're charged with too much softness and leniency. To "prevent bad habits" from breeding and show kids that the "adults are in charge," Frost establishes a non-negotiable set of household rules (no sassing, no aggressive play, no picky eating) and shows parents how to enforce them rationally. Each week, she demonstrates the same step-by-step approach to discipline, beginning with a "warning in a low tone" and culminating with a punitive trip to the "naughty mat" (the information also appears in captions that extend the lesson to TV viewers at home). While the punishments on *Nanny 911* vary, the program adheres to the same notion that "ACTIONS HAVE CONSEQUENCES: Good behavior is rewarded. Bad behavior comes with penalties." Frost demonstrates "tried-and-tested" methods for regularizing problem rituals such as bedtime and encourages children to learn personal responsibility by cleaning their rooms, picking up their toys, and so on; *Nanny 911* is even more focused on developing a work ethic in children, who are given their own wall charts to keep track of chores. To ensure that the regimen will be properly implemented in her absence, Frost monitors the home from a distance via remote camera for a few days; if Mom forgets a disciplinary step or Junior decides to climb out of bed, it's all caught on camera. In the final review session, these mistakes are noted and the process is fine-tuned.

Like other TV interventions, *Supernanny* circulates strategies for informal learning through the acquisition of guidelines and strategies. In doing so, it utilizes procedures (the home visit, video replay, practice and review sessions) that have become increasingly common on television. All of these procedures encourage "real" people to objectify their lives in order to pursue the care of the self. Through television, the self becomes something that can be studied, reflected upon, surveilled and therefore recalibrated. The process of observing is redoubled on *Supernanny* as the student relies upon surveillance cameras in the home to watch over her household and to manage the family, a process that is crucial to observing the self ever so slightly "from a distance" in order to see what needs to be done. This pulls the nanny/teacher (who has observed the family's problems on video) and the parent/student out of the immediate situation only to reimmerse them as both actors and watchers. The teacher governs at a distance, and the student is disciplined while being proactive and "free," or governed while governing. This process is important also because it allows for a customized plan for particular families and individuals. While contemporary TV operates within an economy of mass customization, the impulse to design programs, plans, and rules that are *specific* to individuals and families requires observing and demonstrating in the ways mentioned above what is most suitable and acceptable to particular individuals – even as TV viewers themselves watch at a distance, and are slightly removed from the process of customization. Customization occurs not only because TV has the capacity to create these games of observation – tests with oneself, guided by experts – but also because TV has become part of networks of support that extend beyond the TV set to web sites, magazines, and books.

Supernanny adopts a paternalistic role in the name of facilitating self-empowerment. The goal is for parents to learn to manage on their own, so Frost can move on to other needy families. The program promises to equip parents with the skills they need to improve their lives as well as their families, and in so doing allows for a range of viewing strategies, from emotional identification with the harried mothers to relief that one's own children are not quite as out of control as the ones being documented by the TV cameras. However, none of this prevents the program from operating as an informal technology of government, a role that is facilitated by the parenting tips dispensed on the *Supernanny* web site as well as Frost's bestselling how-to parenting book (*Nanny 911* features a similar web site and how-to merchandise). What is important about the program as a life intervention is how it links care of the self (and of one's children) to a template for government that draws from residual welfare strategies but is actualized within the logic of commerce. It is worth emphasizing that the responsibilized, rule-abiding and (eventually) self-governing children *Supernanny* teaches parents to help produce are the sort of citizens-in-training that neoliberalism depends upon.

Chapter 3

Makeover TV:
Labors of Reinvention

In spring 2005, the TV makeover program *What Not to Wear* presented a special episode called "Worst Dressed Women in Government." Filmed in Washington, DC, it casts a critical eye on women who work for the capital's public sector bureaucracies.

Hidden cameras zoom in on the style faux pas of an entire city filled with ill-fitting pantsuits, oversized floral dresses, and dated hairstyles, implying that big government produces a static work culture, an "iron cage" with little incentive for self-fashioning or fashion change. The woman with the dubious achievement of being crowned the best example of this institutionalized anti-style is treated to a sophisticated new wardrobe, a designer haircut and a professional makeup application. More importantly, she is presented with a set of customized "rules" to guide her in a lifelong pursuit of self-fashioning after the TV cameras have moved on. While *What Not to Wear* offers these services to every fashion "don't" who appears on the program, this woman's need for television's help is explicitly tied to the assumption that government epitomizes an approach to work that is dull, uninspiring, predictable, and permanent – and therefore out of touch with fashion as a signifier of freedom, marketability, innovation, and personality. By developing the woman's capacity to groom and outfit herself to her own advantage, the episode implicitly promises to transform a passive employee into an energized entrepreneur of her vocational future. *What Not to Wear* focuses on the minutiae of personal style and appearance, but its political rationality is in sync with changes in the regulation of work and workers. Like many of the makeover programs that have appeared on television since the millennium, it translates the demands of the neoliberal economy – flexibility, short-term labor, outsourcing, ongoing corporate reinvention, and a shift from production to branding – into people's capacities to carry out the new requirements of work being placed on them. As cultural theorist Valerie Walkerdine explains,

> Jobs for life are being replaced by a constantly changing array of jobs, small businesses and employment contracts. In such an economy, it is the flexible and autonomous subject who is demanded to be able to cope with constant change in work, income and lifestyle and with constant insecurity. It is the flexible and autonomous subject who negotiates, chooses, succeeds in the array of education and retraining forms that form the new "lifelong learning" and the "multiple career trajectories" that have replaced the linear hierarchies of the education system of the past and the jobs for life of the old economy . . . it is argued that these times demand a subject who is capable of constant self-invention. Such a subject is presumed by, as well as being the intended product of, contemporary forms of education and training.[1]

Reality TV's approach to "making over" the self may not be exactly what US Federal Reserve chairman Alan Greenspan had in mind when he spoke in 2000 of the need for "lifelong learning" to prepare US workers for a current economy that values rapid innovation, flexible labor markets, and entrepreneurship: The "heyday when a high school or college education would serve a graduate for a lifetime is gone; basic credentials, by themselves, are not enough to ensure success in the workplace," said Greenspan, who called upon community colleges and vocational retraining and "retooling" programs to bolster the nation's competitive edge and soothe an anxious labor force, an agenda that was adopted by the administration of George W. Bush. Yet, reality TV has developed its own version of lifelong education as a solution to the disappearance of "jobs for life," the rapid obsolescence of job skills, and the social insecurities that accompany these shifts. From programs that teach people how to improve their looks, personality, and social skills, to makeover competitions that transform raw human potential into the next top model, multimillionaire, or American idol, reality TV presents work on the self as a prerequisite for personal and professional success. Unlike vocational training, it presents this lesson inside a pleasurable lifestyle game whose "rules" can be mastered and possibly even exploited by individuals. On *What Not to Wear*, fashion victims accept being ridiculed and bossed around by snobbish experts because their stylistic rehabilitation is offered in the form of a playful challenge that incorporates many opportunities for their own participation, rebellion, amusement, suspense, and reward. Despite its reliance on harsh pedagogical strategies, including humiliation and surveillance, the program acts as if it were on the side of the anxious individual in a larger game of Opportunity, Inc. It offers self-fashioning as a form of self-enterprising, not something the made-over person owes her boss or any other authority figure. *What Not to Wear* illustrates the paradox of makeover TV, in that it prepares the worker to take on burdens of insecurity and disposability in the name of her/his own freedom, and provides them with tenuous resources for navigating the impossibility of this task.

Self-Fashioning in the Flexible Economy

The most obvious example of self-fashioning on television is the beauty/style makeover. Once relegated to the margins of daytime talk shows, this type of programming entered the mainstream with the debut of *Extreme Makeover* on ABC in 2003, and *The Swan* in 2005 on Fox. The beauty/style makeover has also become a staple of many large cable channels, including The Learning Channel, UPN, MTV, and The Style network, which keep episodes of *A Makeover Story*, *Ambush Makeover*, *Ten Years Younger*, *Made*, *How Do I Look*, and other programs in frequent rotation. The beauty/style makeover, which aims to transform "ordinary" people into improved versions of themselves using tactics from cosmetic surgery to stylish new clothes, is often criticized on two grounds: The first is that the programs reject any distinction between content and commerce, so that they effectively serve as "advertorial" for the fashion and beauty industries. The second is that makeover programs perpetuate existing gender and social hierarchies by imposing restrictive notions of beauty and taste on women and the working/lower-middle classes.[2] Both arguments are convincing, but they don't address what is specifically new about reality TV's approach to the makeover, which has, after all, been a theme in Hollywood films, women's magazines, and tabloid journalism for many decades.

Television's cultural conventions, including its use of close-ups and formulaic narratives, make it especially useful for demonstrating techniques of self-fashioning in the form of dramatic stories that incorporate moments of intimacy, disruption, and suspense. The fusion of instruction in the aesthetics of appearance and style with familiar elements of popular fiction produces a hybrid educational/entertainment format that addresses the viewer in different ways from the self-help book or the magazine. The viewer is allowed to observe the diagnosis and "improvement" of others from a distance without feeling as if she/he has set about to learn something. Most makeover programs also allow for multiple and fairly complex viewing strategies that range from emotional identification with the fashion victim, to taking on the rehabilitation work of the experts and judges and possibly judging oneself above the people who are being made over, to ironic detachment, to a combination of these positions. Finally, television's embrace of the beauty/style makeover matters because TV is more in sync with the rhythms of everyday life than other media, and even its niche-oriented dimension is capable of normalizing the makeover as part of an everyday, "real-life" common culture in ways that other media have not been able to accomplish. Partly this has to do with the way in which television has brought a broader range of "ordinary" people together (including men, people of varied ages, and people who do not read fashion magazines) as good candidates for a makeover. However, it also has to do with television's capacity to enter the home as a regularized source of entertainment and information that is continually available for casual observation as well as "appointment" viewing. In many homes, the TV set is habitually on, and the shift toward the constant recycling of its cultural output, particularly on cable channels, means that many TV viewers are likely to be familiar with makeover programs whether they intentionally seek them out or not. TV brings the makeover more deeply into the fabric of daily life, and for that reason is able to circulate its logics and rules more broadly and also more informally than books, magazines, the internet, or other media.

Makeover TV is a more regularized and ritualized technology for "governing at a distance," or the dispersed strategies that guide and shape conduct in liberal societies and enable individuals to perform this role for themselves independently of formal state powers and authorities. In this chapter, we argue that by instilling rationales and techniques for fashioning the self, reality TV also works in indirect (and sometimes contradictory) ways to guide and govern workers and to facilitate their self-government in the flexible economy. Here we

extend our focus on governmentality to several examples of makeover
TV, including the beauty/style makeover and the TV job interview/
talent contest. We situate these formats as cultural technologies for
governing citizens who are expected not only to take care of themselves, but are called upon to perform as what sociologist Paul du Gay
calls "entrepreneurs of the self" within a deregulated capitalist economy
that devalues organized labor and job security. Although makeover
programs are not only (or even primarily) focused on people's vocational lives, they do make promises about TV's capacity to help the
unemployed and/or unfulfilled help themselves as managers of their
"greatest assets" – themselves. They convey the idea that the quickest
route to success is "strategic" self-fashioning, a practice that includes
remaking one's body, personality, and image in calculated ways to
bring about personal advantage in a competitive marketplace. By
bringing demonstrations of the skills and procedures required to achieve
"self-renovation," "impression-management," and "total transformation" into the home as reality entertainment, TV links the makeover
game to mastering the uncertainties of everyday life.

The growth of makeover TV as a forum for displaying and enticing
the labor involved in the stylistic retooling of the self speaks in part
to what Angela McRobbie calls a "replacement of the social with
work." As the public sector and, with it, social services are "relegated
to the margins of contemporary life," she explains, they are replaced
with "competition, the seeking of self-advancement in work, and, in
commercialized leisure spheres, self-improvement techniques." Work
comes to mean more than earning a living: Promoted as the sole means
of ensuring personal security, work "incorporates and overtakes everyday life" and exacts "new resources of self-reliance on the part of the
working population."[3] We saw evidence of this in the entrepreneurial
forms of social work developed by reality TV in Chapter 2. TV programs like *Starting Over* contribute to the official strategies of "getting
people into work" (such as welfare-to-work schemes) that become the
very "definition of government" in McRobbie's analysis. We also saw
how some of reality TV's "suggested" techniques of the self, including
self-esteem, everyday personal managerialism, and lifestyle auditing,
attempt to cultivate the will to work – and to work on the self – as
a way of overcoming public-sector "dependency." The beauty/style
makeover is a less didactic component of the cultural regulation of
work, and while it focuses on external appearances it has much in

common with the governing strategies discussed so far. As the self-help guru, daytime talk-show host and *Extreme Makeover* consultant Dr. Phil explains, life interventions and beauty/style makeovers are intersecting components of the same self-shaping process: one works on the "inside," the other on the "outside."

Reality TV's promotion of self-fashioning as a requirement of work also speaks to shifts in managerial philosophy. In her study of the "career guides" turned out by the self-help publishing industry, Micki McGee traces a shift from the "organizational culture of the 1950s, where people were trained to work in hierarchical corporate context," to the present, when workers are expected to manage themselves and, increasingly, to achieve security "by identifying with capital" – by imagining themselves as "entrepreneurs, as the "CEOs of Me, Inc.""[4] In his book *Management Challenges for the 21st Century*, corporate management guru Peter Drucker (who has also been instrumental in the "reinvention of government" and was awarded a Presidential Medal of Freedom by George W. Bush in 2002) describes this shift in terms of greater individual freedom, empowerment, and choice. A few decades ago, he writes, a person "was born into a job and into a line of work" and trapped there for life. Today, people have "choices" – they can decide their line of work, and they can change jobs and occupations if they wish. To make effective use of their freedom to choose, however, workers must better understand their individual strengths and weaknesses, and they must "learn to develop themselves." This is essential, for they are now free to plan their own careers – to do by themselves and for themselves what the "Personnel Department of the large organization was supposed to do in the 1950s and 1960s." According to Drucker, the most profound change to come out of this transformation is that workers are now called upon to "manage themselves" rather than relying on their employers to do it: "Managing Oneself is a REVOLUTION in human affairs. It requires new and unprecedented things from the individual, and especially from the knowledge worker. For in effect it demands that each knowledge worker think and behave as a Chief Executive Officer."[5]

According to Tom Peters, managerial strategist and author of "This Brand Called You," becoming an entrepreneur of the self is akin to branding oneself: "Regardless of age, regardless of position, regardless of the business we happen to be in, all of us need to understand the importance of branding. We are CEOs of our own companies: Me

Inc. To be in business today, our most important job is to be head marketer for the brand called You."[6] Like Drucker, Peters translates the burdens of the flexible economy, particularly the loss of job security, into the capacities and desires of workers who are reconceptualized as "free agents." He writes:

> Behemoth companies may take turns buying each other or acquiring every hot startup that catches their eye – mergers in 1996 set records . . . but the real action is at the other end: the main chance is becoming a free agent in an economy of free agents, looking to have the best season you can imagine in your field, looking to do your best work and chalk up a remarkable track record, and looking to establish your own micro equivalent of the Nike swoosh.

Within the flexible economy, the individual is no longer an "employee," "staffer," "worker," or "human resource," but has become his/her own branded commodity. Within this logic, work on the self is the equivalent of building and accruing capital:

> You don't "belong to" any company for life, and your chief affiliation isn't to any particular "function." You're not defined by your job title and you're not confined by your job description. Starting today you are a brand . . . The good news . . . is that everyone has a chance to stand out. Everyone has a chance to learn, improve, and build up their skills. Everyone has a chance to be a brand worthy of the mark.

Beauty/style makeovers are increasingly offered as an important dimension of the process of "self-improvement" required to enterprise and brand oneself in the sphere of work. Reality TV's embrace of the makeover in these terms endorses and enables what Toby Miller calls the "spread of self-fashioning as a requirement of personal and professional achievement through the U.S. middle class labor force."[7] However, we shouldn't generalize too broadly, because makeover programs address their "targets" in different ways and allow them varying amounts of "freedom." *Extreme Makeover* operates within ABC's broader turn to privatized charity and community outreach (addressed in Chapter 1) by providing "worthy" individuals with complimentary cosmetic surgeries, dental work, Lasik eye surgery, professional styling, and recovery "vacations" at the *Extreme Makeover* mansion. It works on the needy, offering instantaneous aesthetic improvement as a form of social service. The idea is that by bolstering their looks and therefore their self-esteem, individuals can jump-start success in other areas of life, including work and dating. To qualify for *Extreme Makeover*'s help, candidates usually must have self-described physical "flaws" as well as life hardships (i.e., death of a loved one, job loss, psychological distress) which they hope to resolve through a personal makeover. As Vicki Mayer notes, people may apply for "unsanctioned" reasons such as obtaining free dental and vision work, but this complexity is flattened by the program's narrative. By facilitating these dual desires (for physical as well as emotional/professional/ social improvement), *Extreme Makeover* dislodges the pursuit of beautification from potential negative connotations (vanity, self-absorption, impossible beauty standards, advertising's exploitative pull) and situates it as an integral component of self-empowerment. When Evelyn, "a 29-year-old waitress and single mother struggling to raise three kids," is offered a tummy tuck, liposuction of the inner and outer thighs, breast augmentation, and "teeth whitened and straightened," it is understood that she will then capitalize on the extreme makeover to overcome (through marriage and/or work) her personal situation. Likewise, for Candace, a "family support worker and mother of two" in her thirties, a lifetime of being teased about her looks has come to matter more in recent years, because she wishes to "re-enter the job market." Candace feels that a makeover will boost her employability, and the *Extreme* team agrees. The program follows a paternalistic approach to the care of the self, as the doctors decide how to improve Candace's appearance and perform their work with little creative input from her. Ultimately, however, it is Candace who must perform the work of recovering from the upper eyelid lift, brow lift, nose reshaping, cheek implants, lower eyelid-tightening, breast augmentation, liposuction on thighs and stomach, and extensive dental work. Her swollen features, bandages, and obvious pain are testimony to the labor she is willing to invest in her future.

Extreme Makeover presumes that the right outward appearance, defined by dominant ideologies and filtered through professional doctors and style experts, can bolster an individual's advantage in an unstable, youth-oriented labor market. For women and increasingly for men as well, looks are also understood as a form of currency in the postfeminist dating and marriage market. *Extreme Makeover* does not invent these assumptions, as much as it enacts an extreme solution to a "truth" that circulates in a range of venues, from popular media to social science. Sociobiologist Nancy Etcoff sums up this discourse in her widely cited book *Survival of the Prettiest*, contending that "good-looking men are more likely to get hired, at a higher salary, and to be promoted faster than unattractive men," while "homely women . . . are truly disadvantaged economically – they are less likely to get hired or to earn competitive salaries at work. They are less likely to marry, and less likely if they do to marry a man with resources."[8] Whether or not Etcoff's claims are accurate is ultimately less important than the way in which social anxieties triggered by a perceived link between appearance and work are being exploited by beauty experts and marketers, who now offer regimens for refashioning that collapse boundaries between everyday life and work. As McRobbie observes, a burgeoning culture of "pampering yourself" with beauty treatments, body-toning programs, and cosmetic surgery is now being marketed as a "resource to be mined for added values which can enhance performance in the workplace." This is said to be especially important in the service sector, which has replaced manufacturing as a source of low and mid-level employment, and which in some segments (including retail) "now expects its workforce to look especially attractive and stylish for what they label 'aesthetic labor.'"[9] Such is the case with Peter, a 25-year-old fast-food manager who feels his looks have "attributed to his solitary life, his stalled career and his shyness," and who looked to *Extreme Makeover* to "break out of his shell and bring out his inner rock star."

The need to remain "up to date" in appearance, particularly for middle-aged populations, is tied to stability and success at work by *Extreme Makeover* and other makeover programs, including those that offer minor treatments and professional restyling services in lieu of surgical intervention. The impetus to signify youth is a cultural dimension of the current stage of "flexible capitalism." As sociologist Richard Sennett describes it, "rigid forms of bureaucracy are under attack, as are the evils of blind routine. Workers are asked to behave nimbly, to be open to change on short notice, to take risks continually, to become ever less dependent on regulations and formal procedures." While flexibility is claimed to give people more "freedom to shape their lives," Sennett contends that it merely "substitutes new controls," including the expectation that workers adapt and retool to meet the continually changing demands placed on them. Youth is valuable to "flexible organizations" because older workers are thought to have "inflexible mind sets" and be "risk averse," as well as "lacking in the sheer physical energy needed to cope with the demands of life in the flexible workplace."[10] According to Drucker, the solution is to "learn to stay young and mentally alive during a fifty-year working life." Just as the worker will have to "learn how and when to change what they do, how they do it and when they do it," they will have to communicate their adaptability and flexibility by cultivating a youthful appearance.[11] *Extreme Makeover* assists by footing the bill for facelifts, hair transplants, and other procedures in the hopes of boosting stagnant careers. In one episode, Samantha, a 55-year-old high-school counselor and single mother with a long history of "trying to make ends meet," turns to *Extreme Makeover* for a "new lease on life." She wants to advance her career, but is worried that "no company will invest thousands of dollars" in an employee who looks as old and tired as she does. When Samantha is granted a face lift, neck lift, and full dental restoration, it is under the assumption that such techniques will bolster the worth of her image, which has become so important to the ethos of worker-as-brand/commodity. When Arthur, a "self-employed business development consultant" in his late fifties, lost his "job, his wife and his savings in a short period of time" and experienced an "emotional roller coaster" that took a negative toll on his looks, he also turned to *Extreme Makeover* for help. According to the program's narrative, having made the decision that it was "time to pick himself back up," Arthur hoped the makeover would "be the bridge that [would] help him get his life back on track." When two decades of stress and overtime as a crime-scene investigator appear on the face of 48-year-old Peggy, she too is rejuvenated by *Extreme Makeover*. The program completes its work in time for Peggy's "upcoming work anniversary party," where she is revealed to her colleagues as an earlier version of herself, whose years of experience have been erased, and who is ready to begin anew.

Makeovers as Instructional Games

Ten Years Younger (The Learning Channel) takes a more participatory approach to the aesthetic management of age by fusing techniques of self-fashioning to conventions of gaming. The program eschews surgical techniques but requires more involvement and "maintenance" work from the made-over subject. At the beginning of each episode, an individual is asked to stand in a glass box on a busy public street or in a shopping mall, while random passersby guess their age and comment on what is it about their appearance that "gives it away." The average guess becomes the starting point for the style experts, who claim to use "simple, nonsurgical techniques to take a decade off the participant's looks in just ten days." The voyeurism inherent to the glass-box ritual, coupled with the ostensibly uncertain outcome of the race to rejuvenate the individual, provide an entertaining context for dispensing advice that can be customized and carried out through personal regimens at home. *Ten Years Younger* differs from *Extreme Makeover* in two important ways: First, it demands more learning from the individual, who must become informed about the latest dermatology and dental treatments as well as the way in which makeup application techniques, hairstyles, and clothing can be utilized in precise ways to signify youth. This lesson is extended to the TV viewer-pupil at home, who even when focused on the entertainment dimensions of the show inevitably learns something about a whole spectrum of anti-aging techniques. Second, *Ten Years Younger* links the need for a youthful image to personal fulfillment as well as survival at work, and this breadth, combined with a focus on minor improvements rather than extreme overhauls, creates a wider address for its "empowering" advice and services. The need to maintain a pleasing appearance, and to deal with signs of aging as they come up, is presented as an ethical obligation to the self in ways that evoke Foucault's analysis of the care of the self in ancient Greece. As Foucault argued, the ancients were enticed to work on and "master" themselves in practical as well as aesthetically pleasing ways, so that living one's life became akin to creating a work of art. *Ten Years Younger* also presents aesthetic work on the self as a "quality of life" issue that anyone (with the help of experts) can master and enjoy. Unlike ancient Greece, however, the care of the self that is promoted by *Ten Years Younger* and other makeover programs is inseparable from commerce. The required props – spa services, cosmetics, designer clothes, and so on – ensure that the rewards of self-fashioning are dependent on the marketplace, even as the individual is also required to labor in their proper application and strategic use. Self-mastery over style becomes reliant on the ability to correctly choose from a vast display of consumer goods. In addition to excluding those who cannot pay for it, this entrepreneurial approach to the care of the self works in tandem with the discourse of personal responsibility, which means that the invitation to pursue self-fulfillment through "acts of choice in a world of goods" can become a burden in disguise. Within the context of the flexible economy, as McGee argues, the mastery involved in "engineering one's image" can't really be separated from the impetus to "commodify oneself . . . [by] keeping oneself marketable in a volatile labor market, or mastering the contingencies of the labor market."[12]

What Not to Wear, which originated on the BBC and also appears in a US version on The Learning Channel, illustrates the entrepreneurial aspects of self-fashioning on television in two senses. The more obvious way is by serving as a forum to display brands, stores, labels, and product placements (including *What Not to Wear* merchandise), and therefore consumerism in general. The program also seeks to instill self-entrepreneurialism through micro-practices of self-fashioning that aren't easily reducible to the spread of consumer culture, however. Stylish contemporary images crafted via the right clothing, hairstyles, makeup, and accessories become strategic resources for maximizing performance within and across social situations, including work. Individuals nominated for the style makeovers by friends, family, or co-workers are secretly filmed then confronted by the program's hosts, who promise them a new wardrobe and professional styling services if they agree to acquire fashion sense. The program is built on a pseudo-authoritarianism in which the hosts ridicule the fashion victims, force them to model their most dated and ill-fitting clothes, toss much of their existing wardrobe in the garbage, instill the rules of their "new look," and monitor from a distance as the pupil shops for the appropriate outfits. However, this is done in the name of fun, and the gaming element takes the edge off the disciplinary dimensions of the program. *What Not to Wear* relies on strategies of close supervision, humiliation, and surveillance only as a means to an end, which is the creation of a self-governing subject. The targets must be taught how to fashion themselves as a means to making the most of themselves, and this prod toward personal empowerment (not unlike the rhetoric surrounding welfare-to-work schemes) justifies the need for harsh tactics.

The self-work exacted by *What Not to Wear* relies on video technology to draw the participant into the makeover process in sophisticated ways that printed media cannot accomplish. The made-over

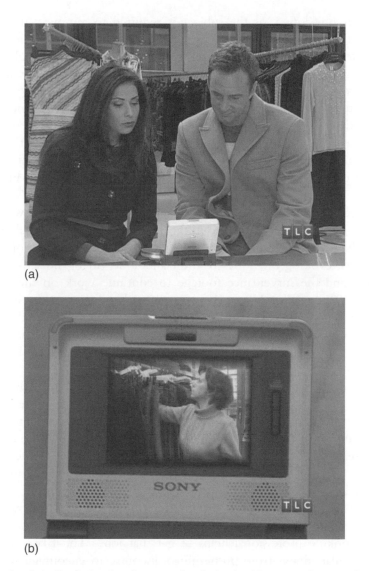

Illustration 3.1 Professional stylists use closed-circuit video to make sure shoppers follow fashion rules on *What Not to Wear* (Granada/BBC for The Learning Channel, 2005)

subject is recorded watching the surveillance footage of themselves while the experts point out their fashion faux pas in a joking tone that, nonetheless, forces a "live" reassessment of the self and a consideration of how one is perceived through the eyes of others. The self becomes objectified, as the subject is required to assume a detached view of him/herself, which allows the process of expert-guided self-work to begin. The subjects are then told to record personal video diaries at home, in which they document their responses to the make-over process, not all of which are positive. Snippets from these diaries are interspersed throughout the episode, adding an element of authenticity and complexity to the pedagogical process, as feelings of embarrassment, shame, and insecurity are often voiced during the self-recordings. The subject is also recorded and observed "at a distance" so the experts can monitor her/his progress. The grainy surveillance images are displayed on a monitor for the trainee and the TV viewer at home to see as well, all of which lends a feeling of being watched and "watched over" throughout the training period. The subject is then charged with internalizing all of these objective and personalized strategies, evoking memories of the clandestine video, the self-created diaries, and the surveillance footage to continue work on the self in private. While *What Not to Wear* was an early adopter of the integra-tion of self-shaping and video, many other shows now use similar hidden camera and surveillance techniques, so that television itself has become part of the makeover process in ways that were unimaginable only ten years ago.

The manifesto *What You Wear Can Change Your Life* by BBC hosts Trinny and Susannah explicitly situates the beauty/style makeover as a cultural technology for empowering women to empower themselves. "So many of us trundle through life not making the most of ourselves because we are lacking in self-confidence, convinced that clothes don't matter or have no idea where to begin," they write. Fortunately, "every lady on our show has turned into a gleaming example of con-fidence . . . [Women] know that at the end of the day the way we look can influence so much in our lives. Looking sexy makes us feel sexy. Looking professional helps us get that job." The BBC version, in particular, draws from postfeminist discourse to encourage women to see beyond what "they hate about their bodies" and make the most of their looks using little techniques, such as choosing the correct hues and styles for one's body type. This advice is not intended to dismantle "ways of seeing" women as objects to be looked at in the sense theo-rized by John Berger, but it does encourage them to become entre-preneurial surveyors of themselves who are able to "minimize" flaws and "maximize" assets using every technique available, including the "art of camouflage." The pursuit of aesthetic self-mastery is to be accomplished by adhering to a customized set of "dos and don'ts" established by style experts who take into consideration the woman's age, lifestyle, occupation, and body type. Not unlike the self-managed worker, she must accept these rules and learn to enforce them upon herself in order to reap the rewards of the makeover game, which extend beyond the traditional pursuit of male approval to accomplishment and "choice" in the professional realm. The "competitive workmates can be kept in the dark as to why you look thinner, sleeker, more sophisticated," advise Trinny and Susannah. "This is your secret weapon."[13]

The US version is even more concerned with remaking women and also men whose personal style hinders their capacities to achieve satisfaction and success at work. Colleagues often nominate such targets, enable the secret filming, and are present during the final reveal, further bolstering the informal association between the TV makeover and the workplace. The need to keep one's appearance contemporary emerges as a major concern in these episodes, and people who are "stuck" in a time warp are a recurring theme. Donna, a 47-year-old "sales rep for a printing company on Long Island," cannot hope to progress beyond talking to "clients on the phone" in her seasonal items and 1970s leftovers, "including sweaters with pumpkins, fall leaves and ice skaters." *What Not to Wear* intervenes, "culling the most horrific items and forcing her to face how bad these clothes look on her in a 360-degree mirror." Donna is sent shopping with "strict new rules and $5,000, before a complete hair and makeup overhaul." However, as is often the case, uncertainty mounts because "Donna's been dressing like a Christmas tree for a long time. Can she learn simplicity and style – on one short week?"

People who are new to work or who are experiencing stalled careers are also recurring targets for a personal style makeover. A would-be professional who is nearly "30 years old," Dave's problem is that he is still wearing clothes he bought when he was in college. They're worn and out of date, which prevents him from projecting an adult persona. In her mid-twenties, "Morna still dresses like a slouchy college student. She works for a major cosmetics company in Manhattan's classy Rockefeller Center – but in billowing skirts, worn-out sandals and an actual headband." Shannon "works as a telephone salesperson, but she's about to leave her desk and come face to face with her customers," which raises the issue of her appearance: Her work colleagues, who have nominated her for the makeover, are worried she "won't be making commission unless she looks more professional." Kerry, a "33-year-old opera singer on the edge of a flourishing career," performs wonderfully but looks as if she's "just come off the farm" with her "balloon-like sweaters, ill-fitting pants, 99-cent panties, and 'virgin' hair that has never been cut or colored." The clock ticks: Can the stylists "manage to help the opera diva hit the high note?" In all of these episodes, *What Not to Wear* introduces an expert-led behavioral regime for empowering oneself at work by learning (quite literally) to dress the part within a compressed time frame that brings a sense of urgency to this mission.

What Not to Wear promotes consumerism, but not in the sense suggested by the political-economic critique of makeover TV. Following a long line of advertising criticism, concerns about "advertorial" and the glorification of shopping tend to presume a passive subject whose consumption is fueled through a manipulation of unconscious desires. In fact, *What Not to Wear* promotes a deliberately "rational" approach to consumption that seeks to correct irrational and "impulse" shopping, particularly among women, and therefore has much in common with the history of consumer education as a cultural technology for guiding wise purchasing habits. *What Not to Wear*'s similarly pedagogical role is to bring into being the rational and autonomous individual upon which liberalism is based – a consuming subject who is "free" to advance his or her private interests within the marketplace. This "freedom" is crucial to the concept of liberal modernity, contends Don Slater, to the extent that "private, individual resources were also defined in terms of the interests of the individual, which only he could know and which he had every right to pursue. Consumer choice is merely the mundane version of this broader notion of private, individual freedom."[14] Through its training dimensions, *What Not to Wear* extends this historically male, bourgeois model of liberal consumption to the female masses, the object of advertising-induced gullibility and irrationality within so much critical discourse. It promises to bring women into liberalism's conception of the enlightened, self-governing individual – provided the program's self-fashioning rules are learnt and followed. The paradox, as Foucault noted of liberalism in general, is that the "freedom" to practice rational and wise consumption with an eye toward advancing one's self-interests remains contingent on ever specialized technologies of consumer expertise.

The elaborate set of customized rules to be followed, which encompass everything from selecting the proper cut of pants for one's body to seeking out acceptable color palettes for one's skin tone and hair coloring, turns shopping into a form of work that is rarely pleasurable for the subjects being made over by *What Not to Wear*. The shopper (who is closely observed by the experts via a remote camera) must not succumb to uninformed impulses or whimsical desires, nor is she to waste time "just looking." She must instead carefully evaluate every potential purchase on the basis of its capacity to bolster the strategic fashion regimen that has been established for her. Price and brands are non-issues (the TV program is after all paying), and in that sense "rational shopping" becomes another way of valorizing expensive merchandise on the basis of expert-valued attributes (quality, cut, etc.) as opposed to the meanings, identities, and associations that link brands to consumer desire in the vocabulary of advertising. On *What Not to Wear*, shopping ceases to be a recreational venue for escaping the drudgery of work (as in the leisure-time activity of "going to the mall") or for fulfilling oneself through symbolic commodities, and becomes instead a route to carefully building an image that is salable in the marketplace of work. The subject must be taught to make calculated choices about consumer products in ways that evoke Wendy Brown's argument that under neoliberalism, "all dimensions of human life are cast in terms of a market rationality" that includes not only "submitting every action and policy to considerations of profitability," but also the production of all human action as "rational entrepreneurial action."[15]

What Not to Wear and similar makeover programs extend the consumer training provided by commercial women's magazines, which have long taught women what to buy in the pursuit of outward beauty. As Ann Cronin argues, consumerism can be seen as a "technology of the self" in that it promises women "self-transformation and appears to validate women's choices," even as it fuels an impossible imperative to "be ourselves" by "doing ourselves" mediated by makeup, fashion, dieting, and exercise. *What Not to Wear* also addresses the female, in particular, as a subject with an "ethical duty to monitor [her] appearance" through consumption. However, it situates the exercise of consumer choice within a slightly different combination of

strategic realism and entrepreneurial self-work. Women are not encouraged to "buy" (or buy into) a fantasy identity as they are through
magazines, which offer airbrushed models as feminine objects of desire.
However, nor are they allowed to reject femininity by adopting an
alternative or subcultural style or worse, genderless "nonstyle." The
US version of *What Not to Wear* in particular targets young and matur-
ing punk rockers, Goths, hippies, and others who "need" to let go of
alternative images. Such candidates are the most likely to rebel against
the rules imposed by the experts, before warming to their "new look"
once it has been assembled for them and valorized by "amazed"
friends, family, and work colleagues during the final reveal. Women
who do not shop at all (one episode featured a woman who bought
all her clothes at thrift stores and was shocked to discover the price of
urban retail fashion) present another challenge for the experts, since
their unfamiliarity with consumerism provides no basis for behavioral
intervention in personal shopping and styling. Finally, while magazines
promote ideals that no flesh-and-blood woman can really expect to
achieve (although this is beginning to change slightly with advertising
campaigns and fashion spreads featuring "realistic" body sizes), *What
Not to Wear* conveys the "can-do" philosophy that everyone can make
small improvements by sticking to shopping regimens designed to
conceal deficiencies and highlight "assets." Subjects are immersed in
the small details of enterprising self-presentation as determined by
experts, so choice becomes the ability to choose the best option within
a realm of weighted possibilities. As BBC hosts Trinny and Susannah
explain, the TV makeover is intended to help women who "want
their purchases to change their lives and are disappointed when they
don't." They do not need to be thin or beautiful to "empower"
themselves, nor is the program's goal to magically transform women
(or men) into fantasy figures who embody these attributes. Managing
the body becomes a matter of learning how to apply technical knowledge, skills, and consumer tricks (how to make the legs appear longer,
how to conceal a tummy) in the short term, before pounds have been
lost or other long-term changes have been achieved. In all of these
ways, *What Not to Wear* offers consumer training that is more technical, enterprising, and laborious than the "mental work" of imagining
a future desirable self through advertising imagery.[16]

   Like other makeover programs, *What Not to Wear* allows for the
possibility of multiple viewing strategies. The TV viewer is not required

to adopt the subordinate position of an unstylish pupil, but can also participate as a vicarious expert who takes pleasure in judging others and seeing one's own self-fashioning skills valorized. However, this doesn't preclude the viewer from approaching the intricate and often customizable advice on offer as a personal resource, nor does it preclude receptivity to dispositions and habits (professionalism, adaptability, innovation, flexibility, contemporariness) to be achieved through fashion and style. The invitation to learn and, more importantly, to apply what one has learned from the TV program to one's own life is enhanced by the convergence of television with other media. If television is a common and regularized technology of self-fashioning, it increasingly works in tandem with a network of other more specialized cultural technologies, including how-to books, mobile phones, magazines, and the Web. These "converged" technologies are often (but not necessarily) traceable to the same corporate parent, and in that sense self-fashioning on TV is bound up in strategies of corporate cross-promotion and synergy. However, there is more at stake in television's ties to other media than the devising of ways to direct consumers from one product to another within the same network of corporate ownership. Convergence also enables formerly discrete media to form a circuit of cultural technologies for shaping and guiding conduct, with each medium serving as a cultural relay to similar "governing" strategies presented in different (including interactive) forms. This enables the "empowering" mission of the programs by extending advice and ways to apply it to viewers who are no longer expected to merely absorb the TV text, in the old sense of broadcast media. The *What Not to Wear* viewer can purchase how-to style books written by the hosts of the programs, can find articles by them in magazines, and can log onto the *What Not to Wear* sites, where style quizzes, customized tip sheets, before/after photos, chat rooms, and other interactive components bring them more directly into the makeover game as active participants. This is also a complex process, however, that hinges less on didactic instruction than on the playful "empowerment" of the self and others. The BBC's *What Not to Wear* site, for example, draws users into the logic of the makeover as subjects and experts. In addition to a detailed version of the sort of advice circulating on the TV show, the site features "real-life" video submissions sent by fans of the TV program for constructive critique by other users, who take up the role of the advisor who explains "what not to wear" to be "cruel to be kind." Finally, convergence has facilitated the production of a self-governing fashion subject through "on-demand" and mobile services. The capacity to access the web sites (and with them video clips from the TV shows) across boundaries of time and space, from computers as well as mobile phones, along with reality TV's trendsetting move into podcasting and text messaging, has made work on the self a truly ongoing and all-encompassing endeavor. When the BBC encourages *What Not to Wear* viewers to take cell phones into the dressing room so they can access on-the-scene advice before making a purchase, the logic of "rational" consumption as a strategy of self-empowerment escapes any notion of TV's distinct textual boundaries. The ability to "keep in touch" with the program in an increasingly mobile world is presented as another dimension of "empowerment," as well as a heightened obligation to live one's life as a project of self-enterprise.

The Male Makeover and the Feminization of Work

In *The Culture of Narcissism*, critic Christopher Lasch put a feminine face on the "cult of the self" he saw overtaking modern life. In a chapter devoted to work, Lasch traced the collapse of a Protestant work ethic in which "values of industry and thrift held the key to material success and spiritual fulfillment" to a new ethic of "self-preservation" based on self-entrepreneurialism and contrivance. The "rhetoric of achievement, of single-minded devotion to the task at hand . . . no longer provides an accurate description of the struggle for personal survival," he argued. Instead, the upwardly mobile individual advances by "convincing his associates that he possesses the attributes of a winner." Lasch situated this shift within an "age of diminishing expectations" brought about by post-industrial capitalism. Nonetheless, he constructed a deeply gendered moral divide between honest work (male) on the one hand, and crafty self-promotion (female) on the other. If the industrious and self-reliant Robinson Crusoe once embodied liberalism's "ideal economic man," he argued, the new ideal was more akin to the manipulative female social climber Moll Flanders. In more graphic terms, Lasch lamented, "The happy hooker has replaced Horatio Alger."[17]

Reality TV's embrace of the personal makeover also speaks to the importance of assembling a stylized self as a device for enterprising the self in every dimension of social life, including work. This path to self-advancement is partly rooted in historical discourses and practices of femininity, which makes it an all too easy target of contempt by male intellectuals like Lasch. As feminist scholars have shown, the production of femininity is an ongoing endeavor involving constant training and props, and in that sense it mirrors the perpetual self-invention and lifelong education promoted by Greenspan and other officials as the solution to the crisis of "flexible" labor practices. Historically lacking legitimate opportunities for socioeconomic mobility, women have had to rely on bodily and social self-improvement as a means to advancement and security within the heterosexual marketplace, and have often been condemned for doing so (i.e., the gold-digger stereotype). Appearance, manners, charm, and personality could be strategically improved with the help of etiquette books, women's magazines, charm schools, Hollywood films, and other commercial cultural technologies. Feminine self-improvement demanded hard work on the part of the individual, but it also came to require an arsenal of consumer goods. The beauty and fashion industries offered women resources to achieve "self-actualization" even when the structures of society prohibited their advancement in the spheres of higher education and work. According to feminist cultural historian Kathy Peiss, "makeup promised personal transformation, a pledge that sounded deeply in American culture – from conversion experiences and temperance oaths to the appeals of medicine men and faith healers. . . . In the coloring and contouring of facial surfaces, a woman could not only change her looks but remake herself and her life chances."[18]

With the rise of liberal feminism and its postfeminist variations, women have been declared "free" to pursue equal opportunities for advancement through work and are called upon to do so by economic realities, the decline of the male breadwinner ethic, and official government policies (such as welfare-to-work requirements). This has caused a partial rupture in the path to feminine empowerment charted by Peiss, particularly on television. Makeover programs like *What Not to Wear* continue to emphasize techniques of self-fashioning, but they are more apt to situate the art of assembling a marketable self in relation to paid labor, so that wearing the most flattering hairstyle or cut of trousers is not only a way to snag a desirable man but also, and most importantly, a way to find and keep a desirable job. Because women continue to face workplace inequalities and obstacles that

contradict the postfeminist promise of freedom and choice, these residual strategies can be represented as empowering strategies for modern
times. At the same time, makeover pageants like *The Swan* have
emerged to provide extreme versions of the feminine makeover to
women who lack opportunities for succeeding in the contemporary
workforce. Meanwhile, men are being brought into the makeover
game as never before, including the beauty/style programs that now
appear in record numbers on television. Men are now expected to
perpetually recalibrate themselves in the flexible economy, which slides
into the expectation that they also work on their appearance and "soft"
social and personality skills. As anticipated by Lasch's smirking characterization of the "happy hooker," this development has triggered
anxieties about the encroachment of femininity as well as the promotion of consumerism and "superficial" work on the self.

We want to avoid reifying the gender hierarchies that often accompany such concerns by emphasizing the gendering of postindustrialism
– a phenomenon that Lasch recognizes, but does not examine. As
Valerie Walkerdine argues, postindustrial service work, which has
replaced agriculture and manufacturing as the mainstay of employment
for most people in capitalist societies, requires the adoption of characteristics (empathy, nurturance, communication, and "to be looked-at
ness") that have historically been deemed female. It is no coincidence,
given this economic valuing of femininity, that the British Labour Party
went as far as to declare that when it comes to work the "future is
female," notes Walkerdine. What's more, the "self-invention demanded
of workers in the new flexible economy" requires an entrepreneurial
relationship to the self that has much in common with the enticement
to constantly make and remake femininity. What is different is that, as
the stability promised in the traditional work ethic fades, men now
"have to face the necessity of constant self-invention and to produce
for themselves a marketable (feminized) image, perhaps for the first
time."[19] If the female worker is now being positioned as the "mainstay
of the neoliberal economy," the process of "retraining" takes on historically feminine dimensions as well, and it is for this reason that the
makeover can be offered to men as well as to women as a way to navigate the new conditions of work. What has long been demanded of
women – to be adaptable, desirable, presentable, consumable – has been
intensified and extended to the postindustrial workforce as a whole, says
Walkerdine; makeover TV helps to foster these attributes.[20]

Men are a normalized if secondary concern of many TV makeover programs, where they often appear as subjects who can no longer rely on a relatively stable path of upward mobility and therefore need to constantly work on themselves to compete or advance at work. The postindustrial feminization of work is especially apparent on *Queer Eye for the Straight Guy*, which debuted on Bravo in 2004. On this program, five gay men make over heterosexual men by teaching them grooming, style, culture, decorating, and gourmet cooking and by introducing them to a burgeoning array of male beauty products. These skills and products are presented as "naturally" belonging to gay urban lifestyle experts whose sexual difference is conveyed by stereotypically feminine attributes, such as knowledge about beauty products and an interest in fashion. However, domesticity and the care of the self is also shown to be learnable by heterosexual men who need a boost of encouragement in their personal and professional lives. In part, this must be done to meet the demands of the postfeminist middle-class dating market, where women who are now expected to earn their own living as opposed to depending on male providers may expect partners to look attractive and share in historically feminized quality of life responsibilities. However, the makeover game is also tied to self-empowerment at work in ways that bring men into the feminized domain of the pursuit of the marketable self as a "technical achievement."[21] Many episodes seek to transform underemployed or unrealized males into successful purveyors of their occupational futures by helping them to join the metrosexual market by developing a stylish new look, providing an education in the new male beauty and grooming products, and providing a crash course in social and cultural skills (manners, etiquette, "people skills") that have historically been coded as feminine. In an episode that demonstrates how "to-be-looked-at-ness" has also come to matter as a strategy of self-advancement for men, Jesan needs the Fab Five's help to break into the quintessential female dream job: fashion modeling. However, he is working three menial service jobs, which leaves him little time to pursue his dream, and on top of that he lives in a room in a boarding house. Jesan's inability to advance in his chosen line of work is presented as a common problem, and in that sense the episode partially disrupts the characterization of the individual as a free agent in the new flexible economy. However, Jesan's difficulty "breaking in" to the highly competitive world of male modeling is easily solved with a crash course in fashion, culture, and grooming that is customized to his professional goal:

> Many of us know what it's like to have a job but not get closer to the job. You know, the dream job that you believe will make you deliriously happy; the kind of job that you look forward to doing every day. That describes Jesan's situation perfectly. Lucky for him, he has the Fab Five . . . to get his modeling career off the ground.

As a heterosexual man (his girlfriend is repeatedly mentioned, as is always the case on *Queer Eye*, which constantly affirms normative heterosexuality), Jesan must learn skills and techniques stereotypically associated with femininity as well as homosexuality in order to transform himself into an entrepreneurialized "object of desire." In addition to learning how to groom and fashion himself to make the most of his good looks, he must be taught how to primp and preen before the camera, and to "sell himself" to clients, by a professional modeling agency. He also must learn how to strategically manage himself in "the business" by acquiring the social and self-promotional skills needed to meet and impress clients, book gigs, and socialize at "model central," a hangout for models and agents. Having presented Jesan with guidelines for success not only in the male modeling but in the larger postindustrial feminized workplace as well, the Fab Five sent him on modeling appointments, where it will be up to him to use his newly acquired skills to "win over" potential clients.

Like other TV makeover programs, *Queer Eye* fuses expert diagnoses, video surveillance, and hands-on examinations with humor and suspense to present guidelines for living within an entertaining format that bears little resemblance to the slow-paced somberness of bona fide "educational" TV. The program governs through a process of self-objectification in that the trainee is forced to step outside his social and cultural "habitus" to examine himself from the vantage point of the experts, and to assess his own progress in implementing the advice and techniques they provide. The format also facilitates a rationality of governing at a distance, in that the experts progressively recede into the background, relying on remote video technology to "watch over" without being seen as the trainee works to practice and implement new grooming, cooking, decorating, social, and wardrobe skills on his own. Both processes are extended to TV viewers at home who, although one step removed from the TV makeover, are offered additional resources to carry out their own customized version of self-fashioning. The television text is only one component of the expansive *Queer Eye* project, which includes a how-to book and a web site where TV viewers can obtain archived fashion, beauty, decorating, and domestic advice as well as episode summaries, video clips, and complete product guides. Multimedia and mobility are also constructed as being very important to the converged *Queer Eye* experience. Reality TV pioneered the fusion of television programming and portable media devices such as video iPods, PDAs, cell phones, and computers; as one executive explained, "entertainment has to be able to find people wherever they are, and in forms that can be easily customized and digested." This turn toward portable nuggets of content has implications for the self-work inherent to makeover programming, as it provides opportunities to bring the viewer/user into the reinvention logic of the makeover game more directly than the viewing experience alone. *Queer Eye* viewers are enticed to subscribe to wireless updates as well as podcasts with promotions such as "Want to make yourself better on the go? Download weekly Hip Tip Podcasts and you're on your way to a better you. Every week download ten new tips from the Fab 5, transfer them to your MP3 player and listen to them anywhere you want (within the law that is)."

As Walkerdine argues, the feminization of work has not unraveled gender inequalities, because it is easier for men to learn to perform an entrepreneurial, stylized version of self-reinvention than it is for women to legitimately acquire and project attributes such as brilliance and competency, which have historically been coded as inherently male. When women attempt to "perform" intelligence and authority, they are more apt to be perceived as pathological than self-entrepreneurial, especially if they lack class status, notes Walkerdine. Women who do not have access to higher education, family networks, and social/cultural capital as entry points to the professional middle class on their own "merit" are offered another route to personal and professional empowerment by makeover TV. The debut of *The Swan*, a serialized makeover program that culminates in a beauty pageant, illustrates the double bind that working and lower-middle class women face as postindustrial work becomes feminized and techniques of femininity become valuable skills to be acquired and exploited by men as well as women. Each week, *The Swan* aims to completely transform a female "ugly duckling" through extensive cosmetic surgery procedures as well as dental work and compressed exercise, diet, and grooming regimens. Unlike other makeover shows, which strive for a "realistic" surgical outcome, *The Swan* remakes women who typically lack college degrees as well as professional careers into the living embodiment of "to-be-looked-at" femininity. The program ups the ante on the TV makeover game by mobilizing a team of surgeons, dentists, personal trainers, stylists, and life coaches to transform an ordinary female into the personification of sexualized beauty, as characterized by hourglass figures, enormous artificial breasts, high cheekbones, plump lips, flowing hair (created through extensions), gleaming white teeth, and fancy evening gowns. In this sense the program draws from, and intensifies, a history of the promotion of makeup and costume as potential "class levelers" among women. While the doctors are reified as magicians of science, the woman must also contribute to the transformation by following a strict low-calorie diet and exercising constantly under the close supervision of a professional dietician and fitness trainer. Each episode works on two women simultaneously; by the end of the episode, they are reevaluated by the professionals, who determine which one of them will be allowed to compete in *The Swan* pageant. The woman with the "most dramatic improvement" goes on to the next round. The other is sent home, armed with her new-and-improved femininity, to resolve personal problems and hardships (unemployment, marital trouble, financial difficulties, poor self-esteem) introduced earlier in the episode, provided, of course, that she is able to keep up the intensity of *The Swan*'s regime. Because only one woman will ultimately win the title of most beautiful each season, the makeover game retains its competitive element, despite its bold claim to make any woman into an object of desire through the combination of surgery, expertise, and supervised self-work.

Reality dating programs are another place to observe the postindustrial feminization of work, which, as Walkerdine notes, involves adopting historically feminine personality and social attributes in addition to "to-be-looked-at-ness." Dating show contestants must work on themselves to win over others in a strategic game of romance. Work seeps into social life, as the contestants navigate the sexual marketplace as highly calculating and self-enterprising individuals. *Joe Millionaire* (2003, Fox) set the tone when it dressed a blue-collar construction worker in fancy clothes and coached him in fine wine, grooming, fashion, and the art of conversation so that he was able to "pass" as the son of a wealthy financier. Each week, "Joe" passively-aggressively eliminates one of a cadre of beautiful women competing for his attention by awarding a prize of fine jewels to those who are chosen to progress to the next round. The women, who believe they are competing for a relationship with a wealthy man, fantasize on camera about the luxurious lifestyle they expected to enjoy as a result. They also spend much screen time styling themselves and strategizing about their performance in preparation for the group activities and individual "dates" leading up to the weekly elimination ritual. This is not surprising, for within the dating game format, women and men who are serious about winning are expected to work on themselves, evaluate themselves, and reinvent themselves when called for, as explained by *The Reality TV Handbook*, a compendium of advice for would-be contestants:

> The most difficult part of dating on a reality show is that you will likely have only one chance to convince your date that you are exactly who she is looking for. When you have the opportunity to be alone with a potential love interest, you must stand out from your competitors. If you choose to be yourself, then you are putting your faith in the hands of fate – if you are meant to be together, you are meant to be together – and there is little advice that can be offered to keep you in the game. But if you want to boost your chances, dating advisor Eve Hogan and psychologist Dr. Barry Goldstein recommend employing the following techniques to convince your date that you're the One: Make eye contact, create similar interests, attempt to finish your date's sentences, laugh and touch your date, be appreciative of your date.[22]

Dating games epitomize what Lasch characterized as a calculated ethic of "self-preservation" creeping into every dimension of social life. "Beneath the concern for performance lies a deeper determination to manipulate the feelings of others to your advantage," he wrote of the changing nature of work. "The search for competitive advantage through emotional manipulation increasingly shapes not only personal relations but relations at work as well; it is for this reason that sociability can now function as an extension of work by other means."[23] What Lasch, writing in the 1970s, didn't fully recognize was the changing nature of post-welfare liberal governance, which offers self-enterprise as a resource to individuals who are increasingly obliged to take care of themselves, look out for their personal interests, manage difficult situations, and make strategic choices in the name of their own "freedom" and empowerment. As Walkerdine (paraphrasing Rose) argues, "the imperative to be free within liberalism and developed within neoliberalism demands that under neoliberalism we live our life as if it were in furtherance of a biographical project of self-realization." Dating games enact this strategy of government, which mirrors the management of skilled femininity in its emphasis on recalibration and self-invention. What we are seeing in dating programs that is new is that men also have to worry about capacities to be made over, and to win others over, through their looks and personalities in addition to or instead of traditional markers of male desirability, such as wealth and professional accomplishment. In addition to *Joe Millionaire*, the dating genre has produced *Average Joe*, in which men who "lack" desirable physical attributes must work hard to win the favor of a beauty queen. This requires exercise regimens and professional make-overs as well as continual reflection about personal "strategy" and self-presentation. On *Mr. Personality*, the male contestants are forced to wear latex masks that conceal their faces; only the TV viewer can see what they look like. With looks out of the picture, they have to work more intensely on their personalities and develop acute "soft skills" (such as being a good listener) that are also part of the "flexible" political economy.[24]

The place of gender in the makeover game was made particularly clear by *Beauty and the Geek* (WB), a hybrid makeover/dating program. The premise of the program hinges on the double bind referred to by Walkerdine, in that beautiful young women are paired with brilliant but socially and physically awkward young men, with the idea that each will help transform the other into better individuals. The men, who all had college degrees, many from prestigious universities, and who were pursuing "smart" career tracks ranging from rocket science to mathematics, are to learn such skills as decorating, grooming, fashion, and the art of personality. They are challenged to break out of their one-dimensional "geekdom" by making over a bedroom, singing karaoke, and learning about spa services. The women, who are introduced on camera as cocktail waitresses, models, and service workers, are thin, buxom, and skilled in techniques of femininity, including makeup, clothes, and flirtation. They are presented as not only uninterested in academics, but incapable of smartness (jokes often revolved around the women's mispronunciations and misunderstandings of basic terms and concepts). To prepare the women for a life beyond beauty and socializing, the geeks attempt to provide a concentrated tutorial in science, politics, finance, and other "intellectual" matters. While the men are able to refashion themselves fairly well, the women are much less convincing in their adoption of "geeky" attributes. No matter how much tutoring they receive, the flexible logic of the makeover game can not reverse the discourse of femininity from which it draws: *Beauty and the Geek* can bring young men into the process of self-invention through restyling and charm instruction, but it cannot transform women without social, educational, and cultural capital into successful knowledge workers.

Branding the Self: TV Talent/Job Searches

The televised talent/job search is a form of makeover TV to the extent that experts, teachers, and judges seek to transform raw human potential into coveted opportunities for self-fulfillment through the realization and expression of talent. Such programming ranges from the amateur talent search revitalized by *American Idol* (Fox) to programs that attempt to discover new talent (usually in the business, fashion, or performance sectors) by immersing contestants in a grueling training regimen and/or competitive elimination process (*Making the Band*, VH1; *America's Next Top Model*, UPN; *The Cut*, CBS; *I Want to Be a Hilton*, NBC; *The Apprentice*, NBC; *Project Runway*, Bravo; *American Inventor*, NBC). Both strands are entrepreneurial in many senses, including the way in which unpaid labor becomes a commodity for exploitation by the culture industries, who profit not only from the TV shows and related merchandise, but also from the consumer goods and services (CDs, fashion, advertising campaigns) produced through the shows as incubators of talent. Talent/job searches are entrepreneurial in another way as well: Within the flexible economy, they work to produce what du Gay calls the governing rationality of the self-enterprising worker.[25] TV governs from a distance through these ventures by circulating techniques for "self-steering" in the new labor economy, and by enacting processes of governing the self at work.

According to Sennett, the changing nature of work produces three mighty challenges for contemporary workers: The first is what he calls the compression of time, which requires the embrace of new strategies for "managing short-term relationships, and oneself, while migrating from task to task, job to job, place to place." The second challenge is to remain marketable in an economy that values potential ability and a capacity to multitask over the ideal of "learning to do one thing really well." Since the "shelf life of many skills is short," workers must retrain frequently, and they also work to discover and develop new talents and abilities inside themselves. Finally, the worker must learn to "let go of the past," says Sennett. In the flexible economy, "work is not a possession, nor does it have a fixed content." It "becomes a position in a constantly changing network," and while people may compete for position in the corporation, no "one location is an end to itself" and no one "owns" their place. As past experience and prior service become less valued, the worker is drawn into a "self-consuming passion" to keep themselves mobile within the labor force. While this process has something in common with the "constant search for new things" endorsed by consumer culture, it is "larger than simply being so ambitious one is never content with what one has." One consequence of the ongoing corporate reinvention and restructuring that defines the current economy is that "work identities get used up – they become exhausted," which requires the worker to embrace constant reinvention as well.[26]

Illustration 3.2   Would-be models must work on their looks as well as their personalities in the competition, *America's Next Top Model* (10 × 10 Entertainment for UPN, 2005)

Sennett does not believe that most people desire to, or are capable of, operating this way. "A self oriented to the short term, focused on potential ability, willing to abandon past experience − is an unusual sort of human being," he writes. Reality TV's talent/job searches enact an intense version of the model of work Sennett describes as a game, and reward people's capacities and desires to meet the challenges and expectations being placed on them. On *I Want to Be a Hilton* (2005), a competitive game hosted by Kathy Hilton, wife of hotel heir Rick Hilton and mother of celebrity socialite Paris Hilton, contestants whose actual occupations include motor vehicle clerk, telephone salesman, bartender, construction worker, landscape supply clerk, ranch hand and retail store manager compete for a $200,000 trust fund and a chance to live in a swanky New York apartment for a year. According to NBC, they will also get a crash course on the New York City high life as "Hilton educates the contestants in the do's-and-don'ts of haute couture, etiquette and even how to handle an unforgiving press." More importantly, they will be exposed to glamorous contacts and insider networking opportunities, which can be exploited for personal gain. To remain in the game, however, the contestants must progress in competitive challenges intended to test their potential to "live like a Hilton," from dog grooming and boat rowing to charity work, holding a press conference, and staging a fashion show. Exemplifying the flexible economy of Sennett's analysis, *I Want to Be a Hilton* links the long-standing rags-to-riches fantasy to "portable human skills, being able to work on several problems with a shifting cast of characters." The challenges vary from week to week, so that each training period is compressed, and self-mastery in one pursuit cannot easily be transferred to the next realm. Moreover, in addition to performing as individuals, the contestants must also demonstrate their capacity to work with a rotating team of other contestants, which demands "soft skills" such as listening, cooperation, and an ability to encourage and motivate others. The point of the game is not to master a particular skill but rather to demonstrate potential (as judged by Hilton) in a wide range of capacities associated with performing the work of a socialite. While the contestants are expected to manage themselves, they are overseen from a distance by Hilton, who at end of each episode (borrowing from the corporate model of management Donald Trump established in *The Apprentice*) determines who has "disappointed her" and who will leave the game. Contestants are forced to reexamine their conduct and behavior through Hilton's eyes in ways that parallel the self-objectification process that occurs on beauty/style makeovers. Hilton's point, as she often emphasizes, is not to punish, but to enable what Drucker calls "feedback analysis," or the individual's own continuously monitoring the consequences of his/her decisions and actions at work so that self-management becomes a reality because the worker is able to "adapt and improve." However, not all of the contestants proved willing to engage with this sort of self-scrutiny. Several candidates eventually rejected the enterprising path to mobility offered under Hilton's tutelage, including an African American single mother who, when eliminated, expressed pride in the fact that she had not changed or "improved" herself as suggested. As she stated with relief during her exit interview, "I am still Leticia."

I Want to be a Hilton rearticulates the American Dream of mobility by joining it to the new requirements of ongoing adaptability, flexibility, innovation, and potential for change. Other talent/job games do something similar in that they often demand working in teams that change constantly and performing across numerous (often unrelated) challenges, and require the ability to learn new skills quickly, change strategies, and recalibrate oneself on short notice. While the material prize (a chance to apprentice to Donald Trump, a professional modeling contract, entry into the fashion business) offered by television is one motivator, many programs present work as its own reward in the sense described by Sennett. This way of thinking about work can be traced to the managerial philosophy of "excellence" that emerged in the 1980s and 1990s to motivate workers by promising them more opportunities for self-management. The impetus, as du Gay argues, was to shift the purpose of work away from material rewards, and toward a promise of self-fulfillment that joined the individual's self-enterprising capacities to productivity and other corporate goals. McGee shows how a related discourse of "do what you love, the money will follow" began to permeate job advice guides during the "downsizing" of the 1990s, which presented the "passion of work" as substitute for material compensation, security, pension plans, and so on. Career advice books began to argue that "shaping one's work life ought to be conceived of as an art," which promised individual creativity and agency as the upside of the flexible economy. At the same time this was happening, an "artistic mentality" was providing an "ideal vehicle for motivating a demoralized, downsized, and otherwise dissatisfied labor force," notes McGee. Drawing from Andrew Ross's study of dotcom workers, she argues that artists provided an "ideal work model" for the postindustrial work force because their passion for what they do motivates them to tolerate long hours for low (or no) pay and they are used to a "freelance" mindset of contingency. In essence, the "new model of artists/workers . . . creates a voluntary army of people who will work for fun."[27]

Many TV job/talent searches are tellingly set within the creative cultural industries, another testing ground for flexible labor. As McRobbie argues in her study of fashion designers, the "talent-led economy" of self-expressive work demands "capacities for inexhaustible resourcefulness, resilience and entrepreneurialism" that (as with the art world) set the stage for the future of labor. However, such capacities still do not guarantee success in a "lottery economy," where opportunities for success are limited.[28] McRobbie argues that the stock rags-to-riches fantasy has mutated into a less predictable mediation of success and failure, in which seemingly random factors such as "bad timing" loom large. For McRobbie, this uncertainty is tolerated because, as with the arts, creative cultural work is presented as a reward onto itself – a self-fulfilling enterprise. Similarly, while the would-be fashion designers who appear on *Project Runway* (Bravo) and *The Cut* (CBS) seek to advance their careers, their passion for their chosen line of work is what rationalizes their devotion of boundless (unpaid) labor to a competitive game with only one prize. The prize awarded by *The Cut* is a position with fashion mogul Tommy Hilfiger's clothing company, where the winner will design his or her own collection under the Hilfiger label. The contestants compete in weekly challenges that range from making fashion statements out of garbage to ethnic "trendspotting"; at the end of each episode, one contestant is deemed "out of style" by Hilfiger and sent home. As with other job games, Hilfiger governs from a distance. Contestants work in teams without direct supervision, but they are also required to participate in an objectifying evaluation process. Design is only one component of time-compressed challenges that measure entrepreneurialism, teamwork skills, and the capacity for self-expression within the Hilfiger brand. As Paul Smith has shown, Hilfiger's fashion empire was built on a flexible model of capitalism in which the "mass customization" and branding of goods is valued over their production, which is outsourced.[29] On Hilfiger's TV program, contestants must simultaneously tailor their creative labor to fit Hilfiger's market niche, and "brand" themselves as distinctive commodities worthy of corporate investment. In this sense, the creative talent competition illustrates McGee's argument that "the primary way individuals seem to imagine achieving any measure of safety and security" in the new economy is by "identifying with capital – by imagining themselves as entrepreneurs, as the "CEOs of Me, Inc.""[30] While Hilfiger is dismissive if not cruel to contestants who fail to demonstrate "potential" to bolster themselves in the service of the Hilfiger brand, uncontrollable circumstances (including the fact that only one person can win) are shown to play some role in the competition, and this also differentiates *The Cut* from conventional upward mobility myths in the sense theorized by McRobbie. No matter how passionate, adaptable, industrious, cooperative, talented, and enterprising the contestant, failure is not only a possibility but a probability in a "lottery" economy. As with work in the real world, there are no guarantees – a fact that *The Cut* and other TV job games illustrate more than any other type of reality television.

America's Next Top Model (UPN), a job game in which young women compete for a professional modeling contract, brings together many of the techniques, strategies, and rationalities examined in this chapter. On this program, women live together while "enduring a series of tasks in a highly-accelerated modeling boot camp to see if they have what it takes to make it in the high-profile industry." Each week, they participate in challenges that have as much to do with the actualization of personality, perseverance, and self-enterprising skills as they do with beauty. Professional stylists, designers, agents, and models serve as coaches to the aspiring models, and as judges who continually evaluate the quality of the products (photograph, video) produced through their labor. The program was conceptualized by Tyra Banks, who presents her own story of overcoming poverty to achieve supermodel fame as a template for the women to emulate. Banks, who also has a talk show and a line of merchandise and has been profiled by *Fortune* magazine as an up-and-coming media mogul, attributes her stardom to her entrepreneurialism: "I see women in the mall or on the streets who look ten times better than I do," she claims, "but can they sell a product?" Likewise, on *America's Next Top Model*, the potential to sell products (including oneself) is valued and measured through challenges that range from improvising a commercial to hanging from wires for a fashion shoot (which caused a contestant with a fear of heights to break down in tears). The woman are also put in situations where they must quickly put together a look or persona using brand-name makeup, clothing, and other props for the camera, in order to demonstrate their ability to tailor their various assets to meet the shifting demands of spokeswomanship. According to Banks, the contestant "who passes all the tests" wins the game. Within the context of the flexible economy, *America's Next Top Model* demonstrates, through ongoing educational techniques and examinations, that no woman – not even a fashion model – can rely on "to-be-looked-at-ness" alone, but must constantly invent, cultivate, and promote multiple assets and talents. As widely noted in the media, Banks "relishes debunking the glamorous illusions of supermodels to reveal herself as a cellulite-prone, baggy eyed average girl." She regularly "appears on camera without makeup" to show women what can be accomplished through a combination of ingenuity, toil, and enterprise. Known for what she calls a "tough love" philosophy, she often screams at those who disappoint her – not to punish them, but to motivate them to improve or face elimination.[31] Banks encourages the women to envision themselves as "CEOs of Me" in the sense advocated by managerial gurus, which means seeing oneself as a branded commodity that requires perpetual reinvention: "Your product just happens to be your physical self and a little bit of your personality too," she explains. "When they don't want it anymore, don't feel discarded. Just know that your product is just not hot anymore. Know that you'll have to revamp that product or go into another field."[32] If the techniques and attributes of femininity are presented as strategies for navigating the insecurities of work, *America's Next Top Model* brings the process full circle.

Chapter 4

TV and the Self-Defensive Citizen

In 2004, producers for a prospective program for the Discovery Channel solicited applicants for a new twist on makeover TV: the "home security makeover show." The program debuted a year later as *It Takes a Thief*, an instructional game in which former criminals show just how easy it is to break into private homes, however secure the owners think they are. According to the program's publicity, personal security has become a serious and ongoing concern in which there's always "room for improvement" – or, in the parlance of a "home security makeover," always rooms for improvement. Each episode demonstrates not only how "vulnerable" the average homeowner is to a break-in, but "how upsetting life would be without prized possessions." To empower the participant (and, by extension, the TV viewer at home) to prevent such an occurrence, the program offers a "free" security upgrade and advice on avoiding future intrusions. Fusing improvement-oriented logic of the makeover to the "problems" of security and risk, it proclaims, "How Safe is Your House? Not as safe as we can make it!"

This chapter shows how instrumental TV has become to strategies of assessing and managing risk in the current stage of liberalism. In previous chapters, we touched on the role of risky behavior in the "interventions" and makeover programs that promise to turn needy individuals into purveyors of their own successful outcomes in life. Here, we trace TV's relationship to more specific security issues and risks, including financial risk, personal safety, and "homeland security." Expanding our focus on the role of cultural technologies in the "reinvention of government," we show how the increase of technologies for managing risk and security (including reality TV) has dovetailed with the privatization of welfare and the promotion of personal responsibility, as well as with heightened attention to terrorism and national security issues. We show how individuals are enlisted to understand and manage risks in all of these spheres, by following and implementing advice as well as by purchasing products. Rather than assuming there is "room for improvement," as TV claims, we analyze the current reasoning about risk, asking whether the new technologies, experiments, and solutions have made our lives safer and more secure, or whether their proliferation is symptomatic of greater insecurities.

Is it fair to claim, as has German social theorist Ulrich Beck, that we are now living in a "risk society"?[1] Is contemporary life more full of risks than in the past? If so, how do we verify this claim? Do we now live in a heightened state of risk because we have lost the traditional forms of social support (as Beck argues), or because we lack faith in the State to be a provider of social welfare and security? Or conversely, to what extent has the urgent sense of being "at risk" been manufactured by the sheer number of programs for risk assessment and management that have emerged? And do the procedures for verifying risks (i.e., the ubiquity of surveillance cameras and data collection) produce insecurities which, in turn, require further solutions and refinements of "outdated" procedures? Has the value and importance of risk management taken on an urgency in the United States since September 11, 2001? And if so, how?

To understand TV's relationship to changing strategies of security and risk management, it is useful first to review liberalism's long-standing preoccupation with strategies of both welfare and security. Foucault is particularly instructive about liberal government's early formation around programs of security and risk-management, and some of the most noteworthy and compelling elaborations of Foucaultian accounts of power and government have turned to liberalism's twin preoccupations with risk and security. Foucault's historical studies of early modern forms of power frequently dwell upon the emergence of programs and institutions of *public health* and *social medicine*.[2] Programs of public health were multifarious, including programs targeting various kinds of conditions, environments (particularly in cities), and populations considered to be unhealthy and capable of fostering the spread of unhealthiness. This is a crucial point because it casts "health" as not just a matter of overcoming physical ailments but as a more heterogeneous sense or "state" of well-being which is achieved or threatened throughout daily *living*. This is also a crucial point because it underscores how programs with a positive uptake (i.e., preventing the spread of disease or helping the unhealthy) simultaneously operated as programs of social management, regulating environments and populations.[3] And in this way, programs for managing public health and administering "social medicine" became a central objective and technique of liberalism as governmental rationality.

Foucault also noted that the "health of the modern state" *depends upon* the welfare, well-being, growth, and energy/productivity of its citizens. In this respect, the modern idea of *welfare* is intertwined with the care that government exercises over individuals and populations, "looking out for" and "watching over" citizens by protecting them from unseen risks, as a shepherd watches over a flock. Liberal government's role in instituting rules and regulations is rationalized as assuring healthy behavior *and* controlling unhealthy or risky behavior. Furthermore, the rules and standards for assessing and managing the healthiness of citizens are the way that health and unhealthiness are verified – made observable, explicable, and a fact according to modern techniques for measuring and assessing. The health of the *polis* (the citizenry and their environment) and of the *metropolis* (expansive and densely populated cities) has depended upon the rules, standards, regulative agencies, curative sciences, and improving technologies (e.g., public sidewalks, sewage systems, street lighting) for keeping the *polis* orderly in all those places where bodies interact in potentially "unhealthy" ways. Pollution, disease, poverty, deviance, and criminality all became separate but interrelated targets of programs for assessing and managing public health. Putting criminals in prison, exiling lepers, delivering the insane to asylums, and installing street-light grids had the effect of linking a healthy life to orderly life and of moving perceived social ills or problems into environments where abnormalities could be observed and "cured." Developing the technologies for monitoring or "watching over" the various and changing threats to public health, therefore, has been a deeply governmental technology, and we discuss below how contemporary TV continues this practice, even as it has become instrumental for a new rationality about government.

Assuring public health, rationalized as protecting a citizenry from risks, has been central to modern conceptions of public safety. The modern idea of *police* and *policing* (as one role of the State) developed out of this positive role of government as looking after, safeguarding, and watching over citizens, and developing techniques for making their behavior rational, orderly, and knowable. "Policing" may be too strong and narrow a term to describe the various ways that the "health" of citizens' lives is managed and regulated. But the term is useful not only because it underscores the semantic tension between policing and policy/diplomacy but also because it emphasizes how welfare is always a matter of risk assessment and management. In this sense, the administration of public welfare and well-being has been tantamount to the administration of public safety and security. The *civility* – the proper, moral conduct – of modern societies has depended upon these techniques of guaranteeing public health as a matter of public safety and security. While the modern conception of a police force has to do with the authority of the State to enforce rules and regulations that prevent, discourage, and quarantine unhealthy/risky behaviors (malaise, sickness, criminality), liberalism has sanctioned policing as necessary for the health and welfare of its citizens. Government thus operates "at a distance" in two senses: administering the rules and regulations for keeping society healthy, and administering public health and safety through multiple programs and associations throughout society, which collectively make the *security* of society and citizens – a "social security" in the broadest sense – the responsibility of the State as well as the private programs and citizens comprising a civil society.

How a society's security is achieved brings together the administration of public safety and public welfare as a "safety net." In this respect, the responsibilities of liberal government have developed in two (albeit connected) ways: guaranteeing various *liberties* and *rights* of citizens (formalized in constitutions) but also protecting against various *risks* (the "social obligation" of state-government). Exercising the political freedoms valued by liberalism (and the economic freedoms valorized under capitalism) involves calculating and managing risks to maximize protection and minimize exposure. In the "security society," liberal government constantly develops, legislates, and experiments about how best to manage the insecurities of citizens (to guard against factors deemed risky and to protect against *exposure*), but also how best to maintain its own authority and expertise to manage these insecurities.

For the most part, the current stage of liberalism (a "neoliberalism") involves a deepening and widening of the arrangement that Foucault has discussed. However, there have been some noteworthy changes.

Building on our arguments about TV's relation to forms of privatization and personalization of welfare, this chapter considers many forms of privately provided security as social welfare, as well as the ways in which these programs are being acted upon by state agencies and administrations, and how a Homeland Security has formed around the considerable networks of securitization. This line of analysis considers how civil rights and liberties (as well as privacy) are being redefined, regulated differently than in the past, and even trumped, by both public and privately administered programs of securitization. While the rights of citizens are formalized in constitutions, the security of citizens is a matter of *social contracts*, many of which are now formed informally through private providers and with oneself. While we will analyze current efforts by the State to protect citizens from risks (as matters of national or "homeland" security) through public–private "partnerships," much of our analysis examines the expansive networks of private, personalized, and customizable security services and technologies now available, and their contributions to the securitization of the social.

As we have seen, the current governmental arrangement for welfare citizenship has occurred through private, market-oriented outsourcing and citizens' daily reliance upon private providers for social welfare and security. As Rose has noted about the current stage of liberalism, "the social logics of welfare bureaucracies and service management have been replaced by a new "configuration of control agencies – police, social workers, doctors, psychiatrists, mental health professionals – [that] become connected up with one another in circuits of surveillance and communication designed to minimize the riskiness of the most risky."[4] Increasingly this requires citizens to act on their own behalf by managing their own risks with the private resources available to them. In this sense, "advancing" liberalism involves not just reinventing *government* but reinventing citizens' relation to a *security society* through new plans, experiments, and demonstrations of risk assessment and management. This has involved changing the relation of citizens to the resources for assessing and managing risk by making risk more observable and intelligible, and by training citizens to be the guardians of their own security throughout daily life. Whereas Foucault's writing about risk management in a security society helps us understand liberal government's deep, historical tendency to cast the *State* as "watching over" the health of its citizens, the current governmental arrangement emphasizes a new rationality about the State's implication in private and personalized *networks* of support, resources available to targeted lifestyle clusters. Furthermore, the new role of these private networks necessitates rethinking Foucault's argument about the State as watchman over a healthy society; in these times (as discussed below) corporate health, and the health of private "support networks," become a measure of a healthy State and society.

There are three general ways that the programs for managing the wide variety of contemporary risks have been integral to "reinventing government," and we outline them briefly using the events surrounding Hurricane Katrina – events that do not represent the full range of contemporary risks but that help clarify what has changed and help introduce the following sections about TV. First, risk management has been part of a *federalism* that favors "empowering" regional and local government to act as "first responders" to current risks, with the federal government cast in a "supporting" role. The lack of timely response to the devastation of Hurricane Katrina in 2005 is an infamous example of this current reasoning about the role of federal and local government in managing intersecting risks. Thousands of volunteer "first-responders" (doctors, firefighters, and police) from various municipal and state agencies around the United States made themselves available, even though many were turned back by federal authorities in Louisiana. The lack of coordination and the failures between federal and local responses (particularly regarding the proper role of the Federal Emergency Management Agency) became a catalyst for further risk assessment and refining security techniques of national and local administrative agencies, though still within the federalist model of security planning and response.

Second, programs for managing and assessing risks have been part of "*public–private partnerships,*" with the federal government again in a "supporting" posture. The response to Katrina elevated nonprofit agencies, such as the Red Cross and Habitat for Humanity, to the first line of a civil defense, even as the Red Cross's blatant cost-overrun and widely reported inefficiencies demonstrated its precariousness as a *primary* provider of civil defense. As explained below, mobilizing and acting upon private programs of risk assessment and management is fundamental to the Bush administration's "compassionate conservatism" *and* Homeland Security that link public welfare and public safety, and the secular and religious roles in "saving" people. However, experiments such as "compassionate conservatism" and "Homeland Security" could not be possible without a relatively robust (and relatively recent) network of private programs designed to assess and manage risk. The "cleanup" after Hurricane Katrina mobilized various branches of these private networks of risk management which already have become part of what counts as a "support service" in the lives of different populations in the United States. This network includes private agencies assessing risk to personal property and finances – insurance experts and claims adjustors (working in communication with building and health inspectors), a real-estate industry, and credit providers, debt counselors, and financial advisors. This network of personal property and financial risk management operates (often on the same populations) with networks of managers of personal health – the nexus of doctors, psychiatrists, mental health professionals, and social workers discussed by Rose.

Third, the reinvention of government assumes, encourages, and increasingly requires that citizens assess and manage their own risks. This occurs in conjunction with the increasingly expansive array of private–public programs in the first and second networks described above, and it certainly involves TV. As discussed in Chapters 2 and 5, the paramedical expertise of Dr. Phil McGraw and the "team efforts" of the crew of *Extreme Makeover: Home Edition* both became televisual solutions to healing select families/households. They provided a model for how, privately and individually, to restore a public's health, to manage a newly risky population that lacked personal possessions, and to provide a plan for securing their lives in a region that may yet be affected by future hurricanes. These TV demonstrations and interventions not only operated in "partnerships" with nonprofit agencies (many listed on the web sites for these TV programs) and with counseling networks (like those Rose mentions), but also in consort with the Bush administration's proposal for Enterprise Zones, wherein homeowners (rather than those who never owned homes) are supposed to build their way back to a healthy and stable life – albeit still within the shadow of a fragile levee system. Katrina thus became not just a TV program, but a laboratory for testing and demonstrating the latest experiments in risk assessment and management as "life interventions." There were the "live" demonstrations of private citizens being prevented from assisting flood victims because federal and local "first-responders" considered their rescue actions to be unsafe (!), and then there were the life interventions of the TV experts, who arrived after the flood, with a plan and a program to manage future risks and to secure financial futures. The following sections consider TV's instrumentality within these three fronts of the current governmentalization of safety and security and within other kinds of risks.

Managing Financial Risk as "Self-Accounting"

Reality TV has emerged around several crises in the global and US financial markets. The first was the sharp downturn of the US stock market in 1999 after several years of intense investment, much of which was directed to the "dotcom" enterprises and startup ventures (businesses developing computer hardware, software, and services, and a variety of "smart" technologies). As Mark Andrejevic has pointed out, reality TV exploited an emerging link between TV and the Web, coopting and repurposing successful online entrepreneurs such as "Jenny-cam" and "Dot.com Guy," which made money by providing direct and paid access to the live web sites.[5] According to Randy Martin, in the late-1990s investing also became personalized, faster, and more common among the investor class through computer software and online brokerage resources that fueled a syndrome popularly referred to as "day-trading."[6] The sharp downturn of the stock market was a televised saga, not only on news programs, but specifically on several TV networks that had emerged during this period to provide round-the-clock "investor-news."

The second crisis, the collapse of the World Trade Center in New York City, was a more dramatic TV event. The Trade Center had become a financial hub in a global economy, replacing the Empire State Building as the vertical icon of New York and as the skyscraper that King Kong scaled in the remake of the eponymous film. The attack on the Trade Center sparked a chain of fear in the United States that profoundly affected the confidence of investors and consumers. To rally US citizens in the days following the attack, President Bush urged citizens to return to shopping centers (presumably to shop) and to take vacations at resorts such as Disney World. As a TV event, the attack on the Trade Center was replayed over and over, demonstrating a "present danger" and "new" threats to national security that partly involved financial insecurities.

The third crisis was another TV event: the much publicized collapse of the energy-trading company, Enron, a few months after September 11, 2001. Enron was a company that benefited enormously from action by the administration of George W. Bush in the early 1990s to deregulate local public utilities. It was one of the most recognized philanthropic resources in Houston, Texas (the site of Enron's corporate headquarters), and was heralded (even outside Houston) as a new model of corporate and employee management, listed as one of top Fortune-500 corporations in the United States for over five successive years, and one of the most recognized and active contributors to the election of George W. Bush (and, according to Bush, a successful model of corporate government and corporate citizenship). And for a few weeks in late 2001, Enron had the dubious epitaph of being "the largest bankruptcy in history . . . and in the world." For a company that in 2000 had about 21,000 employees, reported assets of over $100 billion, and a stock value of $90 a share, the Enron bankruptcy totaled roughly $25 billion, reduced its stock value to about 30c a share, and wiped out most of the personal retirement funds of employees whose financial future had been pegged to stock options in the company. The company's collapse was hastened by a series of revelations in 2001 about its elaborate shell-games and financing schemes involving primarily its management of energy and broadband distribution and a network of subsidiaries. Following in the immediate aftermath of the first two crises, Enron became the most vivid demonstration of the problems in oversight accompanying the new regime of deregulated public utilities (as public services); Enron's collapse exposed lack of oversight in accounting, trading, finance, and investment. And Enron demonstrated the problems of the neoliberal models and rationality/ responsibility of corporate governance that privately controlled the social security of its employees, as corporate welfare-citizens. In the end, the company became a failed experiment in risking the financial futures of employees, of Houston's citizens who were not employed by the company, and of millions of citizens in the United States whose pension managers had invested in shares of Enron. Moreover, in early 2002 the bankruptcies of WorldCom (the second largest telecommunications company) and Global Crossing (also a telecommunications company) relegated Enron's bankruptcy to being the "second largest bankruptcy in history." Though bigger than Enron's, these latter two bankruptcies attracted relatively less media attention.[7] Bankruptcy seemed to matter less as TV spectacle than as the "new normal" – the weekly reality – of TV.

Cumulatively, these events (in part as media events) contributed to a state of panic and unease, which vividly demonstrated the ripple effect of financial risks and linked financial risks to other kinds of risk – to an environment of risks and risk-taking. However, while the bankruptcies may have heightened public unease about being exposed to financial risk, and public uncertainty about the trustworthiness of the experts and authorities who "watch over" the new arrangements of public utilities, public accountancy, and the pensions of citizens whose financial futures are tied to corporate health and risk-taking, TV and other media have continued to prepare and empower citizens about how to live with risk – how to seek out reliable resources and how to better their chances of weathering or surviving in the current climate of risk-taking. In this sense, the events became public examples of the new state of heightened financial risk as well as the need to develop ever more effective and reliable resources for calculating and managing risk privately and by individuals. This environment required not only more but more customizable programs for maximizing protection and minimizing exposure, and made the assessment and management of financial risk profoundly part of daily life – a regular and self-regulating activity in one's life. While there are books, magazines, and web sites that offer customizable resources for an individual's management of personal finance and risk-taking in this environment, the seriality of TV programs has proven to be particularly well suited for regularizing financial self-management – for integrating financial management into one's daily life. An individual seeking aids in financial security and monetary risk-taking may have the "freedom" and the "independent" disposition to seek out reliable resources, but TV is a medium that is best suited to helping consumers help themselves by regularizing regimens of financial self-actualization through serialization.

As Randy Martin has argued, the realm of personal finance offers one way of thinking about the current expectation (in and around TV programs) to put one's life in order, to effectively manage oneself and one's family and household, to take an active role in tending to one's financial future and security. Personal finance (i.e., checkbook-balancing and other record-keeping) is a fundamental feature of the well-run, well-governed household. Describing what he calls "the financialization of daily life," Martin argues that making finance a part of personal routines makes it integral to an array of programs for self-actualization. In that sense, personal finance as the model, necessity, and reward of putting one's house in order bleeds into the various ways that one lives one's life as an ethic involving personal choices, risks, and responsibilities. And if we see finance as central to personal and domestic activities, we also need to recognize that the private/personal world is no less monetarily set or fixed than the outside world.[8] Even though we cannot always predict how certain investments will pay off, just as we cannot predict with certainty the direction of markets and economic trends in the world out there, we increasingly have been provided with ways of ordering our financial lives and our financial selves. While we may not be able to predict financial outcomes with certainty, we can (and are encouraged) to have fun with the games of finance and to take control at least over how we "invest ourselves."

The financialization of daily life has involved various kinds of services and programs (and even games) over the late 1990s. Particularly significant has been the emergence of day-trading as a practice whereby individual investors could (more or less) bypass the traditional financial investment services in order to act as his/her own broker.[9] It is no small coincidence that this trend occurred as a particular professional class and lifestyle cluster began to exploit online services and computer software to manage their own financial accounts as well as their personal financial investments. By the very late 1990s and early part of the 2000s, the risks of day-trading had been matched by the rapid growth of web-based services of personal finance and investment that made TV matter in slightly new ways. TV also became an extension of the contemporaneous proliferation of "do-it-yourself" guidebooks about managing personal bankruptcy, investment, taxes, insurance, retirement, and finance (e.g., *Personal Finance for Dummies*, currently in its fourth edition). Companies such as Ameritrade, which developed on-line divisions for "self-directed accounts," and E-Trade.Com, which had grown over the 1990s primarily as a web resource for personal investors, contributed to forging the link between TV and online trading by advertising frequently on TV programs and channels, particularly the growing number of financial programs discussed in this section. Ameritrade Plus promoted the "Power of Choice" as a reference to the freedoms of self-directed accounting, and in a TV advertising campaign with Sam Waterston during 2006 the company put forth a political–financial Declaration of Investor Independence: "Independence is the spirit that drives America's most successful investors." A 2005 TV ad-campaign for E-Trader software and services represented the exuberance of a man's successfully making trades from his personal computer at home, with the slogan, "Become Master of Your Domain," as the ad's narrator reminded TV viewers about its professional support network accompanying its software. These TV ads for web products and services collectively linked the "empowerment" of self-directed, interactive media (e.g., Ameritrade Plus web site's "Risk Quiz" for "evaluating your risks") with the routinization and discipline found through TV's serialized financial programs.

The trend toward personal investment-service companies that have forged a link between web- and TV-based resources became a basis for launching two 24-hour financial TV channels, the Bloomberg Network and CNBC. Both are, after CNN, global TV networks devoted entirely to investment news and tools.[10] The Bloomberg Network's title refers not only to its global TV, radio, and podcasting network but also to an array of investment services and products. CNBC emerged over the 1990s alongside NBC's other cable-news network, MSNBC, a joint venture with Microsoft (since divorced), and NBC's effort to capitalize upon the connection between the web and TV.[11] While both networks' programming schedules are vivid examples of TV's emerging place within the financialization of daily life, CNBC (more than the Bloomberg TV network) exploits TV's capacity to fit into the routines of daily life. Its daily offerings have included a morning show ("Morning Call"), a midday show ("Power Lunch"), and a close-of-the market program ("The Closing Bell"). If traditional TV was organized around the daily lives of households, these two networks signal two changes to the rationality of programming/scheduling for "financial TV": that there is always money to be made in a world which is eternally risky (24 hours a day) and that the daily life for a personal investor-class of viewers is organized around the major global trading venues such as Wall Street. That both networks continually run banners with trading information and stock-market fluctuations across the bottom of the screen (and often devote one vertical side of the screen to more information) makes these channels' "live-ness" an effect of the rationality of financial management and of the part that live financial TV plays in the organization of the daily lives of personal investment managers. As Martin has noted,

risk-taking is about living "in the moment,"[12] and TV's finance channels make risk-taking and risk management an ongoing game with
ever new strategies that private investors can use to participate throughout their day, or the channels simply provide background (investment
muzak) to create the proper mood for playing the game.

As technologies of the financialization of daily life, these two TV
networks separate (or rather, honor) finance as a distinct discipline/
game, even as the networks represent other activities through the lens
of finance. It is not just that these networks (as TV networks, multimedia networks, and networks of resources) help introduce into daily
life, and for private investors, a rationality about risk analysis endemic
to corporate management, with corporate managers and professional
investors providing the expertise on the networks' talk shows, and with
"financial news programs" providing the lens for understanding any
event in the world, as in business magazines and newspapers. As technologies of the financialization of daily life, they bring the rationalities
of corporate management to all sectors of government, especially
private life, family, and household. As we saw in previous chapters,
the link between education and game is crucial to the current stage
of TV – to TV's reinvention as a technology of government and citizenship. And the development and success of these two networks are
one dimension of this linkage, making investing and risk-taking about
fun and entertainment as well as about education and discipline.

The educational thrust of finance-TV is decidedly a commercial
enterprise, but it also is about shaping a productive, energized, risk-
taking citizen through a particular kind of citizenship training – one
that provides the rules, strategies, and technologies of self-investment
and self-accounting, as a path to self-actualization through "financial
independence." Acquiring sound financial education and becoming
plugged into networks of financial advice and motivational training are
crucial for a political and governmental rationality that has emphasized
breaking "pernicious" cycles of dependence on state forms of welfare.
The link between online and televisual self-investment and self-
accounting thus has recently involved the formation of "universities"
for active, "independent" investors. Like other kinds of online universities (which, as of 2005, could receive federal grant and tuition
support), and after the model of "adult" or "continuing education,"
these "universities for private investors" usually are extensions of the
network of a particular financial advice service, where advice and

training services straddle multiple media, including TV. Ameritrade, the Bloomberg Network, and Donald Trump all have launched their own online "universities." These universities consist of "lessons" or "classes" that are self-directed and that resemble both a menu of advice-hyperlinks and "twelve-step" programs common in self-help training. Trump University developed alongside Trump's TV series, *The Apprentice*, his series of books offering financial and investment advice, and his appearance on QVC (the shopping channel), where he articulated the educational potential of the book series to that of the TV series. And, as discussed in Chapter 5, *The Apprentice* was used during 2005 in seminars at some of the most prestigious business schools in the United States.

Because the finance-TV channels, as part of networks of personal financial services, cater to an investor class and lifestyle cluster that is predominantly male and affluent, their models of citizenship and their techniques of economic citizenship training cast their clients as being "at risk" in slightly different ways than other programs that cater to a class who is economically at risk. This is a complicated distinction, however, since both classes and lifestyle clusters require resources for being active and productive citizens within the current governmental rationality that values self-reliance and enterprise. In this latter sense, risk in the current security society is not restricted only to a class that cannot quite manage its own finances. The breadth of exposure covers more of the population, even though different classes and lifestyle clusters require somewhat different resources and TV.

One of the most noteworthy finance-TV programs that bridges this divide is Suze Orman's. Orman is a dynamic, energized financial advisor who stresses the importance of "financial education" as key to "turning one's life around" – or, as she puts it, to "changing the course of one's financial destiny." Beside being a prolific author (including *Nine Steps to Financial Freedom*) and active on the lecture circuit, Orman has had two TV programs – one on CNBC (*The Suze Orman Show*) and one on QVC (*The Financial Freedom Hour*). Orman's programs are geared particularly to female investors, representing a convergence of neoliberal and third-wave feminist valorization of women's financial independence and self-reliance. However, her CNBC program is primarily a call-in program, similar to radio call-in helplines, that attempts to solve the financial problems of men and women. (She commonly refers to female callers as "sisters.") While there has been

Illustration 4.1   Personal finance guru Suze Orman teaches women to "empower" themselves through money management (CNBC TV for CNBC, 2006)

"paid programming" by authors and professional investors in non-primetime TV since the 1980s, Orman represents a new legitimacy of expertise because of her programs' articulation of "self-worth to net-worth" and of financial self-help to "life interventions" as social work. As part of the schedule of programs at CNBC, Orman's program for financial self-recovery involves learning how to invest wisely but also how to manage daily financial responsibilities, frequently by a class that has difficulty making ends meet. As in radio call-in programs offering financial advice, Orman's CNBC program recommends how to design a very personal regimen of financial self-accounting, helping those who have the desire and capacity to help themselves, and apologetically but firmly explaining to some subjects that they are beyond help. Even in these examples of citizens who are at risk, her message often laments the lack of financial education in public schools, as part of a standard curriculum to prepare citizens for the rest of their financial lives in the United States.

The rationality that Martin attributes to becoming a good citizen through self-accounting and self-investment certainly applies to Orman's televised advice and lessons to aspiring entrepreneurs or those at risk. However, finance-TV also negotiates the relation between education/rationality and the fun/pleasure of risk-taking. TV's instrumentality as citizenship training depends as much upon viewers learning the *responsibilities* of self-investment as upon enjoying what is *fun* — even sexy — about self-accounting and the world of personal finance. In early 2006, an episode of *Wife Swap* (a program wherein wives with apparently incommensurate values trade families) swapped a mother/wife who was fanatical about managing household finances with a mother who was unable to control her shopping impulses, not only for herself but for her only child. (The first season of HBO's *Big Love* in 2006 also played upon this stereotypic binarism, that women either are unable to quell their urge to spend and shop or are fanatical shrews when they do attempt to balance the family ledger.) In the thrifty household, the entire family is held to a strict regimen that values saving, with two daughters having to save their allowance in order to help pay for the family's annual vacations. The other household is represented as less restrictive and rational about savings and expenditures, but also as continually stressed by the challenges of bill-paying. As in other episodes of *Wife Swap*, this one seeks to claw back the two paradigms of feminine self-investment into a model of a healthy balance between rules and pleasure.

Similarly, *The Apprentice* is both a game and a series of lessons through which the rules of entrepreneurialism are learned and rehearsed. In that some reality TV programs such as *Wife Swap* are games with oneself (journeys to greater self-accountancy in the episode discussed above), *The Apprentice* is a vivid example of how the game with oneself is turned into a game about the risks of being an entrepreneur and/or corporate manager on an intensely stressful, but fun, *competitive* playing field. As a game of training good, reliable, and effective corporate citizens to recognize risk and to weed out risky players/partners in games of management, *The Apprentice* also is a televisual experiment/demonstration in solving the problems associated with Enron — with Trump being the successful paradigm of wise self-investment, a counterpoint to Enron's former chairmen who were unable to reinvent themselves for any reality TV series except the collapse of Enron.

US TV has a long history of game programming, with some of the earliest TV game shows having continued already successful radio game shows. And while TV gaming has always and obviously been about risk-taking, the design and technology of gaming meets certain requirements of a new governmental rationality. This is not simply a matter of perpetuating a capitalist ideology of risk-taking subjects but of TV's reinvention to make gaming an extension of networks and "programs" that are explicitly about preparing players to ride the waves of increasingly intense financial risk and responsibility in their daily lives. Recent primetime TV series such as *Deal or No Deal* may reformulate earlier TV game shows (with new hosts, flashier sets, and seemingly larger monetary prizes), but the rules and mattering of the game pertain to a different arrangement between TV and the resources of self-investment. So, NBC scheduled *Deal or No Deal* in early 2006 as its lead-in to weekly broadcasts of *The Apprentice*, with Trump as a "surprise" guest-cum-financial advisor to a contestant laboring over whether to take a risk in the premiere episode. If *Who Wants to be a Millionaire?*, one of the early ventures in the current reality TV syndrome, allowed contestants to make one phone call to help them answer a question, *Deal or No Deal* allowed a free call to seek free advice from a financial expert whose authority is serialized through books and TV programs. Furthermore, if TV (arguably more than other current media) has the capacity to demonstrate how finance can be fun (i.e., a game with rules and strategies), then it is worthwhile recognizing that CNBC reruns broadcasts of *The Apprentice* and has cast the hyperkinetic Jim Cramer (a successful stock investor in the late 1990s) as host of *Mad Money*, a financial advice program in which Cramer wears costumes to convey the fun of learning about finance.

The impetus to design and refine demonstrations, experiments, and games of risk-taking also helps explain the trend in TV poker during the first decade of the twenty-first century. TV poker has been programmed across multiple channels – from sports channels to Bravo to CNBC, whose packaging of poker is entitled *Heads-up Poker* and has become part of that network's menu of "investment tools." TV poker may be the most minimalist, least contrived game of risk-taking on TV, as well as the purest way that current TV represents the democracy of becoming an expert in games of speculation and minimizing exposure. (Most TV poker programs emphasize that anyone can play.) However, that TV poker, unlike forms of online poker and videogaming, is made part of TV's serialized style of programming, and linked (as programmatic) to/through various TV channels, each designed for particular lifestyle clusters, makes TV poker slightly different from earlier TV game shows or online gaming.

These examples collectively have made TV an extension of programs for financial self-help – for the self-accounting citizen – even as the forms and technologies of citizenship-formation vary slightly across the lifestyle clusters comprising contemporary TV. In this respect, an invested (self-actualizing) self is integral to a form of citizenship that is valued and required by the current governmental arrangement. As Martin rightly notes, "financialization is ubiquitous, but never automatic,"[13] and we would add that the same could be said about economic citizenship today. TV continues to play an important role in aiding citizens who are expected and required to maximize their capacity to become self-accounting (and in that way, accountable) citizens. TV, as financial planner and advisor, offers programs of financial empowerment – not in their promise of instant wealth through winning a competition but in lessons learned along the way. Risk-taking always requires that one hone one's strategies. However, finance-TV also operates as support system for those "at risk" – and this includes a professional middle class as well as those populations exposed to mountains of credit-card debt. All are exposed increasingly in a governmental rationality that requires citizens (in an ownership society) to "own up" to their financial futures, though not equally or through the same technologies. Financialization *acts upon* TV's programs and capacity for regularizing (making part of daily life) a regime of self-actualization, and in that sense TV allows citizen-subjects to act "by themselves" *through* support networks of planners, advisors, games.

A paradox of this arrangement is that as citizens find themselves less as citizen-recipients and more as self-actualizing citizen-consumers, they are expected to make more choices. In turn, the choices valorized by government likely results in a preoccupation with uncertainty and risk. Which resource should one choose? From which company? These are questions that make the reinvention of government a formula for embedding risk-taking further in daily life.

Care of the Self as Spying on Oneself

We considered financial risk first because it is a kind of risk often associated with "welfare." However, as Martin argues, "financialization . . . insinuates an orientation toward accounting and risk management into all domains of life."[14] We would add that managing financial risk is *one* (but not the only) objective of "life strategies," of TV's programs of self-actualization, and those programs' implication in a regime of safety and security. Furthermore, neither the rationalities of self-management and self-empowerment, nor the security society and the provision of welfare within it, are reducible to matters of financial risk and exposure. This is a lesson of Foucault. Rationalities (the ordering of life and knowledge) do not derive only or principally from economic logic; finance is one of many ordering activities and knowledges.[15] Governmentalities form around and seek to contain various and changing kinds of risky behaviors, environments, and populations. Welfare involves many kinds of social securities. In this section, we consider the variety of programs through which recent TV, as governmentality, calculates and seeks to manage various kinds of risks and achieve various kinds of security.

The proliferation of programs, on and beyond TV, that offer guidance and personalized techniques/solutions for managing various kinds of personal risks suggests, among other things, that we have a lot to be prepared about these days and that security is something that we achieve and practice throughout our daily lives. Given TV's capacity to technologize the everyday through programs and regimens, TV is in part about endless, daily preparation and readiness – about *watching ourselves through TV*. More precisely, we become aware of various kinds of risk through TV, and we *watch ourselves* through various kinds of televisual preparation for evaluating and managing various kinds of risks. The current security society has made TV matter in this way – linking the injunction to provide for one's own welfare (to "watch over oneself") with the injunction to "watch ourselves" by conducting ourselves properly, not only by recognizing and avoiding risky behaviors but, in so doing, seeing to our personal safety and security.

To the extent that one prominent vein of reality TV involves gaming, tests, and contests, risk-taking is spread out over various genres and programming rationales. Aside from performing risk in TV's tests (with others or with oneself), there has been a resurgence of crime drama since the late 1990s that showcases the most modern (if not preternatural) technology for surveillance and forensics. These programs are not only one of the most successful forms of TV fiction at a time when reality TV has become the new and increasingly dominant paradigm of US TV, but the new generation of TV crime drama, despite its rather residual production values, shares reality TV's preoccupation with surveillance technology as integral to a new regime of security. The "special investigation" units of the various primetime *CSI* series regularly showcase surveillance and other investigative technologies using "artificial intelligence" to recognize criminality that otherwise would elude human sensory perception. The emergence of "profilers" as protagonists in recent TV crime drama not only parallels the widespread adoption of this practice in real-life criminal surveillance, which relies upon behavioral and demographic matrices for sorting among vast possibilities and for verifying true identities, the practice also coincides with the games of profiling in reality TV (e.g., *American Idol* or *The Apprentice*), where candidates representing the most promise (and the least risk) are vetted from thousands of applicants based on technical and/or aesthetic standards. The figure of the forensic psychologist in TV crime drama also extends the authority and rationalities of the "real-life" helpers, guides, interveners, and clinicians in TV designed as welfare and social. The reliance upon computer-based ("smart") technology for gathering forensic evidence and for conducting biometric and behavioral classification is so integral to narratives about control "at a distance" that many investigators in this recent generation of crime drama are cast as psychics, with extraordinary powers for seeing and knowing facts, as in ABC's *Alias* and other outgrowths of *X-Files'* paranormal detective fiction.

Our interest in nonfiction TV, however, emphasizes not simply that TV represents "real-life" security programs, or that it makes these programs ideologically acceptable, but that TV operates as a technological resource for measuring one's risk and for achieving certain forms of security. The care of the self through TV increasingly involves spying on oneself, and spying on oneself is productive of a certain regime of safety and security in the current security society.

Andrejevic is right to note that the hardware and software of surveillance technology has become integral to the mode of producing and consuming reality TV.[16] He discusses how the plays of voyeurism and exhibitionism are materially part of a process whereby consumers' interactivity with reality TV formats leads them, or requires them, to use web sites and telecommunicative devices which programmers in turn use to gather information and data about their customers through "cookies" and other tracking software now regularly deployed by commercial web designers. Through their interactivity with TV's web sites, consumers thus become productive of information about themselves. As Andrejevic puts it, they go to work for TV programmers in their leisure time, perpetuating an "economy of surveillance."

Andrejevic's conception of contemporary TV as integral to an *economy* of surveillance and interactivity (an economy of "mass customization") does not go far enough, however, in considering how TV's various programs of self-surveillance are being adopted as part of governmental rationality that also expects or requires citizens to watch after and over themselves. How, in this sense, are economies of surveillance not just about making money, or about making consumers productive of information that creates monetary value; how are these economies also about making citizens whose application of self-monitoring programs are productive of a new regime of safety, a new arrangement for assessing and managing various kinds of risk, for being ready, within the current security society?

While there are indeed commercial dimensions to TV's game culture, current TV programs also have become preoccupied with providing "security systems" and preparing citizens to use them. Learning the techniques of safety and security in part involves learning how to avoid risky behaviors. Consequently many of the TV programs discussed in previous chapters involve learning about the risks of living one's life as one has been doing (overweight; with a badly chosen fashion statement, unruly children, lack of a proper motor vehicle, limited job prospects, etc.), without the proper resources or training for pulling oneself up by the bootstraps provided by TV.

As discussed in Chapter 3, the process of watching oneself, or secretly watching oneself through the eyes of others, is a common technique in these programs' design as learning regimens. In programs about dating and other forms of social interaction and relationship, subjects frequently watch themselves on camera or watch the actions of others' reactions to the subject's actions – a play of watching and reflection that is supposed to help the subjects gauge risks, slightly at a distance from the live action. These games and laboratories of controlled risk-taking and self-monitoring also include the TV viewer, making the programs' learning and preparation sessions at different degrees of distance.

A program that blends the surveillance game and experiment with forms of life intervention (and whose title most pithily sums up TV's current design of self-monitoring and self-accounting) is the A&E Network's *Spying on Myself* . In this series, subjects "go undercover," disguised by professional makeup technicians and by former "CIA operatives" and monitored by hidden surveillance cameras, in order to surreptitiously learn the truth about their relationship with a friend, employee, or family member. Episodes in 2006 included a young man's encounter with his estranged father, a writer trying to understand why his future mother-in-law does not like him, and a businessman seeking answers to why an employee quit. As *personal detectives* performing a life intervention on themselves, the disguised subjects act out games/experiments of insecurities about personal relationships (observed "undercover," slightly at a distance). As such, the program casts the practices of self-surveillance as integral to overcoming insecurities.

The syndicated series *Cheaters* documents the clandestine love affairs and infidelities of its subjects, also through hidden cameras and disguises. The program's web site states that the program is "dedicated to the faithful and presented to the false-hearted to encourage the renewal of temperance and virtue." Advertising during the broadcasts and on the program's website promotes a panoply of surveillance technology and services designed for keeping tabs on one's spouse or lover (e.g., the "PC Detective" for "recording what your lover does online"). *Cheaters* results as often in allowing subjects to watch out for themselves as in leading subjects to confirm their suspicions and fears about the secretive worlds of friends and family.[17]

It also is worth recognizing that risk-taking has become a rewarded dimension of performing various tasks on TV. Aside from games of extraordinary risk-taking, such as *Fear Factor*, that emphasize a squeamishness about risk, there is a prominent vein of reality TV that demonstrates the *pleasures* of physical risk-taking. MTV's *Jackass* and *Viva la Bam* both are proto-documentaries of slightly absurdist experiments in risk-taking, almost exclusively by young men. (One wonders whether the program considers women to be incapable of achieving "jackass-ness," though Oxygen's *Bad Girls Club* has been a recent formulation of how that identity might apply to young women, or how young women negotiate "acting up.") The riskiness of the performances in *Jackass* results in part from whether the performers will get caught in public places, as when a young man disrobes and then dances to the music in a stereo store before the manager removes him or the police arrive. As exhibitions of risky behavior and rule-breaking, these series are as much about the pleasures and little, personal rewards of risking oneself in the current security society and of risking failure as they are about why anyone watching the program should *not* follow their lead (or be concerned about governing "the jackass" within). The beginning of each broadcast of *Jackass* thus begins with a warning that viewers should not attempt any of the experiments in the program.

Factoring fears and insecurities may be most directly at stake in the vein of reality TV oriented toward testing, under controlled conditions, individuals' capacity to endure and manage extraordinary stress. However, many of contemporary TV's games and experiments in risk-taking emphasize the ordinariness and banality of safety and security. (Arguably, TV that stages spectacular risk-taking – withstanding repeated electric shocks or eating large insects – ratchets up the threshold of what counts as ordinary and banal risks, but even series such as *Jackass* document the little pleasures in inventing and taking risk amid the everyday urban and suburban landscape.) Collectively, these programs advocate and provide practical advice about preparedness for various kinds of unsafe occurrences.

TV channels oriented toward women regularly include "public-service" guides for women's management of various safety concerns in women's lives. One of the most vivid examples of this vein of women's TV is Lifetime's *What Should You Do?*, a safety program whose motto is "Be smart, be ready, and be safe." *What Should You Do?* provides enactments of women facing everyday risks, laced with tips from safety experts. These life-risk lessons include managing household risks (e.g., detecting carbon monoxide), avoiding risky public encounters (facing armed robbers, fending off carjackers, preventing gas-station fires, and escaping safely), being a helper (learning how to administer CPR or to deliver a baby), and (last but not least) "not getting lost in the wilderness." The path to women's empowerment through a TV channel designed for women's needs thus entails practical instruction about helping women protect themselves and others. A contradiction of formulating women's *empowerment* in this way, particularly with respect to the exhibitions of pleasurable risk-taking by men in programs such as *Jackass*, is that empowerment results from managing risk and demonstrating sobriety, responsibility, and "good citizenship," rather than the thrill of risk-taking.

One of the most regularized programs of daily safety is the Weather Channel. While this channel began during the 1980s as 24-hour studio-reporting and on-location reporting (primarily of US weather events), during the 1990s its programming became more diversified. By the current decade, it began offering personalized "weather alerts" for subscribers of their online or text-message service. Its primetime schedule has showcased *Storm Stories*, a series reenacting weather events and disasters around the United States. This program has been both story and scientific demonstration of risk-taking, of the role of local responders to the needs of citizens, of the resourcefulness of citizens having to act "on their own" in "natural disasters," and of what not to do – each broadcast ending with one of the channel's weathermen explaining how these calamities could occur anywhere and at any time, and thus require constant, daily vigilance and preparedness. There is now no purer example of TV as daily program/regimen for being alert to the possibility of emergencies and local, personal disaster – or rather, of how weather affects one's lifestyle as endless, daily planning. Both the TV channel and its web site offer advice on health, travel, recreation, home and garden, and planning for "special events." Each topic involves taking various precautions; the channel's provision of health advice concerns allergies, skin protection, air quality, aches and pains, mosquito activity, colds and flu, and general "fitness" concerns (e.g., whether it is safe to take one's morning run). The channel also offers suggestions for customizing various "safety kits" for disasters and emergencies owing to earthquake, extreme heat, flooding, hurricane, lightening, tornado, wildfires, and winter weather. The Weather Channel now promotes itself as the national authority on various weather risks, referring to itself in the aftermath of Hurricane Katrina as "America's Hurricane Authority." As explained below, this form of public outreach by TV is significant because of the "public–private partnership" that the channel has entered into with several federal emergency-relief agencies.

Preparedness for emergency and "disaster" has become central now to the Weather Channel's and other TV networks' role in the current security society. How could living with disaster (of being totally exposed, with a "change of the weather") be anything but the central preoccupation of a neoliberal reasoning about maximum freedoms, do-it-yourself forms of welfare, and the Weather Channel as one of the most reliable sources for public security? In 2005, the Weather Channel launched the series *It Could Happen Tomorrow*, which enacted through a compilation of found-footage and digitally manufactured images the effects on various US cities of a climatological disaster (e.g., unusually high tornadic activity that lays waste to much of Dallas, Texas). More than early prototypes such as *Storm Stories* or TWC's everyday reporting, *It Could Happen Tomorrow* underscores the risks of weather to the security of the nation and to entire urban populations. In this respect, it is as much about mobilizing large populations of citizens as about helping individual citizens design personal disaster and emergency plans. The Discovery Channel offers a similar program, *Perfect Disasters*, for which viewers are encouraged (through the channel's web site) to test and grade themselves with a Hazard Quiz: "Would you survive?"

The survivalist objectives of this genre of emergency-preparedness program is noteworthy, not only in light of its relation to other forms of factoring fear and testing one's resourcefulness to survive away from home (e.g., *Survivor* and *Survivorman*), but also because of the current expectation that citizens watch out and over themselves, their families, and households. These latter programs make more ordinary and programmatic the techniques of figuring out (through TV) how to design a personal support network in case of an emergency and how to cope with risk when TV becomes the primary provider of personal security. However, in this respect, even these daily regimens of practical preparation for ordinary emergencies intersect with current TV's game culture, where good citizenship involves always factoring the odds so that one can be the last one standing.

Experiments in "Home Security Makeover"

Considering TV's place within the current securitization of daily life requires understanding how its programs intersect with the safe and secure environment that viewers inhabit. To speak of securitization as practiced within a governmental *arrangement* refers not only to the formal and informal agreements about rules and proper conduct, but also to the material distribution and emplacement of technologies for managing the life of individuals and populations. It therefore is necessary to consider some of the ways that TV acts within the current arrangement – particularly from and across particular places (spheres of activity and government) that are understood to be risky in certain ways or to require certain forms of security.

No consideration of TV can ignore its long-standing relation to conceptions of domesticity, the design of houses, and the organization and running of households. As Raymond Williams famously pointed out, the emergence of TV cannot be understood merely as the outcome of an evolution of technologies but as part of a widespread regime of mobility and privacy – what he referred to as "mobile privatization."[18] One might also consider, however, how TV's emergence within mobile privatization occurred through a particular regime of safety and security, and how TV is now being reinvented to accommodate the "advancement" of this project.[19] How have past and current regimes of mobility and privacy, wherein various tele-technologies such as TV developed, become attuned to technologies and programs of safety and risk management designed to make the performance of freedoms responsible and thus governable? How has the expectation of this performance fallen upon "homemakers," whose achievement of "home" (and particularly a home that is safe) relies upon domestic sciences and domestic appliances – including communication appliances? And how has the securitization of one's house and all that it holds made the home a site of active citizenship and management, not only a sphere where one watches over oneself and one's things but also where one's life is lived as a *moral economy* – the personalized regimen and system of rules that govern family life and simultaneously allow a resident to feel most free, most *oneself*, and most "at home in the world"?

While there are book series such as *The Complete Idiot's Guide to Home Security* that parallel the do-it-yourself guidebooks in personal finance discussed above, TV programs concerning home safety and security – particularly those concerning the current role of TV in securing house and home – are as much a part of current TV's mission in public "outreach" as extensions of the do-it-yourself programs from other media. There is a swath of TV programs across various channels intended to prepare viewers to recognize and protect themselves against a variety of personal and household safety risks. One example of this trend is *Your Home: Make it Safe* on the Do-It-Yourself Network, a home decorating network that, as its title suggests, is the paragon of possessive individualism for a middle-class household capable of affording the program tier where cable and satellite companies usually locate this channel. Doing home safety yourself (or rather, through this program) involves awareness of, and lessons about, how to operate and where to place standard security devices (alarms, extinguishers, lighting, first-aid kits), how to secure doors and windows, how to "childproof" one's home, how to "escape safely," and how to design "the look of a secure home."

One of the most remarkable convergences between reality TV's games, makeovers, behavioral experiments, and programs for securing households has been the Discovery Channel's *It Takes a Thief*. This program, which extends to an interactive web site providing safety plans, checklists, and tips, has recruited two former (now rehabilitated) thieves to break into typically suburban houses in order to demonstrate to the homeowners and to the program's viewers steps needed to improve home security. Unlike *Cops*, which during the 1990s documented urban police responses to everyday crimes and disputes perpetrated by "at-risk" populations living outside the US suburbs, *It Takes a Thief* offers a different awareness to suburban homeowners about the vulnerability of the suburban household. Homeowners and the TV audience watch a recording of the thieves' operation captured by surveillance equipment, which often becomes one of the remedies for these "exposed" houses and insecure families. The nonprofessionals are then advised by security experts and the thieves-turned-advisors about a variety of safety measures ranging from common, inexpensive techniques and devices to home makeovers. Each broadcast concludes as the homeowners undergo a second break-in attempt that tests/demonstrates the reliability of the new security system. As "life intervention," this program documents an intervention on body and property that is at risk. As a staged test and demonstration, the care of the self occurs through the program's objectification of risk – of watching and assessing (observing for themselves) an actual (albeit staged) record/experiment of a house's exposure to and subsequent protection from intrusion. Like some other makeover series as "life interventions," *It Takes a Thief* also reproduces the new paradigm of TV "program" as a personal/household *regimen* that will be lived (or in the case of houses, lived in) beyond the specific episode and experiment.

The economic status and lifestyle of the households selected in *It Takes a Thief* make them receptive to and capable of affording a variety of "smart" technologies, such as digitally programmable sensors, cameras, monitors, and relays. Today, the idea of the "smart home" has become synonymous with the idea of a safe home, and the current lessons in the benefits of acquiring "smart" household technologies and appliances regularly links their value to the improvement of household safety and security. For instance, *Your Home: Make it Safe* offers entire episodes and web-site links to learn about purchasing, operating, and arranging "smart technology" for safety purposes. Historically the

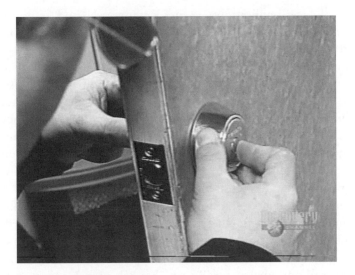

Illustration 4.2 Professional burglars illustrate problems and techniques of home security on *It Takes a Thief* (Lion Television for Discovery Channel, 2006)

emergence of cable and satellite TV, alongside the initiatives for "reinventing government," have converged with the fashioning of households organized and programmed through an assemblage of often interlocking digital appliances. These digital appliances' capacity to monitor and to run/manage various domestic tasks was tantamount to a new rationality about freedoms at home and of being at home away from home, and thus became integral to an emerging political reasoning that valued citizens' self-sufficiency and self-directedness – a "neo-liberalization of the domestic sphere."[20] This ideal and rationality have been fundamental to companies such as Invensys Home Control Systems (IHCS), which since the late 1990s has designed and installed home networks for remote sensing and remote control of the household's various programmable appliances – networks that IHCS promises will allow inhabitants to customize/personalize home management and to run her/his household at a distance, away from home or at home. The intelligence of a household – a regimen of applications and a rationality/science of home management for achieving "domestic freedoms" – thus has become a means of securing the household. Freedom, as the achievement of privacy and mobility through an array of technological applications, carries certain risks and responsibilities and is thus an objective of personalized risk management, at home and away from home.

These integrated services and systems of home-management technology have coincided with the growth of home-security services, so that wiring/networking houses to detect multiple threats and risks (e.g., home invasion, fire, or personal injury) requires emergency assistance.[21] While home-security services have relied on programmable equipment, sensing devices, and telecommunication with remote dispatchers and municipal emergency services, some of these services (e.g., Bolt Home Systems) also have designed and installed home-entertainment and home-communication systems, further making the implementation of home safety and security integral to the hardwiring and software applications of communication and entertainment activities. And as evidenced by *It Takes a Thief* and the safety-demonstration programs of home-makeover TV on channels such as Home & Garden and Do It Yourself, the smart household is a *habitus* (a sphere of productivity reliant upon property, technical competence, and cultural capital) that has been most energetically reproduced, managed, and safeguarded by a particular social class and lifestyle cluster. In the first episode of *It Takes a Thief*, the security experts-cum-housebreakers target a house that is full of luxury items.

One other connection worth making is between the home-management services, home-security services, and TV cable and satellite services. The current injunction that households provide for their own security (albeit through services) has required cable and satellite companies to expand their role in helping households monitor and manage the risks of particular media that enter the home. TV safety "outreach" involves a paradox whereby the federal government allows the cable industry to police itself by providing the technology that allows customers the "freedom" to regulate access to TV at home. Most national cable companies, such as Insight Communication, promote their menus of devices protecting households from unwanted TV programs (e.g., filters on digital cable-boxes, DVR filters, "traps" installed upon request, and V-chips, which were mandated by Congress for all TV sets above 13 inches built after January, 2000 and which block programs according to the industry's eight-tier rating-system). In 2005, the cable industry initiated an awareness campaign, "Cable Puts You in Control," touting this menu of self-regulative options.

The cable industry's self-regulating devices for households, however, are just one facet of a robust ensemble of services, networks, hardware, and software designed to protect households from undesirable media. In 2005–6, The Learning Channel broadcast *Hackers*, a program that (in a variation of *It Takes a Thief*) represents risk-taking strategies used by computer hackers, the risk they represent to personal computing and households, and the tactics that can be deployed to secure one's household from their intrusive activities. Furthermore, the self-monitoring features of contemporary media technologies are often represented as essential for assuring the security of all one's property. In a TV advertisement for AOL antivirus computer software that ran during 2003 and 2004, AOL's ability to insulate a two-story colonial, suburban house from undesirable and polluting elements was represented through a scenario involving gale-force winds (carrying various objects) that collapse one of the house's walls, making it vulnerable to the outside. The commercial depicted "*fire*walling" as a link between the threat to one's personal computer and the threat to one's house and household.²² Learning how to use one's personal computer or TV and DVR systems involves learning about how to protect them, and one's personal information and intellectual property, through these security programs. Paradoxically, TV and its imbrication in domestic communication networks threaten the privacy and moral economy of households even as these media provide the solutions and technical support for managing those threats.

The value of these technologies has been readily articulated to a "pro-family" political rationality that considers the household as "at risk" by the circulation of TV and other media. Family Safe Media, which promotes itself as "preserving family values in a media-driven society," offers an array of technologies for the self-regulating media household: filters for DVD players, TV and video-game "time managers," a profanity filter (titled the "TV Guardian"), remote controls for kids (titled "Wee-mote"), a computer time-manager (titled "PC Cop"), power-plug locks, filtering-tool software (the "Net Protector" with accompanying "porn-addiction info"), mobile cameras and monitors, phone-line locks and blocks, and TV-channel blockers (the "TV B-Gone"). That this "pro-family" political rationality is so attached to the vast array of self-regulating technologies and to the expectation that households should regulate media for themselves underscores the extent to which mobilizing citizens to actively manage the security of home can be a matter of legislating morality. The efforts of Family Safe Media may be considered more overtly politicized than what occurs in most households, but their efforts also remind us that learning how to use the communication technologies "safely" and "wisely" in the everyday running of households is as much ethical as political. The "life interventions" or "home makeovers" that Family Safe Media seek uphold a political rationale about self-government ("helping families protect themselves") as much as they affirm that self-regulating media households are *moral economies* for regulating *proper* conduct.

Maintaining the "smart" household is increasingly part of a general economy of safety and security equipment and operational know-how. Smart technologies have become an integral part of services for do-it-yourself safety and security. Companies such as KeepSafer, WEMA ("We Monitor America"), the Home Security Store, Smart Home, Safety Depot, and Security Depot all sell various kinds of video monitoring devices and systems, along with a variety of other security and safety hardware and manuals. The web site for Safety Depot (www. shop.safetydepot.com) provides "steps" for redressing various kinds of household risks, and links for securing each standard room in a house – "room-by-room product navigation." Security Depot (www.asecuritydepot.com) offers web shopping for several thousand kinds of personal- and home-safety equipment. The equipment in these stores is also commonly available now through the major hardware retail chains in the United States, such as Home Depot, Lowes, and Office Depot. And the circuit between these security equipment and service providers and TV's home-security makeovers has become stronger, as *Extreme Makeover: Home Edition* has undertaken two home makeovers that included new home-security systems sold at Sears and as the onscreen experts in *It Takes a Thief* appeared as the keynote speakers for the 2005 International Security Conference (a trade show attended by manufacturers and distributors of the latest personal-security technology).[23]

Although this section has dealt primarily with TV's role in securing its traditional site, the home, it is worth adding that home security also matters beyond the household – and precisely because video screens are no longer restricted to domestic use. TV is also increasingly part of networks of surveillance and of safety education that extend into domains of daily life beyond the home. The portability of video-monitoring devices allows individuals to monitor and manage their household's health from a distance. Closed-circuit video systems have become an ubiquitous, though generally invisible, technology for monitoring risky behavior on city streets and in a wide variety of commercial spaces.[24] The design of public and commercial space increasingly accommodates these systems. The forms of personal data-collection have multiplied and also are part of the design of convenience and speed in day-to-day living: the use of credit cards at different locations in our daily life provides a record of both our purchases and our paths. As home security becomes part of networks and services that extend beyond the home – rationalized as providing greater freedoms/mobility and safety/security – they therefore provide all the conveniences of home away from home.[25] In this respect, the paradox of TV's reinvention through safe media and media safety is that self-regulation is a means to greater personal independence, and that greater mobility requires that citizens be willing and able to assess and manage their own personal risks, and see to their own security, as if they were always at home.

The Many Responsibilities of the New Citizen-Soldier

Amid the growing number of stores, services, and programs discussed above that offer a wide range of safety equipment, there have been a few specialty outlets, such as Safer America (www.saferamerica.com), that market gear suited to catastrophic emergencies – equipment such as gas masks, radiation detectors, full body-protection suits, "family survival kits," and Life-Cenders (a "personal escape system" comprising rope and harness for emergency escapes from the windows of multi-story buildings). Ten years ago, marketing such safety products was less common, and probably perceived as more strange, than today. However, they still do not comprise the kind of equipment that is demanded by a large group of consumers and households, or figure in daily use, as preparedness for emergencies and catastrophes is mobilized through resources such as the Weather Channel. At the same time, the products offered by Safer America, rationalized as responses to terrorist threats through books such as *How to Tell Your Children about Terrorism*, also vividly underscore the normalization/domestication of safety equipment formerly used only by professionals such as firefighters, riot squads, decontaminators, and soldiers. Collectively these sites for safety resources comprise a professionalization of the culture of everyday home safety, and the shaping of a new citizen-soldier.

In the recent Congressional debate about US border and immigration policy, a few congressmen proposed, in addition to erecting a network of fencing along the US–Mexican border, building a network of surveillance cameras that could be accessed in real time by anyone with a personal computer. The system could mobilize "real" citizens to aid the Department of Homeland Security and regional border-enforcement agencies in watching out for illegal entries into the United States. And while this experiment in border management and national security may never come to pass, it acts upon the kinds of services, networks, and programs discussed in this chapter.

The formation of a Homeland Security and the Bush administration's declaration of an "endless war on terror" in the immediate aftermath of the September 11, 2001 attacks *acted upon* the various initiatives and experiments for reinventing government that had been occurring since at least the 1980s. As Homeland Security Director, Michael Chertoff, stated in 2006:

> as we rise to meet the threat of terrorism, we must face each day with . . . a commitment . . . to "think anew" and to "act anew" . . . We must draw on the strength of our considerable network of assets, functioning as seamlessly as possible with state and local leadership, first responders, the private sector, . . . and most certainly the general public.

If a Homeland Security has made sense and gained traction in the United States, it has done so not only through the increasingly common practice of outsourcing to private companies the tasks delegated in the past to the US military, but also through mobilizing and acting upon an array of public–private partnerships and the private-outreach programs oriented toward various kinds of security. It has done so not only by mobilizing the national guard to conduct new kinds of operations (fighting a war overseas, patrolling the streets of New Orleans after Hurricane Katrina, or preventing illegal immigration) but also by expanding, repurposing, and acting upon the array of technologies and programs through which nonmilitary citizens have been expected to look after their own welfare and security – to be the new first line of defense. In these ways, the formation of a Homeland Defense and the waging of a war on terror have become central to the current governmental rationality about freedom and security as intertwined objectives.

One of the support networks into which Homeland Security has inserted itself is the Citizen Corps, whose web site enjoins citizens to "Be Informed, Be Prepared, and Take Action!" True to the federalist rationality of other current "public services" during the Bush administration, the Citizen Corps' response to emergency management and preparation is decidedly local and "do-it-yourself," with the federal government in an exhortative and "supportive" posture. The web site for Citizen Corp (www.citizencorps.gov) not only represents links to the Department of Homeland Security but to a menu of volunteer programs, such as Community Emergency Response Team Program, the Fire Corps, the Neighborhood Watch Program, the Medical Reserve Program, and the Volunteer Police Service. And within the current penchant for linking social welfare with civilian defense and self-defense, it both professionalizes and paramilitarizes citizens as "first-responders," creating a "corps" of citizens. It also articulates the nurturing of "community" as a public good with the *actively* defensive and protective techniques learned by citizens. To this end, the Citizen Corp is organized as a network of Citizen Corps Councils, the community-based administrators of both local and national security.

Maximizing personal freedoms, "supported" by minimizing government ("constraining government spending" as "economic government"), also has expanded one's exposure to risk, which in turn requires greater vigilance and ever updated and more robust micro-strategies for calculating and managing these risks. According to the *National Strategy for Homeland Security* (a rationale by and for the Department of Homeland Security, July 2002), "our free society is *inherently* vulnerable" (emphasis added). Or put another way, the strategies for waging an endless war on terror have become a way of rationalizing the campaign to maximize self-sufficiency.

The link between the recently formed Department of Homeland Security and TV and other media is one dimension of the State's current experiments in governing through private and personal security programs, and is an increasingly dominant dimension of the current security society in the United States. As much as the Bush administration's creation of a massive new federal program has been questioned as anathema to the neoconservative and neoliberal valorization of "small government," the department has become a paradigm of government service whose idea of service is to make citizens responsible rather than to foster dependency.[26] It thus actively seeks to energize private resources and citizens to look after themselves through do-it-yourself resources found on the Web and TV. The Department of Homeland Security's "Ready.gov" campaign, which seeks to educate and prepare citizens for various kinds of emergencies and catastrophes, relies heavily on citizens taking the initiative to seek out resource networks and on linking citizens to web sites for privately provided security materials and services. In this respect, the Department not only relies upon media programs but operates through procedures similar to TV outreach, stitching itself into relay systems for active citizens and, as was the case in the aftermath of Hurricane Katrina, chastising citizens who were not responsible in recognizing risk and in learning about how to manage their own individual survival. Or, as the former director of the Department of Homeland Security, Tom Ridge, stated at a Public Preparedness Symposium:

> Our goal is to achieve seamless protection; a nation knit tightly together by shared vigilance, readiness and communication. Vigilance, readiness and communication. And nowhere is this more important than in the area of emergency preparedness . . . If you've ever watched the Weather Channel when they talk about some of those individual stories in the midst of some of these horrific natural events and how the people actually saved themselves because they knew what to do before the event occurred and they just did it; it was a reflex. They had it prepared. They had thought about it and did it.

While the FCC has long required commercial TV to reserve bandwidth for "emergency broadcasting" (a practice that made TV responsive to programs in "civil defense" during the Cold War), TV's new role as "emergency broadcast system" is about expanding the range of risks and the services for do-it-yourself security.[27]

Although there have been recent TV dramas that represent efforts by the US government to combat foreign "terrorist" activities in the United States (e.g., *48 Hours* and the made-for-TV movie, *Homeland Security*), there have been a larger number of programs that demonstrate survival skills – at home or away from home. Series such as *Survivor, Survivorman, Road Rules,* and National Geographic Channel's *Worlds Apart* (about US families who abandon their comfortable and lavish homes in the United States to share a home with a family in an "underdeveloped" part of the world for several weeks) all involve learning survival techniques required when facing the risks of leaving home, and the current Homeland. TV's educational programs about recognizing personal risk and learning safety techniques are the everyday engines of a Homeland Security's campaign to make citizens productive of their own security. Chertoff's claim above, that the Department of Homeland Security is about *reinventing* government, depends upon future programs of home *makeover* such as *It Takes a Thief* and other "home-security makeover shows" in which the care of the self involves testing a household's threshold of risk and capacity for security. Perhaps Director Chertoff's claim that the Department of Homeland Security is committed to "thinking and acting anew" refers not just to the department's place within the current efforts to "reinvent government" for a new security society (one designed for "an endless war on terror") but to Homeland Security's "extreme makeover" after its failures responding to Hurricane Katrina – its first major national emergency and its first live-action televised demonstration and test of its capabilities. Four years after the formation of a Homeland Security in the United States, it's become difficult to tell how the title and mission of Homeland Security (as mobilizing a "home front") is entirely separate from a home security makeover show – how "national security" involves anything but the everyday technical achievements of personal "home security."

Chapter 5

TV's Constitutions of Citizenship

Governing Ourselves through TV: New Constitutions

In an episode of ABC's *Supernanny* broadcast in 2006, Nanny Jo Frost assesses and seeks to redress problems that a single mother is having running her household and managing her three young children. Midway through the episode, she advises the mom on the need for a "family routine." The nanny rationalizes this solution by stating that the mom needs to "take ownership through a household constitution." She then formulates and posts on a wall a set of "house rules," a private contract or covenant by which all of the family members are supposed to abide. Living by this contract is enacted and enforced as a game, through which the children are rewarded for playing by the rules, and mom is rewarded by having her household returned to her control. Later in the episode, the nanny addresses the viewers directly in a "public service" announcement, explaining how they can learn from what they've seen and why they should formulate their own household constitutions.

This chapter considers reality TV as a resource for *constituting* households, neighborhoods, and other spheres of everyday government. We use the term "constitution" to refer to television's role in *enacting* and *shaping* (constituting) spaces and populations.[1] *Supernanny*, for example, offers demonstrations in *re*inventing a healthy household. The term also suggests the extent to which TV presents itself as a resource for establishing the rules and standards (constitutions) of belonging and participation that make the group a comity, or a peaceful and orderly association where the rights and differences of all citizens should be respected. Constitutions are a basis for liberal government's emphasis on fairness, collective participation, rights, and limits of government. While the "household constitution" established by *Supernanny* is not a constitution like those formulated by cities or nation-states, it similarly establishes the rights and rules for living and governing fairly and judiciously in this house. In this respect, the household constitution is a technical way of maintaining not only order and respect but also mutuality and fairness at home. Unlike city or state constitutions, the household constitution is also drawn up with citizen-subjects (the family members), even though it is designed and explained by a privately contracted expert – a "governess." As Foucault demonstrated, liberal government developed out of, and through, the government of children, families, and households. This takes on a new dimension in the present political epoch, however. As one way of helping private groups "take ownership" of their governance, TV's private constitutions have become integral to the administration of the current stage of liberalism in the United States, and a new model of citizenship characterized by George W. Bush as an Ownership Society.

The household is arguably the smallest framework for group governance in the daily lives of most people. As comity, a neighborhood is also a sphere where sociality and mutuality depend upon common institutions and administrative bodies with more or less formalized *guidelines* for making collective decisions, managing differences, acting civilly, guaranteeing pleasant and friendly association, and being a "good neighbor." A neighborhood covenant, like the "house rules" in *Supernanny*, is also not exactly a constitution designed and administered by elected legislators, policy-makers, judges, and civil servants. A neighborhood covenant is a *privately* designed and administered set of rules for members of an association – members whose relation to these rules makes them citizens not only of the laws of the State, but of the neighborhood constitution as well. Increasingly, neighborhood covenants, or the rules affecting condos or gated communities or (what is left of) public housing, have become common ways of governing the places where everyday life is lived.

While not all households and neighborhoods abide by the same rules or are as invested in developing a group constitution as the families who appear on TV programs like *Supernanny*, TV has come to play an important technical role in this new regime of privately administered government. What should we make of TV's current strategies for constituting households, neighborhoods, workplaces, and towns as forms of private association and membership, and as forms of group government? How does TV's practice of staging "citizenship tests" as experiments in group government matter within the current governmental rationality? And, what does this trend have to do with the discourse of "reinventing government"? To address these questions, we need to consider briefly some of the general objectives of our analysis. This book does not seek to understand or explain liberalism as a monolithic, universal form of government. Instead the book recognizes a paradox about liberal government: its aspiration toward making rational and fair (through the provision of rights and laws) a government for *all* citizens, even as the constitutions of government (over time and around the world) have not advocated the same set of rights and laws. As such, liberal government aspires to a *universalism* (i.e., government "for all") that is *specific* to local constitutions.

But how local and specific? Liberalism's historical and geographic specificity — its diversity — is not simply the variety of *national* constitutions of government. Understanding liberalism purely as government by the State involves recognizing at the very least the interplay between government of a nation and government of regional and urban administrations.[2] There is another kind of interplay, however, between the State forms of administration and the "nongovernmental" programs of governance. Our focus here is on the multiplicity and diversity of *private constitutions* through which governance is made rational and administered, in and beyond nation-states. These would include the private government of households, of universities, condo associations and gated-communities, corporate management, sports associations, NGOs, and so forth. Sometimes, these privately administered constitutions comprise *networks of government*. Each of us may be subject to the rules and covenants of multiple private entities. And sometimes, the constitutions of private government are in conflict with one another, or with the laws and codes enacted and administered by the State.

One way of understanding the longevity and ubiquity of liberalism, particularly liberal government's diversity, is by considering how the State *acts upon* the variety of formal and informal guidelines and contracts administered by private associations, households, and personal regimens.[3] The introduction of liberal government in Afghanistan, for instance, may have been encouraged by the United States (an extension of a US model of liberalism, or an imagined stage for "advancing" liberalism in the Middle East), but the formulation of an "Islamic constitution" in Afghanistan underscores the local and *specific universalism* of liberalism's constitution. Government by the State is constituted through religious and cultural institutions that authorize specific forms of association, participation, and membership in Afghanistan. The double meaning of "constitution" that we have adopted, however, allows us to emphasize another point: Liberalism's *survival* (or "advancement") has depended upon the ongoing demonstration and testing of a State's formally constituted laws but also of the informal *civic laboratories* – venues for civic pedagogy – and for experimenting with and testing the rules and guidelines of the private associations comprising a civil society.[4]

One way reality TV operates within current strategies of government in the United States is through the technical constitutions of household, neighborhood, and other private entities that comprise civil society. In this respect, our focus is less on how TV programs advance a "neoliberal" *ideology* than on the practical demonstrations about the rules and techniques for membership and participation in private groups. These are techniques that are encountered daily and are continually tested and customized, through TV and other media. While "good citizenship" may involve a particular relation to the State, it also is performed daily through the rules and government of "healthy" households, "good" neighborhoods, and the other private entities that comprise what currently is considered a "civil" society. These are rules and informal guidelines for belonging, proper behavior, rights, active participation, and making a specific kind of place to live. Although it is possible to describe "constitutions of the self" (the regimens and programs through which the self is made active – technologized – in particular ways), this chapter is mostly concerned with TV's models, strategies, and constitutions of group government. From that perspective, this chapter considers how "technologies of the self" or "self-constitution" are about the rules and techniques for becoming a good family member, neighbor, co-worker, etc.

Reality TV's testing of citizens sometimes resemble social and behavioral experiments, but they also operate as judicial trials. The relation between "test" and "trial" is not simply blurred in these TV series, it is a point of interface between the series' proto-scientific experiments in individual and group behavior and the series' privatization of the processes of overseeing group government. In this latter sense, some reality TV series demonstrate the privately administered laws necessary to become an active citizen. If group government is to proceed in an orderly way, it requires displays (trials) by its citizens that prove the rationality of government; it requires putting citizen-subjects in front of a privately authorized judge (such as a *Supernanny*) or a panel of jurists who decide which citizens have acted responsibly and within the technical rules of conduct. Like courtroom trials conducted by the State, private trials like those on reality TV continually put on exhibit the virtues of a privately designed constitution and privately administered citizenship.

Although reality TV operates as *demonstrations* and *experiments* in group government, there also is a *ludic* dimension to its experimental-ism and testing of individuals, families, teams, neighborhoods, and towns. The technical means of reinventing government are integral to the rules for playing "citizenship-contests" and the "games of govern-ment." Implementing the household constitution in *Supernanny*, for instance, involves a game of citizenship played by rules. To the extent that TV *educates* about the proper forms of belonging, of managing differences, and of participation by citizens in various spheres of life, this education occurs as playful or sporting task in the current regime of TV. Learning, mastering, and performing the "rules of the game" is tantamount to successful performances of membership and citizen-ship. Reality TV's citizenship game, as a form of entertainment, is thus tantamount to its operation as a social/behavioral experiment (testing the citizens' capacities and limits) and as a trial (testing the worthiness of subjects to act freely and responsibly as citizens).

Welcome to the Neighborhood: TV's Citizenship Tests

One example of citizen education through TV was the long-running PBS series *Mr. Roger's Neighborhood*, whose opening song extolled the eternally "beautiful day in the neighborhood." The series offered a regimen of friendly and gentle advice, demonstrations, games, and exercises for children (citizens-in-the-making) about how to get along in their neighborhoods – about how to grow into good, active, caring, and responsible citizens through TV. Less overtly didactic TV genres such as the domestic comedy and soap opera have played a role in enacting neighborhood – rehearsing the problems, threats, and chal-lenges to the neighborhoods' and households' private rule-making and membership.⁵ As we explained in the Introduction, there is a long history of TV and other media offering instruction in and demonstrations of citizenship.⁶ However, TV's relation to the current regime of civic pedagogy has relied upon decidedly different strategies for demonstrating and modeling citizenship – ones that have become technically part of the political process and the political reform associated with "reinventing government." Neighborliness – daily citizenship and governance – may still involve lessons, as in earlier TV comedy or *Mr. Roger's Neighborhood*, but achieving it now occurs on a decidedly unsettled terrain of the games and contests of group government, one that makes banal as well as ratchets up the political stakes of TV's citizenship tests. These are games and contests that allow players to demonstrate, for judges and TV viewers, how well they can perform the expectations of citizenship according to the rules of a community constitution. Sometimes, TV's new strategies for testing citizenship do demonstrate good government and "good TV," and sometimes they become the object of *political demonstrations*.

On May 10, 2005, ABC announced that two months later it would begin broadcasting a new TV series, *Welcome to the Neighborhood*. According to ABC, the series would involve "one of seven diverse families [who] will win a beautiful dream home on a perfect suburban cul-de-sac in Austin, Texas. But in order to win the luxuriously furnished and opulently appointed house, they must first win over the very people who will be the most affected by the ultimate decision – the next-door neighbors." *Welcome to the Neighborhood* was conceived by ABC as a summer replacement for *Desperate Housewives*, which had attracted a large audience to ABC on Sunday evenings. Both series mixed elements of the sitcom and soap opera in their representation of life around a suburban cul-de-sac. *Welcome to the Neighborhood* also followed the conventions of the game show, typical of many reality TV programs. Like other contemporary TV (e.g., *The Apprentice* and *Wife Swap*), *Welcome to the Neighborhood* was a regulated *experiment* that *tested* and *demonstrated* the limits of real-life subjects, their abilities to perform in accordance with certain rules of the game. However, precisely in this way, the series was an experiment for demonstrating the wise and effective government by neighbors. And this dimension of *Welcome to the Neighborhood* is noteworthy because it became an assessment of what constitutes (in the civic sense) "good" TV and about TV's judgment and ability to regulate itself.

Though each episode may have represented a slight modification of behavior and thought among all the participants, the network's initial statements about the series' production emphasized the catharsis that the homeowners (and secondarily the prospective neighbors) would undergo. The homeowners' interactions with the contestants would test the homeowner's ideological and cultural limits, their ability to enact their vision and ground rules of what a "neighborhood" should be, and thus their ability to maintain the physical appearance and boundaries (the "gated"-ness) of their neighborhood:

> With every encounter with these families, the opinionated neighbors' pre-conceived assumptions and prejudices are also chipped away, and they learn that, while on the outside we may appear different, deep inside we share many common bonds. The judges find themselves learning to see people, not stereotypes. The three neighborhood families who will be judging the competing families all love their quiet, pictur-esque community and are used to a certain kind of neighbor – one who looks and thinks just like them . . . Each competing family ends up taking the neighborhood judges on an emotional journey that opens eyes and hearts. In the end, one family's life will definitely change when they win the deed to the house and move into the pristine home. But much to the surprise of everyone involved, a whole community experi-ences a transformation.

The homeowners shared more than their love of "their quiet, pic-turesque community" and the same residential turf. They all were white, wealthy enough to afford newly constructed 3,500-square-foot houses with four bedrooms and two and a half baths costing $300,000–$400,000. They possessed sufficient personal transportation to live in a recently developed and relatively remote suburban area, a relatively recent Austin, TX subdivision branded as "Circle C." And they were relatively unabashed about their Republican and Christian affiliations, or at least unabashed enough to express and put to the test those posi-tions on national TV. The homeowners selected to participate in the series were the Stewarts (whose patriarch referred to himself as the cul-de-sac's "governor"), the Bellamys (a Republican dad whose chil-dren were less sure of their political orientation), and the Daniels (an avowed Christian family who claimed to prefer "similar" neighbors).

Unlike studio-produced TV series in which the characters' every action is scripted, a reality TV series such as this one involved a slightly different set of management strategies. Producers located proper settings, participants, and conditions in order to produce a kind of televised experiment, in part about effective governance and citizenship. Homeowners acted as private "judges" and "governors" of families actively seeking to become citizens (and future judges) in this neighborhood. The series' producers acknowledged having selected the residents of the cul-de-sac in Circle C Ranch (a subdivision whose population is 80 percent white) not only for their physical propinquity but their demographically calculated cultural orientation. The experiment displayed the limits of the participants' cultural capital, their commitment to the material properties of what a neighborhood should be and look like, and their ability to represent civic virtues that mattered to them individually and collectively. For the homeowners, good governance demonstrated, in this sense, good citizenship. The series also was a political experiment for testing the homeowners' ("neighbors'") abilities to govern various kinds of problems – particularly, how best to govern one's neighborhood, household, family/children, and self while remaining true to the rules and fairness of a democracy game. The series thus tested neighbor-contestants' abilities to remain tolerant, fair, and "open-minded," to keep the process of inclusion and exclusion fair and rule-driven, and to conduct themselves as model citizens – at least a model of citizenship suited to life in the cul-de-sac and suited to life in the United States from the cul-de-sac. Although the series' publicity statement emphasized that the transformation of the neighborhood would be "a surprise to all involved," the experiment (at all levels of its production) also was about learning how best to manage, act upon, and instrumentalize individualism and difference, change and surprise – how best to solve problems within the rules. If Circle C is a new settlement, an effort to achieve and manage a "neighborhood," then the series experimented with the unsettling conditions upon which the settlement was constructed.

This is not to say that the experiment merely pitted owners (as governors/judges) against those who lacked that authority or who were completely unformed as citizens (subjects waiting to be shaped). As political experiment, the series was about the aspiring neighbors actively and voluntarily participating in a game of governance – of testing and demonstrating their ability to play by the rules, to manage their own families and selves effectively, and to complete tasks that represented their commitment to neighborhood government and citizenship, even

178 TV's Constitutions of Citizenship

if they were not yet authorized within this neighborhood to be judges. The aspiring neighbors were selected to represent a more "diverse" population and demographic, a diversity that both perpetuated and complicated stereotypical identities and lifestyle clusters.[7] In one sense, all of these families represented (particularly for Circle C) a compendium of current *family-experiments* in the United States, whose "experimentalism" (deviation from the "normal" family unit) was itself a problem for the forms of self-governance practiced by the WASP-ish nuclear-families populating Circle C.

Given that the aspiring neighbors in this series lacked the economic and cultural capital for readily participating in neighborhood government and citizenship in Circle C Ranch, the series positioned the homeowners as *overseers*. The primary task of the homeowners involved a fundamental paradox of liberal government: developing strategies of government that also are strategies for helping to empower the aspiring homeowners. It was the homeowners' prerogative to *watch over* and *watch out* for, to preside over, take responsibility for, and thus assist those who desire to play by the rules and (by playing/performing well) to become part of the neighborhood. In this sense, *Welcome to the Neighborhood* was supposed to have followed in ABC's Sunday-evening schedule after *Extreme Makeover: Home Edition* – a series which involves the effort by private, technical experts to assist a socially and economically handicapped household achieve its full potential.

Following *Extreme Makeover: Home Edition*, *Welcome to the Neighborhood* even had the potential to demonstrate the strategies of what the Bush administration (in describing its own political experiments) has referred to as "compassionate conservatism" for an "ownership society." Good governance and good citizenship in and from Circle C thus tested and demonstrated the abilities of homeowners, as "neighbors," to help those who actively seek to improve themselves by moving into the neighborhood. As the Bush administration has consistently emphasized, this kind of social welfare depends upon private rather than State forms of care-giving and assistance and upon a citizenry actively engaged in helping themselves. In this respect, neighborhood becomes an objective and a resource for mobilizing what Bush has referred to as "the armies of compassion" and for administering forms of social welfare upon which an "ownership society" (homeownership as well as owning up to one's responsibilities) models good government and good citizenship.

Welcome to the Neighborhood serves as a useful way to begin this chapter in part because it was a series never broadcast. Its failure highlights the experimentalism pervading the new model of "TV program" at various levels – TV as experiments in the best techniques to self-empowerment, as locally and privately administered social service for helping, guiding, and shaping citizens, and in this way as a resource that has come to matter for the current experiments in the arts and science of government. Many factors contributed to the program's failure, and a variation on this particular experiment may emerge in the near future, especially since there is much that is familiar and not surprising about the way that it pushed the limits of "good TV." Since few people actually have seen this program, however, it serves as a reminder that TV programs are more than the sense that they make of the world, or the sense TV viewers make of the program's televisual world. It serves as a reminder that TV programs (even those never broadcast) are objects of intense regulation by various institutions. From the moment that *Welcome to the Neighborhood* went into production, it became the point of relatively intense discussion about how reality TV had broken not only rules and codes of what is considered good or proper entertainment, but potentially had broken the law.

Welcome to the Neighborhood might have become part of ABC's Sunday-night schedule in July, 2005 were it not for interventions made particularly by the National Fair Housing Association (NFHA), the National Low Income Housing Coalition (NLIH), and the Gay and Lesbian Alliance Against Defamation (GLAAD). All of these associations are examples of ways that "neighborhood" is the object of regulation and government by the State as well as by private, "non-governmental" organizations. And all are examples of "citizen groups" whose activism is geared toward "social justice" and "civil rights." The NFHA is a privately supported group reporting noncompliance with the Title 8 of the Civil Rights Act of 1968 (the part of the Civil Rights Act pertaining to Fair Housing and commonly referred to as the Fair Housing Act), which prohibits discrimination in the sale, rental, and financing of dwellings, and in other housing-related transactions, based on race, color, national origin, religion, sex, familial status, and disability. According to Shanna Smith, President and CEO of the NFHA, *Welcome to the Neighborhood* violated the spirit and intent of the Federal Housing Act because the series' game of homeownership and neighborhood governance was inseparable from the production process's violation of federal laws protecting homebuyers from discrimination. Complicating the series' violation of the FHA was the allowance made by various states to administer fair-housing laws and codes. The Texas Fair Housing Act, for instance, covers "most housing [though] . . . in some circumstances, the Act exempts . . . housing operated by organizations and private clubs that limit occupancy to members." While neither ABC nor the NFHA acknowledged that the Texas statute might have allowed the series to stage a game with these rules, the statute is worth mentioning because it underscores precisely how the program worked within a fairly established reasoning about local and state rights. Furthermore, the conflict over the series is an example of how the sanctioning of private governance ("neighborhood government" or "community government") to implement its own rules has increasingly been litigated (in courtrooms rather than TV) to sort out the sovereignty of private government in relation to public/ state government. The Circle-C Ranch subdivision is governed by a "homeowner's association" that administers and enforces rules established by the association for every homeowner. The action by the NFHA thus occurred at the intersection between private government and "political government" – a televisual staging of a game about homeownership in a suburban gated community, in a state sanctioning the sovereignty of "neighborhood rule."

Collectively, the interventions by the NFHA and GLAAD underscore the complicated and multidimensional process of group government, and particularly the complicated intersections between government by State constitutions and government by private covenants that occur in the current stage of liberalism.[8] In certain respects, the actions by these "nongovernmental" overseers, and the subsequent decision by ABC not to air *Welcome to the Neighborhood*, was a newsworthy item from May through July of 2005. The NGOs threatened but never pursued court action, and the network's decision not to broadcast any episodes of the series was arguably a strategy for demonstrating its civic conscientiousness (the network as fair, rational, "socially responsible," and "civic-minded" – committed to the virtues of liberal government). The government of television thus occurred without direct intervention by state institutions of government.

The challenges to the civic virtues of *Welcome to the Neighborhood* (i.e., the problems of "governing the neighborhood" and governing *through* "neighborhood") also pertain to the trend in corporate "outreach" discussed in Chapter 1, particularly to ABC's "Better Community" initiative.[9] While *Welcome to the Neighborhood* would have been yet another TV program through which ABC could have practiced (and promoted its civic virtue as) the new trend in corporate "outreach," the Better Community initiative also served to deflect the kinds of criticisms and political demonstrations directed at the neighborhood cul-de-sac by NGOs such as GLAAD and the NFHA. Such are the current political stakes and contradictions of governing, and governing through, the televisual citizenship of neighborhood and community.

This example needs to be pushed one step further, by returning to one other way that the series' production, experimentalism, and prohibition involved the mechanisms of private and self-government: the Circle-C Ranch Homeowners' Association. The series never directly connected the game of homeownership and neighborhood government/citizenship to the subdivision's form of private government and "self-determination," though homeowner associations have become (since the 1990s in particular) ubiquitous entities governing life in residential areas. The practice of "gating" has become coterminous with the formation of homeowner associations that regulate various kinds of conduct in residential enclaves, and that link these regulations to the formation and maintenance of "neighborhood." The web site for the Circle C Homeowners Association, for instance, states:

> **It's the neighborhood that matters.** From talking to prospective homebuyers, we've learned a lot about what's important to you. You want to live in a place . . . where education is the finest, where lasting friends are made, where security and safety are a part of everyday life, where leisure and recreation are as close as your front door and, most of all, a place where families come first. Every part of Circle C Ranch is designed to provide the people who live here with that extra special something which truly defines the term "neighborhood."

> **Appreciation for a great neighborhood.** One of the best bonuses in our efforts to become Austin's finest neighborhood is the opportunity made for your home to significantly appreciate in value. Our emphasis will always be on the human side of creating a neighborhood, but it's nice to know that as we achieve our goals, the marketplace recognizes the value of such an effort. When you buy a home in Circle C, there will be countless aspects of the neighborhood which you will appreciate; not the least of which will be the true appreciation of your investment.

While neighborhood is an "investment," managing the investment wisely involves oversight, vigilance, and active involvement in various aspects of life – in various ways that neighborhood is enacted, achieved, and valued. The televisual game of homeownership and neighborhood government is not merely a signification, distortion, or simulation of Circle C's games of homeownership and neighborhood government. Rather, these are interlocking and interdependent technologies of government and citizenship. The promotional programs for Circle C are part of a trend in marketing research that uses polling to determine buyers of suburban residential developments who share certain "values" – polls whose questions to prospective residents are used to identify "values subcultures," such as differentiating buyers who are "traditionalists" from those who are "cultural creatives."[10] Furthermore, Circle C's web site offers a constantly updated schedule of games ("fun contests" and participatory events) that are directed toward cementing neighborhood, and thus particular forms of citizenship. The games are, to wed the terminology of reality TV and immigration law, "citizenship tests." As in the TV series, Circle C's events ask homeowners to be "judges" and careful/vigilant players in these games, for instance identifying a photo of a mysterious but common object in the neighborhood – a game not entirely unlike the televisual one involving homeowners' oversight of exotic families in their neighborhood. In this sense, the tasks devised by the producers of *Welcome to the Neighborhood* are not particularly far-fetched, surprising, or limit-pushing. They are integral to the rational governance of citizens in these times.

By July, 2005, at the height of the national and local controversy surrounding *Welcome to the Neighborhood*, the Circle C Homeowners Association's monthly business meeting addressed the negative publicity that the association felt had been generated about their neighborhood – publicity that not only "cast a shadow" over the subdivision but that threatened property values. As the minutes of the meeting that were posted on the association's web site indicated, the controversy became the first order of business:

Quentin introduced the homeowner forum. Homeowner Ryan Garcia spoke on the ABC television series, "Welcome to the Neighborhood". He asked the board of directors to issue a statement regarding the inaccuracy of the portrayal of the Circle C neighborhood by the television series. The board of directors said they would discuss posting a reply on the website and/or newsletter, but would not write a response to the local media. The board suggested that individual letters from residents to the *Austin American Statesman* would have a bigger impact that [sic] a board statement.

The Circle C Homeowners Association's mobilization of its own media technology of governance to respond to newspaper accounts of a controversy surrounding a reality TV series was complicated further by private contractual agreements, made by ABC with the participants in the series, which prohibited the participants (but not the President of the Circle C Homeowners Association) from talking with the press about the TV series. "Governing TV" has become, in this way, a matter of governing, and extending a welcome mat to, the neighborhood. And this process occurs at the intersection of TV's and the suburb's constitutions.

Welcome to the Neighborhood was not only a demonstration and experiment in effective and wise management of neighborhood, estate, real estate, household, family, and self, but it also became the object of political demonstrations about what counts in these times as good citizenship and as fair, reasonable, and wise government – in short, the civic virtues of liberalism. As an unsettled and unsettling event, the TV program in government and citizenship enacted by *Welcome to the Neighborhood* was a "citizenship test" that became a test in what counts as fair, reasonable, wise, and good TV. This is a complicated process, since the failure of certain technologies of government may affirm the usefulness and reliability of other governmental technologies. The "failure" of *Welcome to the Neighborhood*'s strategies and rules for staging "citizenship tests" became part of current TV's experimentation with the rules of citizenship and the techniques of good government by various private groups. Within this field of experimentation, even the failure of certain rules, strategies, games, and tests are lessons to be acted upon.

The "failure" of *Welcome to the Neighborhood* had little to do with its having ventured too far afield from TV's customary design of programs that are games as well as scientific experiments and demonstrations. The impulse toward designing a TV program as social-scientific experiment runs throughout the history of US TV,[11] and in certain respects this tendency has deepened and broadened in the current stage of television. The makeover programs discussed in Chapter 3, for instance, frequently involve calculating improvement and progress through experiments involving subjects' completion of tasks within the framework of a contest. These contests test and demonstrate the subjects' limits and abilities to perform, improving their self-constitution through a set of guidelines made available through TV as program/ regimen. However, *Welcome to the Neighborhood*'s group dynamic, its demonstration of how a private group manages and administers a "neighborhood" (resolving differences, deciding the rights of various families/households, vetting what kind of behavior is suitable to its neighborhood's constitution) set it apart slightly from makeover TV and align it with numerous other veins of recent TV programming. Series such as MTV's *The Real World* and *Road Rules*, NBC's *The Apprentice*, CBS's *The Survivor*, ABC's *Wife Swap*, Fox's *Black/White*, Bravo's *Top Chef*, and TLC's *Town Haul* have been not only some of the most successful recent TV series, but they also share *Welcome to the Neighborhood*'s experimentation with group governance – with enacting provisional, privately administered constitutions. Collectively, these experiments and games of group government have become integral to the idea and practice of "reinventing government."

Games of Group Governance

In one respect, contemporary TV's preoccupation with demonstrations and techniques of private group governance developed out of a paradox of the post-broadcast TV era, which conceived of maximum representation of a national population as best accomplished through a proliferation of channels. The trend toward maximizing representation and toward managing population differences occurred during the early 1970s with series such as *All in the Family*, which weekly demonstrated the feebleness of prior TV fashionings of neighborhood and household (and the dissolution of the idea of "family TV" that had been an organizing principle among US broadcasters through the 1950s and 1960s). The formation of a "public broadcasting" channel during the late 1960s and early 1970s also was rationalized partly around a perceived need to represent more adequately a racial and gendered diversity lacking in commercial broadcast TV. PBS's *Sesame Street* thus became one of the most recognizable ways that public TV could achieve this, and in so doing represent the important civic mission of TV. Since the 1970s, fashioning a pluralist TV thus became intertwined with the formation of cable broadcasting. And in the post-1970s period, televisual citizenship increasingly became an objective and self-justification of new networks – Pat Robertson's Christian Broadcasting Channel (which became the Family Channel); Black Entertainment TV (as TV for African-Americans); Music TV (as TV for youth); the Playboy Channel ("men's entertainment"); Lifetime, and Oxygen TV (as "women's channels") all articulated lifestyle and values as a basis for televisual membership-cum-citizenship.

While we have selected *Welcome to the Neighborhood* as an example of a controversial and relatively unsuccessful experiment in group governance – a selection made partly to underscore TV's experimentalism in reinventing the mechanisms of group governance – there are ample (albeit varied) examples of what counts in contemporary TV as successful group government. One would not need to look further than *Survivor* (2000–present), one of the longest running (and by that standard, most successful) prototypes of TV as experiment/demonstration in group governance. It would be simplistic to attribute the reality-TV syndrome to the success of any one TV program as prototype, but it is worth recognizing that *Survivor*'s emergence as a model of successful TV production has involved staging games of group constitution and group governance involving nonprofessional actor-contestants.

Considered as a game of teamwork and group governance, *Survivor* has been one of the most recognizable and durable examples of demonstrating that good, active, and effective citizenship (being a useful member of a team, and even upholding the team's reputation or honor) requires maximum degrees of self-sufficiency – by the individual contestants and teams. The series ritualistically tests the limits not only of contestants' stamina, resolve, and craft (or craftiness) in completing certain prescribed tasks and surviving/winning, but also of individual players' and teams' tolerance for those unable to carry their load, to be productive and responsible team-players, and to be a good citizen. There are nevertheless certain paradoxes around which the series, as civic laboratory, organizes its experiments in wise and effective government. The series plays upon the tension between individual and collective interests, between the myth that premodern societies are organized around an intense sense of "community" or *Gemeinschaft* (the series' reference to the teams as "tribes") and the myth of a modern possessive individualism and self-interest (*Gesellschaft*), between materialistic pursuits and a world lacking familiar material comforts and appliances (where the need for comforting things is heightened), between a managerialist injunction to be a team player (to pull together) and the relentless rewarding of the entrepreneurial capitalist and the Hobbesian strategist, between the caricature of a premodern world as abiding by a *natural* "tribal law" and the heroic caricature of modern societies as "governed" (guaranteeing freedom as the "natural condition" of man), between a heightened state of insecurity (the jungle) and the promise of financial security for the winner (returning home), and between the civilities and incivilities of participation, belonging, and membership in privately formed groups. Particularly in these last two respects, *Survivor* enacts (weekly and seasonally reenacts) the *birth* of government and the reinvention of new liberal citizen players. Arguably, the absence of neighborhood and neighborliness – far away from the suburban ideal of home – accentuates a need for provisional, seat-of-the pants constitution of group and household.[12] The lessons/ instructions of a "remote island" lacking remote controls (of the kind used to operate TVs and TV households) are decidedly about how to govern through shifting and provisional alliances and through exercises in caring for oneself (i.e., remotely and "at a distance").

Survivor's experiments in government and citizenship also developed out of US TV's post-1970s preoccupation with representing and managing diversity as democratic comity. Not only are *Survivor*'s tests and tasks impelled and punctuated by periodic rounds of voting (more on this in Chapter 6), but of voting members "off the island" who are unable to demonstrate their fitness to remain actively involved in winning/surviving as increasingly smaller groups. Each season begins with a collection of team members (tribal citizens) who are selected by the series' producers often to accentuate interaction between various populations, "values-subcultures," and lifestyle clusters. By the end of each season, however, the problem of governing fairly is put to tests over sheer self-interest and self-reliance, as the group and its managers narrow and become increasingly incapable of being fair. In this respect, the most fundamental game of the series is about testing/contesting the limits of democratic comity in an environment where difference increasingly matters. And even though this game is cast as an exercise/experiment in group behavior and group governance, the series rewards a "survivor" – the most self-actualized citizen player.

As both experiment and game (a test in both senses) that winnows the useful or successful participants from those who are not, *Survivor* perpetuates a paradox about the democratic aspiration of its group governance, and about TV as technology of liberal, democratic government and citizenship. How can the series' enactment of group governance be about equality (mutual decisions) if it also is about selecting who's in and who's out (who is the fittest, and thus who represents the most successful and model-citizen/player)?[13] In the current regime of TV series about group governance, the long group-process of selecting and recognizing a winner (who's in and who's out) is a practice of demonstrating that there are certain kinds of citizens who are more fit than others to become the kind of citizen that the series' games are training. Even though the process involves a game of gradual exclusion, what remains is the fittest – the example par excellence of self-reliant citizenship. This does not necessarily mean that the winner is liked (as was evident with the public ambivalence about Richard Hatch in the first season of *Survivor*), but the winner still warrants admiration as an exemplar of effective self-actualization and group brokering.

Although *The Apprentice* perpetuated many of the features of *Survivor* (in part because of Mark Burnett's involvement as producer of both series), *The Apprentice* offered a different game of group governance in several important respects. First, and most obviously, *The Apprentice* converts the Darwinian rationale about fitness, adaptation, and "natural selection" in *Survivor*'s jungle/paradise to a stage/lab that is unabashedly commercial. Rather than introducing commodities as occasional rewards for contestants competing in a wilderness supposedly untouched by commercial signage (as is customary on *Survivor*), *The Apprentice*'s very fiber (its games, tasks, setting) is about profiting from commercial signage.

At the center of the series (as judge, boss, manager, series-owner, and exemplar) is Donald Trump, which the series casts as arguably the most recognizable US entrepreneur and mogul of the late twentieth century. Before the series began, Trump was a relatively successful real-estate investor and developer, owner of casinos, resorts, and country clubs, and author of several bestselling books on investment advice, money management, and strategies of financial success. In the series' 2004 première, Trump describes himself as a self-made billion-aire, summarizing the erosion and subsequent expansion of his fortune over the 1990s, and associating his personal financial prowess and suc-cesses with a national economic recovery between 1999 and 2004 (a period coterminous with the current reality-TV syndrome). While Trump's personal narrative in the series' première omitted references to his being the son of a wealthy investor and his attendance at one of the nation's most elite business schools, Wharton Business College, Trump and the series repeatedly invoke his personal successes, status, and authority (as author of books about personal financial success-strategy) in order to rationalize the series as games of and rewards for self-actualization. These games and rewards demonstrate that any player supposedly has a chance to become successful playing by his techniques and the series' rules.

While (like *Survivor*) *The Apprentice* is organized as a game with nonprofessional actors, the series casts the game as a learning experi-ence and casts the contestants (*players* and *performers* in the business sense) as there to learn – to prove that they possess qualities which Trump would want and will reward. In this respect, the series is not only a vehicle for displaying Trump's business ventures and brands, but a lab for teaching/producing/inventing an ideal corporate citizen. In this sense, the series is an extension of Trump's books: exercises for the contestants and the viewers interested in cultivating the skills nec-essary to be self-actualizing, self-disciplined, and energetic makers of their own fortunes and financial futures. After the first season of the series, some courses in US business schools were using episodes of *The Apprentice* to teach management skills. And after the second season, Trump developed Trump University, an online curriculum in business strategies and management techniques. *The Apprentice*, however, is populist pedagogy – free, though not commercial-free, for anyone to watch.

Like *Welcome to the Neighborhood* and *Survivor*, *The Apprentice* is a behavioral experiment. The series'/game's design also links its exercises in self-help through investment and management skills to a kind of citizenship and government modeled after and involving management models in corporate organizations. In each season of *The Apprentice*, contestants are chosen to represent geographic, racial, and gendered diversity; in the première episode, Trump declared that he intended to pit male contestants against female contestants to determine whether

(a)

(b)

Illustration 5.1 The tribal council on *Survivor* and the boardroom on *The Apprentice* enact the rules and rituals of private governance (*The Apprentice*: Mark Burnett Productions and Donald Trump Productions LLC for NBC TV; *Survivor*: Mark Burnett Productions for CBS, 2004)

there really is a "glass ceiling" in US corporate management culture – an experiment within an experiment. However, contestants also are selected because of their fledgling business experience (many have started their own companies, though some have only an MBA from prestigious business schools). The contestants vie for a chance to work for Donald Trump for a year by demonstrating on a weekly basis their abilities to manage a group (as a "group leader") that is charged with accomplishing certain business tasks (e.g., selling lemonade, attracting customers to a Planet Hollywood restaurant, designing and market-testing a toy for Mattel, running a charity event at one of Trump's country clubs and casinos). As in *Survivor*, the series tests these young corporate players'–citizens' ability to navigate a paradox: to fend for themselves (to be self-actualizing entrepreneurs and effective "leaders") while exhibiting their ability to be trustworthy workers and team players. Good (corporate) citizenship within current liberalism's mantra of reinventing government requires not only citizens who are *players* but players who are competent in both these respects. And the game played by *The Apprentice* enacts this paradox as a natural and funda-mental tenet of US corporate management's recent emphasis upon "leadership training" (as part of the curriculum of privately sponsored, corporate training as well as of higher education). In a state where good government is less government, then everyone needs to be a leader rather than a dependent/onlooker, though clearly, the game's objective is also to underscore that only one player can be selected to lead the other corporate citizens. Aside from this paradox, *The Appren-tice* affirms the trend toward structuring the workplace around small groups (one example of which is the organizational model of "com-munities of practice" in corporations), and the series experiments with extending this model of corporate small-group management and pro-ductivity beyond the workplace, as when the program tests and has surveillance over the contestant-employees who extend their team-work back into their apartments, where government by the group continues.[14]

That all of the contestants are young (20s through mid-30s) in the first few seasons of *The Apprentice* attests to several implications that have been suggested above but that need to be elaborated briefly. First, casting the corporate citizen-leader as youthful reinforces *The Appren-tice's* premise that the game is training. Even when contestants lose, their closing confessions to the TV audience frequently refer to the important lessons that they have learned from the experience in the game.[15] Losing can be the path to winning if one is self-actualizing. Second, the series represents a population and lifestyle cluster (young entrepreneurial professionals) which are most affected by the current political rationality's expectation that citizens manage their own financial futures.[16] There is little about *The Apprentice* that understands social welfare in any terms except taking personal responsibility. The première episode begins with the song, "Money, Money, Money," whose lyrics invoke the Depression-era phrase, "Buddy, can you spare a dime?" Financial risk and securing one's financial future is central to the game played by young contestants on *The Apprentice*.

In addition to repurposing *Survivor*'s behavioral experimentation with group governance, and *Survivor*'s citizenship tests, *The Apprentice* also "advances" the kind of games played in reality TV for youth. In one respect, *The Apprentice* is a slightly more grownup version of some of the most recognized and formative youth-oriented experiments/games in group-governance (e.g., MTV's *The Real World* and *Road Rules*, and BET's *College Hill*). *The Apprentice* arguably makes sense – is a rational progression – in part because its contestants, and many of its viewers, are a population that has grown up in a TV regimen anchored in part by these programs. *The Real World* (which premièred in 1992) and *Road Rules* (which premièred in 1995) are two of the forerunners of the current vein of reality TV. MTV was the first channel in the United States (and the world) designed primarily for young audiences, and both series were integral to MTV's transformation away from predominantly music-video programming during the 1980s to lifestyle programming during the 1990s. Historically, the success of these programs intersected with the discourse about "reinventing government" that this book addresses.

Unlike older TV soap opera, these programs emphasized the provisional constitution of household. Because all of the cast are out of high school but not exactly beyond the normal age of a college student, the series belong to a history of youth fiction as (and about) rites of passage – of recognizing and assuming "adult" responsibilities. *The Real World* has formulated its lessons from a provisional home, for a population that (by US standards) is usually between the homes of their parents and living "on their own." *Road Rules* has formulated its lessons "on the road" – from a mobile home and within a ritual of youth of this age involving going abroad to learn lessons of responsibility. BET's *College Hill* is set more within dormitory life on a college campus.

While the two MTV series have increasingly involved games and tasks (as part of the trend in the current regime of reality TV toward practicing and exercising abilities and responsibilities), the MTV series always have been behavioral experiments in private group governance by non-actors. In these series, becoming a mature citizen involves learning how to act and perform – not simply as training to become a Hollywood actor but a good performer of citizenship from the home or on the road, a competent social actor/agent as group leader and member.

Since their first seasons, the provisional status of the households in *The Real World* and *Road Rules* are about managing diversity. One thing that makes these households provisional (and certainly a hallmark of these series) is their representation of gendered, class, racial, and geographic diversity – "multiculturalism" for a lifestyle channel. As in the series already discussed in this section, the MTV and BET series are demonstrations/exercises that lead ordinary young people to realize their relation to the rules (house rules and road rules) for getting along with difference. In this respect, the series stage carefully designed experiments in achieving democratic comity, for a population of citizens whose recent eligibility to vote (to be a political citizen in that sense) is intertwined with their eligibility (according to the State) to have sex, to drink alcohol, to drive, to have an abortion without their parents' consent, or to serve in the military. While the series enact scenes of membership, belonging, and association, they do so as informal (and for these young, non-trained actors) relatively unpracticed forms of group decision-making, caring, and leadership. In this respect, they reformulate a long history of educational films for youth about becoming good citizens, except that these TV series are not part of an academic curriculum (i.e., are watched whenever its young audience is away from school and wherever its audience provisionally calls home).

As a form of civic education and exercise, these TV programs' emphasis upon youthful subjects converge with other series. In 2005,

Mark Burnett teamed with Sylvester Stallone to produce NBC's *The Contender*, a variation of the game-experiment wherein amateur male boxers who were selected from across the United States underwent a period of training and then a series of individual bouts between two teams of fighters. *The Contender* interweaves a regimen of self-actualization with exercises in group management. Furthermore, it also emphasizes the racial diversity of the contestants, and their generally blue-collar backgrounds, in making training about citizenship a sport.[17]

Bravo's *Top Chef* (which premiered in 2006) is the most recent of relatively successful reality TV series organized around professional cooking (following *The Restaurant* in 2004, and the Food Channel's programming about contests among professional chefs). Like the reality TV programs of self-care, *Top Chef* rewards a form of entrepreneurialism: a young chef who most impresses a panel of experienced and often famous chefs is rewarded, not simply with money but with financial and other resources for starting her/his own restaurant. However, like *The Apprentice* and *The Contender*, *Top Chef* is also a set of lessons, exercises, and tests in managing a kitchen, where young contestants (with experience as chef-helpers) must work with less supervision while demonstrating their promise as wise and effective leaders of kitchen help. Paradoxically, demonstrating leadership in the kitchen can only be imagined through demonstrations of young contestants' individual work and talents for assembling ingredients, management of time, and attractive presentation. The contestants aspire toward and work as if they were in charge of a collectivity of kitchen help. Because *Top Chef*'s primary performance stage and laboratory is the kitchen rather than the sites of corporate management typical of *The Apprentice*, and because *Top Chef* emphasizes individual artistry and technique as a prerequisite for successful group governance, it affirms that good government is as much an *art* as a highly technical science.

The TV series we've looked at so far are enacted as *tests* of group governance, democratic procedure, and citizenship – tests that combine games by citizen-players (contestants actively competing and striving to win and to reap rewards) and social experiments that test the limits of individual and team endurance, the depth of individual and group resolve, the ability of groups to resolve differences and to act fairly. The game dimension of these series is slightly more pronounced than their scientific dimension as social and behavioral experiments. On

Illustration 5.2   The household is a site of governance on *Wife Swap* (RDF Media for ABC TV, 2005)

series such as ABC's *Wife Swap* and Fox's *Black/White*, however, group government is conducted as a social experiment. These series acknowledge (even accentuate) the seriousness, rather than the play, of managing difference and negotiating their role and responsibilities as citizen–subjects in multicultural association. Unlike the citizen–games that involve vetting who's in and who's out, these series recognize alternative lifestyle, difference, and plurality as conditions (even an objective) of contemporary forms of liberal government and citizenship. In that respect, they are about the limits of inclusivity, about the ability of subjects to *tolerate* the discomforts of living difference and sharing the same space with alternative lifestyles, and about the capacity of subjects to adjust their familiar management solutions to the requirements of the alternative lifestyle.

Both *Wife Swap* and *Black/White* temporarily move subjects into environments that test their ethics and their commitment to a certain lifestyle. The household as stage or lab for these TV experiments not only exposes a set of privately held and lived values but does so within a sphere of family management. As in *The Real World*, the subjects' temporary household becomes, in its unfamiliarity, a stage/set for testing one's accepted practices and lived principles of running a household. The new, temporary arrangement requires testing and modifying one's constitution – the rules of life and order at home, the regimens that have made a house a "home."

Wife Swap, as its title suggests, routinely organizes its tests around two wives (invariably mothers) who trade households with one another. Each broadcast also follows a certain sequence: the introduction of the wives and their distinctive, contrasting habits/rules of household management, the introduction of the wives to their temporary households and families, the effort by the wives to size up and adjust to the governmental rationality of their temporary households, the wives' implementation (often imposition) of a new set of rules for managing various problems perceived by the wives in their temporary households, a period of adjustment, deliberation, and reconciliation in the temporary households, and finally, the return of the wives to their more permanent households – a reunion in which the wives and family members discuss what they have learned from the experiment. Not only does the series examine how subjects adjust to differences, but this adjustment involves learning (and demonstrating to the viewers) paths and techniques of household management. Some of the differences in the first two seasons of *Wife Swap* included a peace activist who opposed the war in Iraq and who trades places with a military-trained mom who supported the war in Iraq; a woman who was unable to control her credit-card expenditures who trades places with a mother who rigorously/fanatically managed the household finances; a devoutly Catholic, Italian-American mother of a meticulously kept household who trades places with a Caucasian woman who was married to an African-American male artist and who apparently devoted little effort to household upkeep; an upper-crust mom who was supported by her husband, left the children and household to the care of paid help, and trades places with a working-class mom whose daily duties involved more strenuous labor than her husband's.

In *Wife Swap*'s experiments and demonstrations about women as domestic managers, the series requires its subjects to develop sets of personally constituted rules (homemade constitutions) and to experiment with the efficacy of their management techniques and skills in the alternative households. In the central part of each episode, the female subjects/managers learn the rules of the host (or project) household and then formalize and impose their own rules. ABC's official web site for the series also prominently displays each woman's rules and "manual." The online manual (which further formalizes the woman's guidelines as a personal constitution) thus serves as a way of representing each woman as citizen and as governess. As citizen, she is a foreign member of a household whose rights she must declare and defend, and *as* governess she is a house manager – not legally a house-wife – who must solve problems accentuated by her presence as for-eigner, temporary citizen, and guest worker. Like the ritualized sequence of steps taken by the women in the broadcast program, the online manual and rules-statement for each woman formalizes a tem-plate for what each woman believes are her codes, rights, and respon-sibilities. (So in this sense, ABC constitutes the coda – as "manual" – by which the women declare their personal constitutions.) Each online manual invariably includes each woman's guidelines for house-hold chores, kid management, kitchen management, shopping, a weekly routine, weekend routine, leisure and social life, relationship with her partner, relationship with her family, relationship with her pet(-s), and (lastly) finances. The moral economy of the household is thus codified as a set of formal prescriptions and declarations – much like (but mattering differently from) a legal contract or constitution.[18]

Similar to many of the series discussed in this section (and in contrast to many of the series discussed in prior chapters), *Wife Swap* conducts an experiment in self-actualization without a guide, coach, or mentor. Series such as *The Apprentice*, *Survivor*, *The Contender*, and *Top Chef* are programs in which group governance is "overseen" by a judge who makes and imposes rules, though usually after the group has made their own decisions. *Wife Swap* presumes and recognizes a woman's techni-cal abilities to manage households, even as it puts in play the ethics of management, and even as it affirms that there is no longer a uniform morality or set of rules, no standard moral economy, of the US house-hold. Constituting a plurality of moral economies is, after all, a central preoccupation of a TV network such as ABC, which tries to address a relatively diverse audience – an aggregation of lifestyle clusters and "values subcultures." A program that formalizes manuals and guidelines (as homemade constitutions) is one way for ABC to solve that problem.

Black/White's experiment in liberal and democratic government involves literally shaping (physically reconstructing) subjects to heighten their sensitivity to and their reflection about racial difference and the requirements of citizenship in a multiracial society.[19] To demonstrate these requirements, the program tests its subjects' (in-)tolerance of racial difference by converting their racial identities. Three Caucasian and three African–American subjects undergo a makeover so that they can "pass" in various locations and can experience what it feels like to have a different racial identity.[20] As in *Wife Swap*, they are made to feel temporary citizens in alien territory, having to learn and navigate the rules, codes, and laws of their *membership* in a free and open society. Like makeover TV, the program followed a process of ethical training and self-actualization through the acquisition of new techniques and technologies. This process occurred through steps taken by each subject and family group to state their civic rights in alien territories (places where they, as racially hybrid subjects, felt uncomfortable going and performing certain tasks). Unlike other makeover TV, however, physical transformation in *Black/White* is temporary. The series may be, secondarily, about putting these subjects (and viewers) on a path to a life lived in greater harmony and understanding toward another race; however, in the last episode of the six-episode series the two patriarchs agree to disagree about whether the other harbors racist attitudes. In this respect, the program is less about training than about observing and testing the behavior, reactions, and tolerance of subjects before they presumably retreat to households and neighborhoods where their membership is more readily validated every day.

We include *Black/White* as part of a discussion of group governance because the subjects are expected to constitute, cohabit within, and collectively manage a mixed-race household, which is located (as one of the cast points out) in a multiracial suburb. In this household, they appear out of their racialized *costumes* and are continually judged and coached by members of the other family about their *performance* as representatives of a black or white population.[21] In scenes staged at their collective home, they are not presented doing housework together; instead household management is overtly a process of hammering out how each one is supposed to act and behave – at or away from home. Aside from these displays of group governance at home, the subjects' staged involvement away from home involves situations where each character participates in forms of collective decision-making: each family (in costume) participates in racially homogeneous focus groups, the son in the African–American family participates (in costume) in an etiquette class comprising white students, and the daughter of the

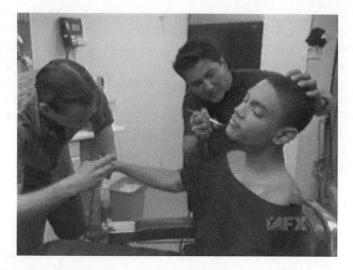

Illustration 5.3 Two families "swap" races on the TV experiment *Black/White* (20th Century-Fox Productions for F/X, 2006)

Caucasian family participates (in costume) in a drama class consisting of African-American students who collectively judge each other's performances.

In *Black/White*, the process for achieving pluralism and racial equality (central to democratic government/citizenship) thus is made to run through commercial and cultural spheres which are just as much about differentiating and rewarding good performances of race and racial citizenship as they are about constituting an environment – public and private worlds – where different races can live together and participate as equals. As noted above, a paradox of democratic participation in the current regime of reality TV is that the path to pluralism is through nongovernmental (private, everyday) spheres where one's performance as a member is assessed, and thus where pluralism turns on who's in and who's out. That *Black/White* represents focus groups as one of the *natural* sites where group decision-making occurs attests to how naturalized and rational this process is within reality TV's mode of producing citizens and staging exhibitions of democracy in action.

Two other programs, TLC's *Town Haul* and Bravo's *Real Housewives of Orange County*, link our initial analysis of *Welcome to the Neighborhood* to this section's discussion of group governance and reality TV's paradox of democratic participation. *Town Haul* (2005–6) shares many of the conventions of makeover TV. Its host and lead expert is Genevieve Gorder, an interior decorator and a host of another TLC series, *Trading Spaces*. In *Town Haul*, the "overhaul" is not of a car, house, or football field, but of a small town – or certain sites whose collective improvement is supposed to improve the town. As in *Extreme Makeover: Home Edition*, the program's producers arrive with specialists to assist in projects, but the producers also actively involve the town's population in accomplishing the various renovations. Each broadcast follows the citizens' participation in remaking their town. *Town Haul* is therefore similar to programs discussed in Chapter 1 that provide a form of welfare assistance through private initiatives and contractors arranged by TV – granting wishes and offering aid to several families in the town as part of the town's improvement. As a program on the Learning Channel, *Town Haul* also intersects with the programs discussed in Chapter 2 that are about teaching citizenship and shaping citizens through demonstrations about self-fashioning and care of oneself.

In both these respects, the program is integral to the discourse of "reinventing government," although (as the program's web site makes explicit) civic action is merely catalyzed by TV experts and professionals; the work and energy comes from citizens-cum-"neighbors": *Town Haul* "is an inspiring look at the power of neighbors to connect and create positive changes in the world around them." And as Gorder states:

> I've always wanted to do a show with people that needed more than just some paint on their walls. TLC has given me this remarkable opportunity to actually move into some of America's most intriguing small towns, and help orchestrate a physical and emotional renovation. I really think this series is going to redefine the meaning of what it means to be a good neighbor.

While other programs may select and then demonstrate the capacity of individual citizens and families to help themselves, *Town Haul* is slightly more ambitious – helping individual families rebuild individual sites that, with the input of "neighbors," gradually and collectively reshape the town.

The program's emphasis upon small towns is significant in several respects. One is that the small town becomes a manageable scale for demonstrating the potential consequences of group and *grassroots* involvement (although "the people" are selected and guided by TV professionals/experts). Also, a "town haul" easily represents a scale of civic action that is imaginable for suburban gated communities or urban gentrifiers who have moved recently to residential developments whose design seeks to re-create a bygone sense of "neighborhood" and "community."[22] Neighborhood and community (the idealization of small-town life in urban and suburban development) also are articulated in *Town Haul* with displays of civic pride. That the producers of *Town Haul* describe their project as empowering neighbors to "connect and create positive changes in the world around them" assumes that the program's outcomes represent an improvement (a "positive change"), and simply on the basis of mobilizing neighbors to "take back" the town, to make the town more neighborly and thus more able to galvanize civic pride.

The program's selection of the particular towns is also significant. Just as individuals and families are selected in many of the other programs discussed in this book, *Town Haul*'s producers select a town worthy of being made over. In its first three seasons, *Town Haul* was set in Jeffersonville, NY, Laurens, SC, and Washington, MO, and these towns were selected (according to a Chamber of Commerce bulletin regarding the latter town) from fifty other locations. All of these towns have relatively modest income levels (with average household incomes ranging between $29,000 and $48,000) and thus are suitably "in need" of assistance. However, two of the towns (Jeffersonville and Washington) were already engaged in initiatives to promote themselves as historically important, as tourist destinations, and as cultural/arts centers.[23] The official web site for Washington, MO provides links to the Downtown Washington, Inc. – A Missouri Main Street Community, where donations are accepted to rebuild its waterfront and farmer's market. The program's web site and the town's web site both note that the town was a stop on the Lewis and Clark Expedition and has no fewer than four Nationally Registered Historic Districts. The program's improvements, therefore, are not only about putting the town on the national map (a group exercise in civic pride) but assisting (through private aid and grassroots action) the town's designation as historically important and valuable. Furthermore, the program's makeover both assists and capitalizes upon the efforts of the town's government, Chamber of Commerce, historical society, and volunteer associations – each catalyzing the other. In this respect, selecting which families/sites are improved is a form of group governance (or more accurately, public–private partnerships) occurring between citizens, local government, local booster institutions, and national TV. Selecting appropriate towns and citizens is itself a process that involves already active efforts to promote and make over the town – a process that makes *Town Haul* instrumental to the reinvention of local governments, and an active local citizenry instrumental to TV as public assistance.

The selection of these small, needy-but-energized towns are also convenient yet vivid sites of a form of community and group initiative galvanized through TV because of the towns' relation to Red States and Blue States – to a map of a political rationality that has emerged during the first decade of the twenty-first century. Without making a claim about the political orientation of these towns, and without affirming that the category of the Red State explains the town, the selection of small towns does tap into (in these times) a political rationality as national map that associates small towns (particularly in the South, Midwest, and Rocky Mountains) with a neoconservative reasoning about the role of liberal government. It is worth noting that two of the three towns chosen to be "overhauled" in the first three seasons (Jeffersonville and Washington) are between 97 and 98 percent white. This demographic feature makes them convenient settings for an idyllic re-creation of a national past, and it makes *Town Haul*'s demonstration of group mobilization (particularly the civic action implied by old-fashioned "town hall" meetings) tantamount to eliding racial difference in the town's reconstitution. The series has yet to include scenes of group deliberations by the towns (in the fashion of town-hall meetings), and relies instead on displays of ad hoc group support – of neighbors recognizing the need to help one another in an initiative in which the supporters and supported have been preselected.

This synergy between the current stage of broadcast TV and the enterprise of local government returns our discussion to why the *Welcome to the Neighborhood* experiment matters. By considering *Town Haul* and *Welcome to the Neighborhood* together, another paradox of a neoliberal practice of democracy through TV is that the "town hall" has been reinvented as "neighborhood association" or "community association" – a private legislative body that administers privately designed constitutions (rules) for groups that have been vetted by the association and that have been the target of marketing efforts to fashion a particular kind of neighborhood as "lifestyle cluster" and "values subculture". Bravo's *Real Housewives of Orange County* is a documentary-styled serial about the private lives of women in Orange County's Coto de Caza gated community. Although this residential development's average income per household ($137,000) makes its lifestyle the antithesis of the towns in *Town Haul*, it too is predominately (90 percent) white, roughly the same number of residents as the towns in *Town Haul*, and just as invested in the idea of neighborhood and community. The residential development's online source of news about itself, for instance, is the "Coto de Caza Community Association Neighborhood News." Orange County is also widely recognized as a bastion of a neoliberal (if not rural neoconservative) political rationality. *Real Housewives of Orange County*'s first season (2006) was largely bereft of scenes of Coto de Caza's rules and regulating authorities. The rules are made in and from households, and the program plays (sometimes with great irony) on the female subjects' and protagonists' group encounters (at local leisure locations). These subjects' lack of apparent commitment to local government and civic activism is, in part, what is at stake in representing their everyday lives and alliances.

It is worth recognizing that, as residents and citizens of a gated community (the real backdrop of these *Real Housewives of Orange County*), the subjects of the program are also subjects of an elaborate set of rules and administrative bodies that regulate their forms of association (including, presumably, the staging of a TV series there). Aside from the Community Association, which has an elected board of trustees, Coto de Caza is governed by various committees (e.g., an Architectural Committee and Beautification Committee). These administrative bodies formalize and enforce rules and bestow awards for various aspects of daily life there: reporting vandalism, timely removal of trashcans from curbsides, parking, safety, best holiday decorations, and dues and penalties paid to the Association. To consider TV as experiments, games, and demonstrations of neighborhood constitutions and group governance thus involves considering how the means of democratic deliberation and participation are an enabling condition of TV series such as *Real Housewives of Orange County*, *Welcome to the Neighborhood*, and *Town Haul* – the subject of Chapter 6.

Chapter 6

Playing TV's Democracy Game

In *Convergence Culture*, Henry Jenkins contends that the recent "collisions" between old and new media, and among new media, are to be welcomed because they afford new opportunities and forms of participation.[1] An old "consumerist" medium such as TV, he contends, can be redeemed through the interactivity of viewers/players. Jenkins advocates what he calls a "politics of participation" which "starts from the assumption that we may have greater collective bargaining power if we form consumption communities."[2] Although Jenkins devotes a chapter to cataloging various commercial tie-ins between advertisers and TV series such as *American Idol*, he also concludes that undue emphasis on the economics of media concentration accompanying convergence fails to recognize that "a participatory media culture is worth fighting for."[3] Jenkins's analysis is pitched between the familiar antinomies – such as corporate power vs. consumer activism – that have guided not only media criticism, but also many campaigns for media reform.

Using somewhat different key concepts, but still affirming many of the premises guiding Jenkins's project, John Hartley has proposed that contemporary TV should be taken seriously by cultural critics, even as a critical engagement with TV requires critics to recognize the enormous popular appeals and pleasures afforded by popular entertainment as "everyday education."[4] Hartley is particularly fond of the trend toward what he calls "do-it-yourself" TV, whose appeal is the empowerment of viewers to express and choose for themselves, and their *freedom* to explore and re-create alternative cultural identities through TV. As he states, "In a period of consumer choice, computer-aided interactivity and post–identity politics, semiotic self–determination [the construction of one's own identity and community through TV] is emerging as a right."[5] For Hartley, this development is nothing short of a new kind of citizenship that viewers form not with the State or "traditional" kinds of community but with media such as TV – a cultural citizenship that he lauds as Do-It-Yourself Citizenship. One of his primary examples of a DIY citizenship is the role that programs on the Nickelodeon channel play in freeing teenage girls to re-create their identities. Examples such as this signal to Hartley the "emancipa-tion" of TV's full cultural and political potential as a communication medium for "independent, autonomous, modes of human interaction unbrokered by control agencies."[6]

   This chapter is partly an effort to consider the paradoxes of an emancipated, self-creating media citizen and a "participatory media culture," and to ask a different set of questions about media power and consumers' agency, in order to imagine an alternative path to political reform through media citizenship and to acknowledge what is difficult about this path. In certain respects, the culture and politics of participation that Jenkins and Hartley envisage being brought to bear on TV are decidedly democratic – predicated upon the "social contract between participants,"[7] or upon a "contract between viewers and media communities,"[8] and driven by consumers and fans who, by building imaginary communities, "learn to govern themselves."[9] For Jenkins and Hartley, the value of the private contract, self-creation, freedom, and self-governance – such as the meaning and performance of democracy – is mostly self-evident. As we have shown, private contracts, self-fashioning, exercising freedom, and self-governance are invoked as justifications and objectives for current initiatives to "advance" liberal government through public–private partnerships and a greater self-responsibilization of citizens; TV in particular is being made over and reinvented to make it more useful within this rational-ity about an active, self-possessive, and entrepreneurial citizenry. Also, as suggested in Chapter 5, TV's current emphasis upon ordinary people playing *games* of citizenship and group governance, enacting and testing privately designed rules, pacts, and constitutions, makes it necessary to avoid generalized valorizations of democracy as a goal and to recognize instead what is complicated about TV's current mattering as a *democratic* form and practice. While Jenkins and Hartley's emphasis on the liber-ating possibilities of contemporary media seeks to counter the view the TV is undemocratic, they fail to acknowledge how the personal or collective freedoms of media interactivity involve a form of self-government (the *government of the self*) that is authorized by a current reasoning about citizenship and civic participation. The active (or "interactive") citizen is an objective of current efforts to reinvent liberal government. Rather than resolving this question by arguing one side or the other, or arguing for a middle ground, it is necessary to rethink the premises upon which this question often is posed, considering why it is such a persistent reasoning about TV and media power and suggesting an alternative set of questions suited to the current "neoliberal" reasoning about self-government and the *government of the self*.

First, the question of whether TV enhances or erodes democracy often tends to treat democracy as a universally recognized ideal and a moral good (what Jeffrey Minson has called a "romantic Republicanism") that can be achieved best under certain conditions – in some nations rather than others. Or it tends to idealize democracy as something that always will produce the same benefit – do the same good – everywhere.[10] Too often, the question of whether TV enhances or diminishes democracy assumes that democracy can be abstracted, not just from specific *arrangements* for governing (interdependent institutions, constitutions, and programs) but also from an *experimentalism* – the ongoing failures, contingencies, and provisional achievement of democracy.

With these considerations in mind, our project does not assume that there is an *authentic* form of democracy that TV has veiled or perverted as *spectacle*. The view that TV is a spectacle of democracy is often cast nostalgically, as if TV has degraded a pre-mass media democracy or fostered the disappearance of a "public sphere." Or recent TV is thought to have spoiled a democratic potential associated with early broadcast TV, resulting in the fall of a heroic age of broadcast journalists such as Edward Murrow and in the rise of a "sound-bite journalism," *The Daily Show*, or the inanity of Reality TV. Against this view, Hartley argues that TV's current incarnation, and its legacy for the future, might best be described as "democratainment" – a term that he does not use pejoratively to describe the new "emancipated" potential of Do-It-Yourself TV.[11] It is incumbent on anyone interested in understanding TV's relation to "states of democracy" to recognize that democracy is not simply a universal ideal but material and technical procedures. As such, democracy is always a provisional achievement, involving on-going failures and break-downs and whose technical procedures provisionally allow citizens to govern themselves actively and responsibly. Democracy as "self-government" is thus reliant upon the technical procedures, such as the ones that we have discussed that mediate the government of the self. From this starting point, we can begin to figure out how televisual techniques and technologies become instrumental within the arrangement, experiments, and rationalities of government, and particularly how these technical procedures and rationalities of government support *particular* democratic states and their constitutions – even as these techniques are continually modified and replaced. Examining these technical and programmatic procedures allows us to understand better *how* participation and citizenship/ membership are rationalized as being "fair" – and how the replacement of techniques is rationalized as "improving upon" or "advancing" the fairness of earlier processes.

Because each of us lives our life through various governmentalities constituted around particular forms and guidelines of participation, membership, and association, it also is necessary to develop an analysis that recognizes the multiple and diverse – sometimes interdependent and sometimes competing – technical procedures of democracy.[12] From this perspective, TV is only *one* of many ways that participation and association are constituted and rationalized, even though TV has been reinvented to accommodate and sometimes link multiple forms of participation and association. Consequently, there currently are multiple constitutions/rationalities of TV – multiple ways of enacting and testing group governance. The proliferation of cable networks and its lifestyle-clusters, as well as TV's intersection with the Web, has multiplied TV's constitutions and the guidelines suited for particular forms of participation and association. This development also has cast the consumer-citizen as actively ("interactively") involved in the process. By focusing on the ongoing invention of procedures for participation, TV can be studied for its capacity to "advance" or "reinvent" democracy. And when anyone points now to the United States as a state of "self-government" and "advanced democracy," this (and the televisual experiments considered in this book) must be in part what they mean and have to grapple with. So rather than asking whether these developments have made TV *more* democratic, it is necessary to ask how TV has been redesigned to accommodate more techniques of self-government and more forms of the democracy game, and how that development has been useful to a discourse and reasoning about the present as being "more democratic" than before.

The trend toward customizing participation around lifestyle clusters has occurred not only through efforts by TV networks to tie TV watching and consumption to more or less formalized "memberships," but also through expanding and accounting for membership that involves particular technologies of participation (e.g., Home Shopping Network membership, Turner Classic Movie membership, or Pat Robertson's Family Channel's solicitation of members and money to its TV congregation). The proliferation of these rules and technologies of membership establish the specific benefits and forms of empower-ment which accrue from membership. It is this trend that distinguishes contemporary TV from a rationality in the 1950s about democracy and broadcasting – about a form of TV that represented or addressed the nation.

TV's diversification and emphasis on choice paradoxically have contributed to an arrangement for insulating from diversity – from those who have limited access to a specific network's membership. As we have seen, reality TV's experiments and games of citizenship often are tests about the rules for playing (and playing fairly), particularly with respect to inclusivity and the problem of rights for all. And so they too are everyday ways of vetting and rationalizing who gets to be a member and participate. However, their contestants already share (have been selected by producers to share) an aspiration to a specific enterprise, community, or neighborhood of belonging.

Too often the debates about TV as a democratic or undemocratic medium fail to acknowledge the paradoxes of participation, agency, empowerment, and fairness through which TV is made to matter.[13] Certainly being able to participate in a democratic process requires membership or citizenship – that participants be of good standing and recognize (are willing to "play" by) the rules of the game. Reality TV series' experiments and games in group governance, as tests of alliances and alliance-building, help rationalize a broader investment by contemporary TV in membership as a requisite for democratic participation.

From these perspectives, democratization does not pertain now (nor ever) merely to the formal procedures of political agency (voting for political candidates and referenda). It also pertains to various spheres and techniques of life management – and in the current regime of TV, to "lifestyle management." The formation of "good citizens" through "good TV" involves an ongoing process of a testing and improvement/advancement, of both contestants and viewers, that makes it impossible ever to generalize about democracy or about TV as democratic or undemocratic. Instead, one needs first to figure out how various ways of *rationalizing* participation and membership matter with respect to the formal and informal, public, private, and personal workings of government. The question should be, what is it that governmental rationalities ask or require of particular members in order to perform democracies? As Raymond Williams noted, "No questions are more difficult than those of democracy . . . , [and that] analysis of variation will not resolve them, though it may sometimes clarify them."[14] And as Gregor McLennan has added, "there is considerable contestation over democracy's content and value . . . partly because each process of democratization serves to highlight (new) issues about what exactly *more* and *better* democracy involves, and (changing) issues about the proper *subject, scope,* and *depth* of political 'self determination.'"[15] Democracy is not, in other words, another instance of false consciousness formed through TV as political/ideological spectacle; it is an achievement that – for better or worse – occurs through specific techniques, experiments, and demonstrations with which members and citizens "enter into their own government" (forms of self-government, and government of the self). But this does not make the objective of analysis to prove (one more time) that TV masks an authentic kind of democracy, nor that the proliferation of TV channels and their forms of interactivity have resulted in a more democratic form of TV. The question is less how has TV failed or succeeded as a type of mass democracy than how is a "mass democracy" made rational and technically conducted in these times, when the injunction for a kind of TV that is "of, by, and for the people" occurs through the pluralization and mass customization of "popular" constitutions, and through experiments that are as much about failure and setbacks as about provisional successes.

TV and the Technology of Counting

To consider democracy as a technical achievement that is predicated upon ongoing experiments and failures, and upon citizen education, involves moving beyond an analysis merely of TV's representation and staging of participation and group governance and looking toward how the citizen-games and citizen-experiments occur through an array of technologies (machines, devices, skills, and logics that currently comprise and have transformed televisuality). Indeed, the reinvention of TV has occurred through various technological means of participation and group-governance – technologies that work in conjunction with the particular kinds of experiments, games, and demonstrations in group governance discussed in Chapter 5. And the linkages between TV's enactment of group governance and other forms of local and national government are complexly intertwined with the adoption of, and ongoing experiments about, these technologies of participation.

This section first considers some of the trends and implications of the recent technology of viewer-citizen participation – technology that is profoundly about accountability, about counting and being counted. Given that democracy is a technical achievement, what are the televisual technologies of voting/counting in recent times? And how is what counts and who counts for full membership and citizenship (active players in group governance) a matter of knowing and mastering not only the techniques and "rules of the game" but also the hardware (the material technology) of citizenship?

TV's "reinvention," and its relation to the "reinvention of government," is a history of technological practice. The proliferation of cable channels in the United States since the 1970s has occurred through specific technologies of viewer participation and interaction. The most widespread transformation since the 1970s has been the reliance upon remote-control devices which allow viewers not only to switch channels from a distance but also to avoid advertising, control volume levels, and (by the late 1980s) to watch two channels at the same time.[16] The remote control became a standard provision of audio and TV manufacturers as well as cable companies for their customers, such that the proliferation of cable channels and remote-control devices was interdependent. Not only did the widespread adoption of remote controls make viewers active in a different way than before their use, but their use was often perceived by TV programmers and advertisers as undermining attention to programming and channel loyalty. And the creation by cable channels of lifestyle programming became a way for emerging cable channels to gain a foothold in the TV market.

In its earliest days, "live" TV in the United States represented interactions onscreen between studio audiences and the onstage moderators, hosts, and performers. By the late 1980s, however, the telephone (which, like the remote control, had become increasingly portable in US households) began to be a resource for viewer interaction and participation with certain emerging forms of TV programming and network. "Home-shopping" programs and networks, in particular, used customer call-ins to make purchases offscreen and to register customer input about the product being sold onscreen. This practice also became common in religious broadcasting (e.g., testimonials and financial contributions on Pat Robertson's Christian Broadcasting Channel and Jim and Tammy Baker's Heritage broadcasting). Radio talk-show personality Larry King also helped convert his radio format for TV, hosting one of the most successful programs on CNN by the late 1980s.

By the late 1980s, TV networks and cable-service providers began to refine techniques for tracking and calculating viewership through these technological appendages to TV watching. Not only could cable subscriptions be counted and used as a standard for program-bundling and fees, but the cable providers became accountants of what viewers watched – and over the 1990s, when and for how long they watched particular programming. The model of "on-demand" programming (a practice that promised viewers more choice and freedoms) worked in a similar way to account for and calculate viewing habits. Satellite TV providers, such as Direct TV and Dish Network, thus promise customers "free choice" among various program-packages designed for lifestyle clusters (e.g., Dish TV's 2006 marketing of packages titled "Dish Latino" and "Dish Family").

Over the late 1990s, TV's reinvention occurred through the conjunction of these forms of audience participation (which also were ways that audiences were calculated and assessed) with Web-based technologies. A report by the Center for Digital Democracy noted in 2001 that "as today's multi-channel television is transformed through computerization and sophisticated set-top boxes, technology is now being put in place with the goal of collecting information from individual consumers and families. This information will be harvested in data profiles, which will be used to target individual consumers with personalized advertising."[17] Mark Andrejevic similarly has noted that reality TV's techniques of voyeurism and exhibitionism, and its "lottery of celebrity" (the promise that anyone can become a star through reality TV's contests), are accomplished through web sites where viewers actively provide/produce information about themselves, thus

making the game of voyeurism into an economy of surveilling consumers and of active, productive consumers.[18] For Andrejevic, the
promise of greater democracy through the internet must be considered
in these terms – as forms of participation and interactivity through
which citizen-consumers are counted.

Without refuting Andrejevic's important insights about TV's current
"economy of interactivity," we want to consider how the procedures
and technologies of participation and "interactivity" pertain to a current
governmental rationality about citizenship and about the necessary
procedures and experiments of democracy – how they pertain to the
"reinvention" of liberal government, which expects that democracy be
conducted through new technical procedures. Paradoxically, for
democracy to be effective it requires new, endlessly updated and
refined technical procedures. Because it is difficult to ascribe to democracy one universal way of being enacted, our analysis of TV seeks to
understand what is expected of democracy now, through current techniques which often are cast as improvements over the past and as
providing a new and improved democracy.

One of the most remarkable examples of TV's current matrix of
remote-controllability and accountability was Fox's *Todd TV*, a brief
experiment involving a subject (Todd) who is commanded to perform
certain tasks, and then rated on his performance, by viewers who send
text-messages (via T-Mobile cell-phones, the program's primary
sponsor). Although *Todd TV* was a behavioral experiment par excellence, with viewers testing Todd's capacity to perform demeaning and
sometimes unhealthy tasks, the program gleefully showcased the capacity of TV for "popular," group governance *by* viewers – viewers who
were encouraged to be interactive and whose vote immediately was
tallied, even though Todd would only perform one viewer's command
at a time. In that sense, the show's self-described objective of "building
a better Todd" not only became a social experiment linking participatory group government with the government of the self, it also articulated the "improvement" of its main subject (Todd) with the
"advancement" of TV, now "better suited" for the citizen-subject of
democratic participation (the interactive TV viewers).

Viewers voting on whether Todd should succeed or whether he
merited celebrity status was not an allegory, spectacle, or debasement
of democracy; it was one enactment of group governance by viewers
whose technology has become integral to a political process and

legitimated by a governmental rationality. And its "advancement" of
TV as technology of democratic participation needs to be assessed in
those terms. Although *Todd TV* was canceled after only a few months,
its design reformulated, on a smaller scale, another Fox program that
was designed as a national election of national celebrity – the reality
TV hit, *American Idol*. *American Idol* is a marathon process of selection
that moves back and forth between snippets of individual performers
and of groups amassed in various cities around the United States. Like
The Apprentice, *American Idol* is a citizen-game refereed by a panel of
experts – authorities in contemporary musical tastes, sensibilities, and
marketability. Contestants perform (and the producers accentuate the
contestants' representation of) various musical genres and those genres'/
performers' relation to particular regions of the country, thus making
cultural citizenship one object of voting and regulation/management
– by the judges and the viewers who submit their votes electronically.[19]
More than *The Apprentice*, however, *American Idol* calls attention to the
role of viewers (as the nation and the people) in *helping* decide which
contestant best exemplifies and represents a particular expression of
cultural citizenship through musical performance and television.
Although citizenship-games such as *The Apprentice* design web-links to
encourage viewer interactivity, *American Idol* thus far has been the series
in the United States that most relies upon the massive mobilization of
viewers as voters. To the extent that *American Idol* is a national event,
its status as event has been its ability to mobilize literally millions of
viewers as voters in a national election.

As voting becomes a standard technique of designing and watching
TV programs (as media such as TV, print journalism, and radio are
reinvented through technologies of "interactivity"), emerging web-TV
initiatives often cast themselves as more democratic than older broadcast media (or even than current cable or satellite TV packages).
YouTube, whose logo appropriates or parodies the logo of *TV Guide*
(the foremost TV programming guide for over fifty years) and whose
motto is "Broadcast Yourself," is a web site organized as a collection
of short video pods purportedly submitted by anyone. Links to each
video are accompanied by a tabulation of the number of viewers who
have watched it and by a four-star rating (voting) system, now standard
features of service-industry and e-commerce web sites such as eBay,
Amazon.com, and Hotwire.com. The most highly rated providers of
videos on YouTube are allowed to create "channels" (collections of

their video submissions) that are linked to "subscribers" and "active groups." Like the Todd-TV experiment, *YouTube* thus articulates programs of self-actualization ("broadcasting yourself") with exercises in group testing and group governance (the formation of "active groups"). *YouTube*'s web site is a visual display of a rationality that organizes, differentiates, and links self-broadcasters and "active groups." *Democracy Player* is a similar site which distinguishes its process and objectives from regular TV (and even alternative web-TV sites such as *YouTube*) by casting itself as built upon a capacity to improve media democracy. Its web site states that the network "promotes" and "supports democracy" through a "free and open-source Internet-TV platform." *Democracy Player*, beside representing itself through the current liberal emphasis upon being a citizen-"player," attributes its democratic possibilities to choice (400 channels as of 2006) made by net-izens who have the technical knowledge to participate and associate in a platform such as this. A third web-TV platform that promotes its usefulness in terms of its promotion of an improved media-based democracy is *Current TV*, whose most recognized organizer is former Vice President Al Gore. According to *Current TV*'s web site, the network "is a national cable and satellite channel dedicated to bringing your voice to television." Like *YouTube* and *Democracy Player*, *Current TV* is primarily a menu of "viewer-created content"; according to the web site, "anyone who wants to can upload a video." Unlike the other two web-TV platforms, however, *Current TV* pays for, and temporarily has rights to, videos that the network makes available. It also makes available only videos approved by "members of the on-line community" (i.e., subscribers who have the right to vote) and uses submitted videos in only one-third of its overall programming.

Reality TV is Technically Part of the Political Process

Just prior to announcing the winner of the fifth season of *American Idol* (2006), moderator Ryan Seacrest proclaimed to the program's audience that the 64 million votes cast for the season's winner had been "more votes than for any president in history." If one is to believe this claim by the producers of *American Idol*, Taylor Hicks (the year's winner) received more votes than did George W. Bush, in either 2004 or the infamous 2000 elections.

Illustration 6.1   The interactive dimensions of programs like *American Idol* are often taken as "democracy" on television (Freemantlemedia, North America for Fox, 2005)

On May 12, 2006, many newspapers across the United States published two stories – one about an alleged snafu involving electronic voting equipment the night before, when contestant Chris Daughtry was eliminated from the *American Idol* competition, and one about an alleged vulnerability of Diebold, Inc.'s touch-screen voting equipment in a Pennsylvania election of political candidates.[20] Thousands of unhappy fans and supporters of Daughtry protested to Fox and the program's production company, claiming that the vote either was rigged or was skewed due to numerous reports of problems with the telephone-recording service that registered votes for specific candidates. In Pennsylvania, a Carnegie-Mellon professor of computer science warned that the Diebold system, whose touch-screen technology had been mandated by Congress because it was supposed to correct the kinds of voting irregularities attributed to punchcard ballots in the 2000 presidential election, still contained inherent vulnerabilities to hacking and thus to vote-tampering.

On July 28, 2006, in the midst of meetings concerning the crisis between Israel and Lebanon, George Bush invited the finalists of the year's *American Idol* competition for a meeting with him at the White House. One TV program reporting on the event cited a poll conducted by a company, Pursuant, Inc., on the evening of the final vote which purported that 35 percent of those casting votes for their favorite "American idol" believed that their *American Idol* vote "counted as much or more" than their vote for president of the United States.

In times that have supported initiatives to "reinvent government" through "public–private partnerships," it sometimes is difficult to distinguish where the techniques and technology of public government end and those of private government begin – where the procedures for voting and counting in elections for public office end and the procedures for membership in private associations or for reality TV's citizenship-games begin. This is not necessarily a recent trend; however, the rationale about reinventing government draws the procedures and technologies of public and private government into a relation that can not be explained by a broad assertion that TV either is or is not democratic – or that TV necessarily erodes or enhances a democratic political process. Nor is it enough to point out that sometimes TV blurs the difference between "real politics" and TV's games or experiments of government. Rather, how is it that the procedures and technologies of public and private government (as political process) operate interdependently, though not necessarily or always uniformly?

To say that reality TV offers *demonstrations* in group participation and governance is to point out TV's little, everyday ways of instructing viewers about the techniques and rules of participation. *The Apprentice* enacts a process of group decision-making and deliberation, culminating in a staged board meeting where Donald Trump leads players through a series of questions that require each player and team to reflect on who should advance and who should be terminated. The demonstration also offers viewers a means, as Trump repeatedly points out, of learning how to manage corporate groups effectively. While *The Apprentice* is not overtly about a "political process" (that is, in the narrow sense of "electoral politics"), its demonstrations of corporate accountability become, technically, interdependent with the procedures for political accountability in the United States in these times. This is not to say only that citizens are governed, or that state government operates, like a corporation; it is to say that *The Apprentice* is one site (and a popular one) where public and private government intersect.[21] It is to point out that the technology and procedures of democracy are spread out over daily life – across various forms and sites of membership and association where one counts and is made account-able. Some forms and sites of participation through voting (election by rules and technologies of counting/representation) matter more to certain populations than to others. This point particularly applies to contemporary TV, where different viewers are more invested in one channel or group of channels than another – or in one program rather than another. TV networks and program producers conceive of their audiences as associations where viewers are expected to actively demonstrate their involvement and membership, through programs that often are experiments and games in deciding collectively who's in and who's out. So given that democracy's enactment is "spread out" across daily life, and across TV's various kinds of programming, each with their own constitutions/rules of participation ("rules of the citizenship-game"), one of democracy's current paradoxes is that the political process is diffuse but that certain technologies and procedures cross over and are shared between public and private enactments of democracy (e.g., between electing a state senator, an American idol, or an Apprentice). Another current paradox is that by enacting democracy through private associations only certain citizens/members get to operate these technologies and to vote on who is included and who is excluded.

The technologies through which various TV networks have marketed lifestyle clusters have been integral to initiatives for mobilizing viewers in recent electoral politics. The oldest and most recognized of these convergences has been the "Rock the Vote" campaign. Begun in 1990 as a drive to register young voters for the 1992 presidential election, Rock the Vote has expanded from its initial and primary connection with MTV to become a multimedia enterprise (even as the number and percentage of young voters has declined since 1992). Historically, Rock the Vote emerged with the discourse about "reinventing government" through "public–private partnerships." The Rock-the-Vote Action Center web site lists an alliance among three kinds of "partners" – nonprofit, creative, and corporate (the latter including MTV, Sony, and other major media companies). Its rationale for its initiatives has articulated a liberal commitment to freedom (e.g., artistic freedoms or media freedoms perceived as under attack during the Reagan and GHW Bush presidencies): "Rock the Vote is dedicated to protecting freedom of expression and empowering young people to change their world."[22] As both a form of media "outreach" and an engine for voter-registration (shaping civic-minded youth), Rock the Vote's techniques of mobilization rely upon the same techniques that MTV has used for other kinds of voting (e.g., MTV programs such as *Total Request Live* and *Rock Countdown*, the latter of which uses a web site where viewers can cast votes for favorite musical celebrities). Following (and partly modeled after) Rock the Vote's public recognition, Oxygen Network used its status as a TV channel for women, and the first TV network designed to educate women about internet use, to conduct a voter-registration drive for women in the 2000 presidential campaign, and has since aligned itself with Declare Yourself, a voter-registration campaign for young women. For the 2004 presidential campaign, Black Entertainment TV (BET) similarly became involved in the National Action Network, a voter-registration initiative for African-American youth. Both of these latter two TV networks were part of partnerships between "nonprofits" and media corporations.

TV's techniques and experts of personal makeover and self-actualization increasingly have become integral to the electoral campaign process during the era of government's "reinvention." In the lead-up to the 2004 presidential election, Dr. Phil interviewed both presidential candidates, George W. Bush and John Kerry, and their wives. Through these interviews (advertised as a "special event"), the two presidential candidates acted upon TV's preeminent laboratory of self-improvement (a TV doctor-cum "life coach" who offers guidelines for correcting one's behavior). And Dr. Phil's life-strategies acted upon the national electoral process – the preeminent citizenship-game and laboratory of national group governance.[23] While presidential candidates have appeared increasingly in entertainment venues on TV since the late 1980s, these interviews represent a more recent convergence of self-help coaches and political government. Dr. Phil also went to Mississippi (and not Louisiana) in the aftermath of Hurricane Katrina, where he counseled victims about "self-matters" and how to restart their lives – challenging them to pull themselves up by the soggy straps of their wading-boots.[24] The web site for these specials solicited donations but also provided "resources" for victims, including the Salvation Army, the United Way, Mercy Corps, Habitat for Humanity, America's Second Harvest, and the USA Freedom Corp. In another Katrina-related initiative, Laura Bush participated in a broadcast of *Extreme Makeover: Home Edition* (which she described as her favorite TV series) set in Biloxi, Mississippi – another demonstration of TV's role in providing the resources by which citizens are supposed to govern and help themselves. The two latter programs in particular are noteworthy for their emphasis upon partnerships between for-profit TV and "nonprofits" that have been rationalized by the Bush administration as part of the "armies of compassion" – assisting, and not doing the work of, state institutions.

These trends in recent TV have occurred amid the proliferation of programs and channels that not only dramatize the work of "public," state institutions but literally extend the technology and procedures of these institutions. We want to be clear about what has changed. TV has long dramatized the work of various public institutions – TV series about police, emergency rescue units, the courts, the military, and national political office. However, since the late 1990s numerous TV channels and programs have emerged that do not involve professional actors but instead draw directly from the proceedings of public institutions. Court TV is a channel that programs hours of court proceedings as well as dramatizations which use video of court proceedings. And although there are past examples of "reality" courtroom TV (e.g., *Divorce Court*), the number of these programs (outside the Court TV Channel) has grown immensely since the 1990s.[25] *Cops*, *America's Most Wanted*, and *To Catch a Predator* are examples of recent TV series that extend the procedures and techniques of local and national police work, with the last two programs having assisted actual law-enforcement efforts to apprehend criminal suspects. The Military Channel programs hours of video made by soldiers and often produced by the US military. The NASA Network programs hours of footage of US missions in outer space. The Weather Channel emphasizes its recent partnerships with the National Oceanic & Atmospheric Agency, the Federal Emergency Management Agency, and the Department of Homeland Security. C-SPAN offers two channels of (sometimes live) proceedings in the US Congress. All of these channels and programs are rationalized as educational and as demonstrations of how "government works." In that sense, they are a new way that TV forges a relation between government and citizens. Most importantly, these developments do not necessarily mark a withering away of government (ceding the work of state institutions to commercial TV), but rather an extension of government – even as this extension in another respect makes government more reliant upon privatized, commercial resources (i.e., upon a kind of "outsourcing" through TV, that matches TV corporations' own "outreach"). They provide a framework for TV events such as Dr. Phil's and the First Lady's "work" in Mississippi as examples of TV's instrumentality within the Bush administration's "compassionate conservatism." Or, as when *The Apprentice* broadcasts arranged meetings between its young contestants and public office holders (such as New York Senator Charles Schumer and New York City Mayor Michael Bloomberg), TV invites the office holders of state government to authorize TV's own exemplary displays of entrepreneurialism, corporate citizenship, and private group government.

The political process in the United States is regularly trumpeted as being responsible for the most "advanced democracy" in the world. "Advancing" freedom and democracy (or at least a US model of democracy) was George W. Bush's mantra for mobilizing the United States to wage a war in Iraq. Once citizens in Iraq "tasted" democracy, there would be no stopping its spread throughout the Middle East. "Exporting" or "advancing" democracy in Iraq has occurred in part through the US CIA funding of the Iraqi Media Network and its first TV channel, Al Iraqiya.[26] This effort to shape the "hearts and minds" of Iraqi citizens floundered during its first year, but in early 2005 it produced a US-style reality TV series, *Terrorism in the Hands of Justice*. Broadcast two times a day and six days a week, the program presented actual prisoners confessing their crimes to a video camera, interspersed by reactions of Iraqis to the bombing/crime attributed to the prisoner. While the series resembled US court TV programs and series such as *America's Most Wanted* (programs which extend an institution of State through TV), and while the series clearly was a strategy by the US government to build or shape a new "civil society" in Iraq, the program also operated in lieu of a national judicial system since Iraqis had not yet voted on a constitution or its first government. Judgment and "justice" through this program therefore denied prisoners due process and legal aid, generally assuming the guilt of prisoners who had been coerced to confess and who often bore clear signs of having been beaten, tortured, or drugged. The program also exhibited a "direct justice," mediated by TV: viewers were invited to act as juries – to call in, vote, express their outrage, report on other suspects, and in this way participate in an exhibition of "democratic" reform and government's reinvention mediated by the country's emerging regime of reality TV. This regime (of TV and democracy in Iraq) is a process wherein citizens who watch particular kinds of TV can be empanelled as jury – to decide who's in and who's out.[27]

To say that TV in the United States is technically part of a political process is not in itself a new claim about TV. Beginning from this assumption, however, requires that one figure out how the political, as process and procedures, occurs within a rationale about government and the sanctioning of particular experiments in democracy. These experiments are designed through TV's "partnerships" and "outreach" with corporate and "nonprofit" groups that collectively serve as the rule-makers and often (as in *The Apprentice*) as referees in demonstrations and games of group governance and citizenship. However, the experimentalism of this process is itself fraught with failure, and we emphasize that TV is a laboratory for democracy in order to emphasize this experimentalism and ongoing effort to test limits and to manage failure. Arguably, failure is what is at stake in contemporary TV's games and demonstrations of group governance and citizenship – programs that are about testing the limits and capacities of participants to decide who is most suited to govern. And, as noted at the outset of this section, the technology of TV's projects in democratic participation and group governance (i.e., how one votes) is itself a series of experiments and failures. There are numerous recent examples of reality TV's *celebration* of failure – of citizens who have lost their civic virtues (e.g., *Jackass, Viva la Bam,* and *The Bad Girls Club*), even as they demonstrate their individual freedoms to take risks and to "act up," at least within the rules that TV has set for risk and misbehavior.

It is not sufficient to see the current interfaces between TV programming and other media as simply a matter of progress and modernization, and particularly as heralding either a refinement or diminution of "democracy." Democracy has always been a *technical achievement*, and the current interfaces among media ("new" and "old") are instrumental to the current interdependencies between the public and private rules and technologies for participating in the citizenship-game – a "reinvention" of democracy and self-government that involves numerous paradoxes. In May 2007, the broadcast of the first televised debate among Republican presidential candidates at the Ronald Reagan Library involved procedures that the broadcast's host network (MSNBC) promoted as unprecedented and as an improvement upon the election process that once occurred on "pre-interactive" TV: candidates would be asked questions submitted through the Politico.com web site by TV viewers, presumably after the questions were screened by MSNBC and Politico.com's producers and relayed to the event's moderator, Chris Matthews. As Andrejevic would point out, there is monetary value added through this event's production at the intersection between TV and the Web. But another issue is that the interactive televisualization of this game of citizenship and democracy not only reinvents the rules and technical procedures of the electoral game; it puts on display the value of the "public–private partnership" in "improving upon" the past limitations of broadcast TV. Here, viewers are not "building a better Todd" but supposedly refining a process to select the best candidate. And, like *Todd TV*, the event affirms in this way the civic virtue of "reinventing government" by "reinventing TV" – by making the televisualization of the political process *participatory* through current techniques that embed political campaign in the playing field or game-board of *American Idol* and *The Apprentice*.

If a lesson to be learned from reality TV is that, by voting (enacting democracy and self-government) through private associations, only certain citizens/members get to operate the technologies and to vote on who is included and who is excluded, then how does enacting democracy today rely upon these private associations? To isolate the MSNBC event as single text or spectacle misses the numerous intersecting networks and technologies of accountancy and polling through which the participation occurs, and how voting through privately organized associations drives and naturalizes the formality of electing candidates for public office. Contemporaneous with TV-initiatives such as MTV's Rock the Vote, Moveon.org and other activist websites have developed voting campaigns for subscribers. Sometimes these campaigns "take the pulse" of their subscribers by asking them how they would vote on particular reforms or candidates, and sometimes the campaigns state that those votes will reveal how the subscribers want the association to devote its resources. In both cases, the voting campaigns are instrumental not just in gauging the will of the majority but in mobilizing subscribers to contact the legislators and administrators of state government, or to vote for office holders. The web-associations serve as portals between a set of procedures technically linking private and public citizenship, and private, subscription-based voting is part of a long process of electing office holders.

One other lesson to be learned from reality television about the current paradox of democracy in the United States leads back to the technologies of membership and participation discussed at the outset of this section – and specifically back to the private, national–popular voting juggernaut, *American Idol*. The show's distributor, Fox TV, is not a network of subscribing members, unless one counts the fees paid by viewers for usually the lowest tier of cable subscriptions, or the fees paid to Internet and mobile phone service providers through which viewers vote. (And these frequently unacknowledged forms of subscription do indeed matter as a prerequisite for playing the game.) In the spring of 2007, a "crisis" of the series was not simply whether the voting apparatus had failed by having excluded thousands, maybe even millions, of voters who were confused about how to vote for particular contestants or were confident that their votes had not been properly recorded (as had happened in 2006); instead the crisis was whether voters would destroy the series by voting for an "unworthy" candidate. The most visible point of the crisis was candidate Sanjaya Malakar's worthiness to be an American Idol, at least according to the codes and conventions of celebrity and musical performance that the show upholds. There were almost weekly reports that *American Idol*'s system for recording votes was being "overtaken" by telephone switchboard operators in India who had programmed computers to automatically and endlessly vote for Malakar – or (according to an only less slightly xenophobic rumor) that a segment of US citizens, the Indian-American population, was voting as a bloc for Malakar. The show's legitimacy as a pure reflection of majority rule, however, was called most into question by disc jockey Howard Stern's quite public campaign to mobilize his listeners to vote en masse for Malakar in order to elect the most unworthy and illegitimate contestant.[28] That the reputed six million listeners to Stern's subscription program on Sirius Radio could affect the outcome from the reputed thirty million votes that *American Idol* records a week (perhaps in addition to the bloc of reputed Indian and Indian-American voters!) was enough to compel Fox to issue a statement vouching for the fairness and legitimacy of privatized Idol-voting in America. At the time of writing, it is difficult to decide whether the "crisis" of Idol election in America is a crisis that should be welcomed or dreaded; most viewers might say that it all depends on which celebrity or media channel (Stern or Malakar) you prefer, or subscribe to. But to the extent that it became (however temporarily) a crisis of fealty in democratic procedures, and that it offers one of the most visible and widely followed enactments of the privatization of national voting, then it is necessary to recognize and map the changing networks and programs (privatized and public) upon which the American Idol is selected and through which it is seen to be endangered, requiring future and somehow more refined techniques for managing. Such are the requirements and challenges for an analytic of governmentality in these times and in this place.

Mapping the televisual linkages between public and private enactments of democracy leads to one other (maybe not so final) event. During the final stages of its 2007 season, *American Idol* conducted its "Idol Gives Back" campaign to raise money for charities by using the show's participatory technologies to garnish financial-aid contributions from viewers.[29] The campaign was certainly a shining example of the kind of privatized welfare provision that has been championed by the initiatives to "reinvent government," particularly by the Bush–Cheney administration. And it proudly articulated the virtue of participatory government (of "government by and for the people") with the neoliberal virtue of the "government of the self" (citizens who actively look after and take care of themselves). So it was no small coincidence that President George Bush and First Lady Laura Bush punctuated the fund drive by appearing through a satellite TV feed (or a video-recording) to praise the show and its viewers. At the conclusion of their address to the Idol nation, the president asked the First Lady whether she thought *he* ought to sing for the audience, and she replied, smiling, "I don't know, darlin'; they've already seen you dance." Mrs. Bush was referring to the couple's participation the week before in a performance by a group of West African musicians in the grounds of the White House – an event widely distributed and often lampooned over TV news and comedy programs and on web sites such as *YouTube*. While the president's appearance on *American Idol* was yet another instance of State government *acting upon* the private laboratories and gameboards of democracy in the United States, it also might have been one of the last means by which citizens (in the United States or India) could vote for or against Bush – even though it certainly would not be the last televisual *stage* for "advancing" liberal government.

Conclusion

For Jenkins's book, discussed at the outset of this chapter, the key to fostering a culture and politics of participation lies in "media education," an endeavor whose goal is teaching viewers and consumers how to be actively engaged with the current media culture. As he notes, "We need to rethink the goals of media education so that young people [and adults] can come to think of themselves as cultural producers and participants and not simply as consumers, critical or otherwise."[30] Education is crucial for overcoming the "participation gap." While Jenkins may be right about rethinking "media education" as a civic enterprise, education and even "media education" are already integral to the current regime of TV. TV does in fact instruct, and now through a practice of game playing and group participation and through a rationality about citizenship and participatory governance that was less pronounced in the days of earlier TV. If anything, Jenkins's argument – like Hartley's – does not press hard enough at the paradoxes of freedom and control, of self-actualization through learning, or of the practice of entering into forms of self-government as self-discipline.

In one sense, our project recognizes the importance of Hartley's intervention that casts contemporary TV, and the future legacy of TV, as a form of citizenship training. Hartley rightly ties TV as civic education to TV's "do-it-yourself" features and to "democratainment" – to TV's twin capacities to educate and entertain. However, unlike Hartley, we see the freedoms afforded by Do-It-Yourself-TV as an objective of a governmental rationality that values self-enterprise, self-reliance, and lessons to be learned in privatized experiments and games of self-constitutions and group government. So if there is to be a kind of media education that is oriented toward the shaping of future citizens (as we hope this book is), we suggest that this education first and foremost begins by recognizing how – in or out of the classroom – we are implicated in forms of learning and knowledge that tie our citizenships to the games and experiments of government. And as Dr. Phil is prone to say, we all "have a lot of work to do." Imagining or performing political reform through new and changing forms of media citizenship is a path complicated by televisual teachers and "life coaches" such as Phil McGraw whose regimen for self-actualization is that "life is not cured, it is managed."[31] Recognizing these complications are a starting point, not an end, for a politics that occurs through the networks, programs, policies, and constitutions of life management, which each of us traverse daily.

Notes

Notes to Introduction

1 Mitchell Dean, *Governmentality: Power and Rule in Modern Society* (Thousand Oaks, CA: Sage, 1999), p. 209.
2 See Michel Foucault, "Governmentality," in *The Foucault Effect: Studies in Governmentality*, ed. Graham Burchell, Colin Gordon, and Peter Miller (Chicago: University of Chicago Press, 1991); Michel Foucault, "Omnes et Singulatim: Toward a Critique of Political Reason," "The Subject and Power," "Governmentality," and "The Political Technology of Individuals," in *Power*, ed. James Faubion (New York: The New Press, 1994); Michel Foucault, "The Birth of Biopolitics," "On the Government of the Living," "Technologies of the Self," "The Ethics of the Concern for Self as a Practice of Freedom," and "On the Genealogy of Ethics," in *Ethics*, ed. Paul Rabinow (New York: The New Press, 1994); and Michel Foucault, "Politics and Reason," in *Politics, Philosophy, Culture*, ed. Lawrence Kritzman (New York and London: Routledge, 1989).
3 Andrew Barry, Thomas Osborne, and Nikolas Rose, "Introduction," in *Foucault and Political Reason: Liberalism, Neoliberalism and Rationalities of Government*, ed. Andrew Barry, Thomas Osborne, and Nikolas Rose (Chicago and London: University of Chicago Press, 1996), p. 8.
4 The latter expression from Gramsci, "The State as *Veilleur de nuit* – Night-watchman," in David Forgacs (ed.), *The Antonio Gramsci Reader* (London: Lawrence & Wishart, 1988), p. 236. Of particular importance to our project in the writing of Gramsci is his conception of the modern State as an "ethical" and "cultural" State. In part, Gramsci used the terms "ethical" and "cultural" to underscore how modern, liberal government operated through (relied upon) an array of private institutions for public *education*. While Gramsci's use of the term education is somewhat vague (or robust), he clearly viewed the modern State, and its reliance upon "the private institutions and activities," as mechanisms for linking moral and cultural uplift, welfare, and caring as technologies of governing populations. For Gramsci, civil society (the "State" and process of moral and cultural uplift)

was thus the objective and the resource of modern, liberal government. The State casts itself and is required to play a supportive role in looking after the welfare of the population and in ensuring a robust civil society – upon which it acts, through which it governs (at a distance), and from which the goodness and caring of the State can be demonstrated. For this reason, Gramsci (following Lassalle) also understood the State/government less as authoritarian than as "night-watch-man." For Gramsci, one of the most fundamental characteristics of liberal government in early twentieth-century nation-states (including Italian Fascism) was its role in watching over and cultivating the private institutions and activities by which society was made civil and moral (and thus was regulated) through education and culture.

5   Nikolas Rose, *Powers of Freedom: Reframing Political Thought* (Cambridge: Cambridge University Press, 1999), p. 27; we draw here from Ron Greene's elaboration of the "modernization" of pastoral power. See Ronald Walter Greene, "Y Movies: Film and the Modernization of Pastoral Power," *Communication and Critical/Cultural Studies*, 2.1 (2005), pp. 20–36.

6   Rose, *Powers of Freedom*.

7   Alexandra Chasin, *Selling Out: The Gay and Lesbian Movement Goes to Market* (New York: Palgrave Macmillan, 2002).

8   Graham Burchell, "Liberal Government and Techniques of the Self," in A. Barry, T. Osborne, and N. Rose (eds.), *Foucault and Political Reason* (Chicago: University of Chicago Press, 1996), pp. 19–36, p. 23.

9   For a critique of neoliberalism as market rationality see Wendy Brown, "Neoliberalism and the End of Liberal Democracy," *Theory & Event*, 7:1 (2003); Nikolas Rose, "Governing 'Advanced' Democracies," in *Foucault and Political Reason*, pp. 37–64, and Lisa Duggan, *The Twilight of Equality? Neoliberalism, Cultural Politics, and the Attack on Democracy* (Boston: Beacon Press, 2003).

10 Rose, "Governing," p. 45; see also Nikolas Rose, *Governing the Soul: The Shaping of the Private Self* (2nd ed., London: Free Association Books, 1999) and *Inventing Ourselves: Psychology, Power and Personhood* (Cambridge: Cambridge University Press, 1998).

11 Rose, "Governing," pp. 47–8; Walter I. Trattner, *From Poor Law to Welfare State: A History of Social Welfare in America* (New York: The Free Press, 1999); John Ehrenreich, *The Altruistic Imagination: A History of Social Work and Social Policy in the United States* (Ithaca, NY: Cornell University Press, 1985).

12 Tony Bennett, *The Birth of the Museum* (London: Routledge, 1995).

13 As Bennett has argued, "culture *emerges* as a pluralised and dispersed field of government which, far from mediating the relations between civil society and the state or connecting the different levels of a social formation, operates through, between, and across these in inscribing cultural resources into a diversity of programs aimed at directing the conduct of individuals toward an array of different ends, for a variety of purposes, and by a plurality of means" (Bennett, *Culture: A Reformer's Science* [London: Sage, 1988], p. 77).

14 That approach has not tended to dwell on the usefulness of TV as a regimen for living one's life. To consider TV's utility governmentally, it is necessary to avoid generalizing about culture, for if we see culture as responsible for "everything,"

we lose sight of what regulates and instrumentalizes culture within historically specific programs and technologies of government. How does culture become an object and a resource of government/administration? How is culture acted upon through the programs, strategies, and technologies of government? Addressing these questions is crucial to thinking about how cultural politics occur through the privatization and personalization of government, and specifically through the self-training of citizens through televisual programs. While television also operates as a system of representation and ideological formation, our focus on governmentalization seems particularly helpful for thinking about media power in these times.

15 The preoccupation with "TV culture" has tended to downplay the technical and scientific applications that occur through TV and other media because they are not the best examples of TV as a popular art, story-form, or cultural form. TV began in the lab (the object of scientific invention and experimentation), and although we side with Raymond Williams's effort to avoid a technologically determinist view of TV's development, we emphasize more than he did TV's mattering and transformation within the rationalities, science, and experimentalism of liberal government.

16 In part through TV, self-cultivation also involves how to watch TV, where to put it, what to do with it, and thus how to manage it, at home and in one's daily life. Home-makeover TV often involves tips for designing attractive and rational "media rooms" at home.

17 This point is elaborated by Barbara Cruikshank, *The Will to Empower: Democratic Citizens and Other Subjects* (Ithaca, NY: Cornell University Press, 1999).

18 It is worth noting that our account differs from treatments of television, which have understood it as a textual practice (narrative and genre criticism), as commercial activity (studies of TV/media industries and advertising), or as a combination of these concerns. While we discuss television as a form of representation (both semiotic and political) and recognize its commercial nature, we emphasize how a wide variety of TV shows operate as advice, guides, and instructions, coordinating and differentiating a set of knowledges and techniques for everyday living.

Our perspective also offers an alternative conception of the TV audience, which is typically cast as consumers/spectators, as those subjected to media's effects, or conversely as active makers of meanings and value. Instead we underscore the tension between the promise of agency, freedom, and "active citizenship" that surrounds the care and management of the self, and the promise of democratic reform (the procedures of democratic participation) that depends upon knowledge/power relations.

19 Our use of the term "civic laboratories" is indebted to Tony Bennett's use of the term to describe museums. See Bennett, "Civic Laboratories: Museums, Culture Objecthood, and the Governance of the Social," *Cultural Studies*, 19:5 (2005).

20 We do not mean to say that TV's programmatic qualities always have uniform and stable effects in the lives of individuals and populations but that TV broadcasting in the United States has been obsessed with experimenting with schedul-

ing in order to foster TV's integration into how individuals and populations organize and run their daily lives. Our analysis emphasizes what has not always been foregrounded in studies of TV and modern media: media as technologies of government and citizenship, and the TV/media program as curriculum, as outline of a performance, as prospectus and agenda, as a plan or system under which action may be taken toward a particular goal. All of these connotations have been implicit in analyses of TV and media but need further unpacking.

21 Nikolas Rose, "Governing," p. 47 (emphasis added).

22 "Despite posing itself as a critique of political government, it [neoliberalism] retains the programmatic *a priori*, the presupposition that the real is programmable by authorities: the objects of government are rendered thinkable in such a way that their difficulties appear amenable to diagnosis, prescription, and cure. Neoliberalism does not abandon the 'will to govern': it maintains the view that failure of government to achieve its objectives is to be overcome by *inventing* new strategies of government that will succeed" (ibid., p. 5; emphasis added).

23 As Rose argues, "Historians of the present [should] avoid substantializing either the present or the past. Rather than conceiving of our present as an epoch or a state of affairs, it is more useful, in my own view, to view the present as an array of problems and questions, an actuality to be acted upon and within by genealogical investigation, to be made amenable to action by the action of thought. As an array of question of this type, the present calls for a style of investigation that is more modest than that adopted by sociological philosophers of history. It encourages an attention to the humble, the mundane, the little shifts in our ways of thinking and understanding, the small and contingent struggles, tensions and negotiations that give rise to something new and unexpected" (Rose, *Powers of Freedom*, p. 11).

24 Peter F. Drucker, *The Age of Discontinuity* (New Brunswick, NJ: Transaction, 2000).

25 Hayek is arguably one of the intellectual reference points for a "neoconservatism" that has emerged in the United States since the 1960s. The last chapter of his *The Constitution of Liberty* (Chicago: University of Chicago Press, 1960), "Why I am not a Conservative," navigates and sorts out the ambiguities of the terms "liberal" and "conservative" in the United States, as opposed to the European, context. He argues that he is more a "liberal" than either a conservative or a socialist, even though advocating a "party of liberty" is complicated by the way that liberalism has been construed in the United States. He views conservatives as too prone to rely upon protectionism (hence their nationalism and provincialism) rather than "free growth and spontaneous evolution" (p. 408). While he acknowledges that the liberalism he advocates is closest to what in the United States is referred to as "libertarianism," he rejects that term, frustrated that there is not *yet* a proper term. Hayek's predicament in the early 1960s is thus one way of thinking about the longing for a "new" conservatism which recognizes that "the chief need is once more, as it was at the beginning of the nineteenth century, to free the process of spontaneous growth from the obstacles and encumbrances that human folly [re: conservatism and socialism] has erected. Hayek's rationale

is, in this sense, consonant with Drucker's advocacy of "reprivatization" – the need and strategy to cure the "malaise" of the early twentieth-century forms of public planning, welfare, and administration, and to do so through *active*, generative terms such as "reprivatizing" and "reinventing" (i.e., through the language of "free growth and spontaneous evolution").

26 "The choice . . . is no longer *either* complete governmental indifference or complete governmental control . . . [We need] a government that can and does govern. This is not a government that 'does'; it is not a government that 'administers'; it is a government that governs" (Drucker, *Age of Discontinuity*, pp. 240, 242). Drucker considered "reprivatization" (not a return to the past, but an uncovering of the *natural* organs of social and economic management) to be a "heretical doctrine" in the 1960s and argued that privatizing government required a new way of thinking. His book was replete, however, with examples beyond the nation-state where privatization was already successful, such as international corporate management and international private–public ventures in space exploration and global communication (e.g., COMSAT) so central to enacting liberal government on the New Frontier.

27 Rose has suggested that Hayek's conceits about freedom and government, and his critiques of the welfare state, took three decades after the 1960s to be "assembled into a politically salient assault on the rationalities, programmes, and technologies of welfare in Britain, Europe, and the United States," but it is just as important to recognize how the discourse of privatization emerged during the 1960s through programs (big and small) to mediate the contradictions surrounding emergent and residual rationalities of welfare, public services, and liberal government. (As we explain below, returning to the 1960s also allows us to consider how TV's emergence became instrumental to and problematic for these rationalities.) The various "rights" movements of the 1960s, for instance, demanded that the federal government look after the welfare of specific populations, even as their discourse of "rights" could be articulated to a rationale such as Drucker's about privatization: "Reprivatization is hardly a creed of 'fat cat millionaires' when black-power advocates seriously propose making education in the slums "competitive" by turning it over to private enterprise, competing for the tax dollar on the basis of proven performance in teaching ghetto children. It may be argued that the problems of the black ghetto in the American city are very peculiar problems – and so they are. They are extreme malfunctions of modern government. But, if reprivatization works in the extreme case, it is likely to work even better in less desperate ones." Rationales such as Drucker's became more central to a post-1960s mobilization of conservatism in the United States through a rights discourse and through efforts to demonstrate that the beneficiaries of publicly administered welfare were best served by and naturally inclined toward privately administered programs.

28 In a 1986 speech, Indianapolis Mayor William Hudnut, for instance, described "entrepreneurial government" as "willing to abandon old programs and methods. It is innovative and imaginative and creative. It takes risks. It turns city functions into money makers rather than budget-busters. It eschews traditional alternatives that offer only life-support systems. It works with the private sector. It employs

solid business sense. It privatizes. It creates enterprises and revenue generating operations. It is market oriented. It focuses on performance measurement. It rewards merit. It says, 'Let's make this work,' and it is unafraid to dream the great dream" (cited in David Osborne and Ted Gabler, *Reinventing Government: How the Entrepreneurial Spirit is Transforming the Public Sector* [Reading, MA: Addison-Wesley, 1991], p. 18).

29 The NPRG helped to justify the Hope VI program for redesigning public housing through public–private partnerships (e.g., with the collectivity of private architects and planners known as New Urbanists) and through the "empowerment" of occupants to "take back" their "community."

30 In his campaign for the US presidency, Bush had stated bluntly his opposition to earlier forms of welfare policy, which he considered to encourage dependency: "The new culture said if people were poor, the government should feed them. If criminals are not responsible for their acts, then the answers are not in prisons, but in social programs. People became less interested in pulling themselves up by their bootstraps and more interested in pulling down a monthly government check. A culture of dependency was born. Programs that began as a temporary hand-up became a permanent handout, regarded by many as a right" (*A Charge to Keep*, pp. 229–30, Dec. 9, 1999).

31 The Bush administration's 2002 *National Strategy for Homeland Security* declared that the department's mission is to "mobilize our entire society." In this way, a Homeland Security (as a primary *reason of state*) becomes the most central means of administering the state's *supportive* role in local, private, and personal techniques for helping, looking after, and taking care of oneself: "The *NSFHS* recognizes the crucial role of state and local government, private institutions, and the American people in securing our homeland. Our traditions of federalism and limited government require that organizations outside the federal government take the lead in many of these efforts. The *NSFHS* . . . seeks to empower all key players by streamlining and clarifying the federal *support* processes" (p. 3, emphasis added).

32 James Hay and Mark Andrejevic, *Homeland Insecurities*, special issues of *Cultural Studies*, July–Sept., 2006.

33 Paul du Gay, *In Praise of Bureaucracy: Weber, Organization, Ethics* (Thousand Oaks, CA: Sage, 2000).

34 See, for instance, Thomas Streeter, *Selling the Air: A Critique of the Policy of Commercial Broadcasting in the United States* (Chicago: University of Chicago Press, 1996); Susan Douglas, *Inventing American Broadcasting* (Baltimore, MD: Johns Hopkins University Press, 1989); and Robert McChesney, *Telecommunications, Mass Media and Democracy* (Oxford and New York: Oxford University Press, 1995).

35 The rationalization of a plan for broadcasting in the United States dates back at least to the formation of the Federal Radio Commission in 1927 and subsequently the Federal Communication Commission in 1934.

36 Laurie Ouellette, *Viewers Like You? How Public TV Failed the People* (New York: Columbia University Press, 2002). See also Michele Hilmes, "Desired and Feared: Women's Voices in Radio History," in *Television, History, and American Culture:*

Feminist Critical Essays, ed. Mary Beth Haralovich and Lauren Rabinowitz (Durham, NC: Duke University Press, 1999), pp. 17–35.

37 "Primary responsibility for the American system of broadcasting rests with the licensee of broadcast stations, including the network organizations. It is to the stations and networks rather than to federal regulation that listeners must primarily turn to improved standards of program service. The Commission [FCC] . . . has a responsibility to consider overall program service . . . , but affirmative improvement of program service must be the result primarily of other forces" (the "Blue Book" of 1946, a.k.a. "Public Service Responsibility of Broadcast Licensees," *Documents of American Broadcasting*, 4th ed., p. 155).

38 Ouellette, *Viewers Like You?*

39 Dwight MacDonald, "A Theory of Mass Culture," in *Mass Culture: The Popular Arts in America*, ed. Bernard Rosenberg and David Manning White (New York: The Free Press, 1957).

40 James Hay, "Rethinking the Intersection of Cinema, Genre, and Youth," *Scope*, July 2002.

41 See Nicholas Sammond, *Babes in Tomorrowland: Walt Disney and the Making of the American Child, 1930–1960* (Durham, NC Duke University Press, 2003).

42 Newton Minow, "Address to the National Association of Broadcasters," Washington, DC, May 9, 1961, in *Documents of American Broadcasting*.

43 Johnson's Message to Congress, H.R. Doc. 68, 90th Congress, 1st Session, Feb. 28, 1967, in *Documents of American Broadcasting*.

44 Ibid.

45 And in this way, Drucker's point in 1968 about "black power" advocates "reprivatizing" the administration of welfare (discussed above) becomes a dominant paradigm for TV's operation as cultural technology. Through the proliferation of cable and satellite channels, TV was "freed" from a broadcast model "limited" to three channels, even though the broadcast-model itself had been rationalized as more liberal than the examples of state subvention typical of the rest of the world.

46 Andrew Goodwin, *Dancing in the Distraction Factory* (Minneapolis: University of Minnesota Press, 1992).

47 Chad Raphael, "The Political Economic Origins of Reali-TV" and Ted Magder, "The End of TV 101: Reality Programs, Formats, and the New Business of Television," both in *Reality TV: Remaking TV Culture*, ed. Susan Murray and Laurie Ouellette (New York: New York University Press, 2004).

48 The current regime of TV education at home has developed as part of (though not always or necessarily in synergy with) the transformations of public schooling (as an older form of social welfare) and the emergence of the "home-schooling" trend as an alternative to public education.

Notes to Chapter 1

1 Felicia R. Lee, "Raising Reality TV Stakes," *New York Times*, Jan. 17, 2006.

2 Laurie Ouellette, *Viewers Like You? How Public TV Failed the People* (New York: Columbia University Press, 2002).

3　Nikolas Rose, "Governing 'Advanced' Liberal Democracies," in *Foucault and Political Reason: Liberalism, Neoliberalism and Rationalities of Government*, ed. Andrew Barry, Thomas Osborne, and Nikolas Rose (Chicago and London: University of Chicago Press, 1996), pp. 37–64.

4　Ibid., p. 39.

5　Ibid., p. 49.

6　Mark Carl Rom, "From Welfare State to Opportunity, Inc.," *American Behavioral Scientist*, 43.1 (1999), p. 157.

7　Rose, *Inventing Ourselves*, pp. 164–5.

8　Ibid., p. 165.

9　Lisa Duggan, *The Twilight of Equality? Neoliberalism, Cultural Politics, and the Attack on Democracy* (Boston: Beacon Press, 2003).

10　Rom, "From Welfare State," p. 155.

11　Ibid.

12　Thomas Streeter, *Selling the Air: A Critique of the Policy of Commercial Broadcasting in the United States* (Chicago: University of Chicago Press, 1996).

13　Rose, "Governing," p. 38.

14　Wendy Brown, "Neoliberalism and the End of Liberal Democracy," *Theory & Event*, 7.1 (2003), p. 3.

15　The Better Community project is described on the Disney corporate web site, http://corporate.disney.go.com/outreach/better_community.html, as well as on the ABC web site, www.abc.com

16　John McMurria, "Desparate Citizens," *Flow* 3.3, www.flowtv.org

17　Extreme Makeover Home Edition, episode summaries, http://abc.go.com/primetime/xtremehome/index.html

18　Sears American Dream Campaign, http://www.searsamericandream.com

19　Martin Gilens, *Why Americans Hate Welfare: Race, Media, and the Politics of Anti-poverty Policy* (Chicago: University of Chicago Press, 2000); Linda Gordon (ed.), *Women, The State, and Welfare* (Madison: University of Wisconsin Press, 1990).

20　Gilens, *Why America Hates Welfare*.

21　Samantha King, "Doing Good by Running Well," in *Foucault, Cultural Studies and Governmentality*, ed. Jack Bratich, Jeremy Packer, and Cameron McCarthy (Albany: State University of New York Press, 2003), p. 297.

22　"Iowa Student Loan Assisted in Making Kobes' Dream Come True," *Le Mars Daily Sentinel*, Oct. 18, 2005.

23　Amy Johannes, "NBC Grants 'Three Wishes' To Promote New Series," *Promo*, Sept. 8, 2005, http://promomagazine.com

24　Annia Ciezaldo, "Reality TV hits home in Baghdad," *Christian Science Monitor*, July 27, 2004.

Notes to Chapter 2

1　John Ehrenreich, *The Altruistic Imagination: A History of Social Work and Social Policy in the United States* (Ithaca, NY: Cornell University Press, 1985); Barbara Ehrenreich and Deirdre English, *For Her Own Good: 150 Years of the Experts*

Advice to Women (New York: Doubleday, 1978); Mimi White, *Tele-Advising: Therapeutic Discourse on American Television* (Chapel Hill: University of North Carolina Press, 1992). Our analysis is different from White's analysis of television's therapeutic ethos for two reasons. First, we see television's turn to self-help as a technology of citizenship that seeks to instill specific conduct and behaviors (including "personal responsibility") rather than ideology. second, we focus on programs that have emerged since her focus on 1980s television, and situate them within changing liberal and neoliberal strategies of governing.

2   Mary Ann Watson, *The Expanding Vista: American Television in the Kennedy Years* (New York: Oxford University Press, 1990); for an analysis of *East Side/West Side*'s engagement with civil rights policy in particular see Aniko Bodroghkozy, "Negotiating Civil Rights in Prime Time: A Production and Reception History of CBS's *East Side/West Side*," in *Television: The Critical View*, ed. Horace Newcomb (New York: Oxford University Press, 2006).

3   Wendy Brown, "Neoliberalism and the End of Liberal Democracy," *Theory & Event*, 7.1 (2003).

4   Nikolas Rose, "Governing 'Advanced' Liberal Democracies," in *Foucault and Political Reason: Liberalism, Neoliberalism and Rationalities of Government*, ed. Andrew Barry, Thomas Osborne, and Nikolas Rose (Chicago and London: University of Chicago Press, 1996), pp. 37–64. See also Nikolas Rose, *Governing the Soul: The Shaping of the Private Self* (2nd ed., London: Free Association Books, 1999) and Nikolas Rose, *Inventing Ourselves: Psychology, Power and Personhood* (Cambridge: Cambridge University Press, 1998).

5   The SageWalk mission is described at www.sagewalk.com; see also http://abc. go.com/primetime/bratcamp

6   Rose, "Governing," p. 57.

7   Ibid., pp. 58–9.

8   Stephen Labaton, "Transition to Digital Gets Closer," *New York Times*, Dec. 20, 2005.

9   Charlotte Brundson, "Lifestyling Britain: The 8–9 Slot on British Television," *International Journal of Cultural Studies*, 6(1): 5–23.

10   Judy Sheindlin, *Beauty Fades, Dumb is Forever* (New York, Cliff Street Books, 1999), p. 112–13.

11   Quoted in Luaine Lee, "Judge Judy has always believed in the motto 'just do it,'" *Nando Media*, Nov. 28, 1998, www.nandotimes.com. For a detailed critique of the court program see Laurie Ouellette, "Take Responsibility for Yourself: Judge Judy and the Neoliberal Citizen," in *Reality TV: Remaking Television Culture* (New York: New York University Press, 2004).

12   Barbara Cruikshank, "Revolutions Within: Self-Government and Self-Esteem," in Barry et al., *Foucault and Political Reason*, p. 231.

13   In addition to Cruikshank see Heidi Marie Rimke, "Governing Citizens Through Self-Help Literature," *Cultural Studies*, 14.1 (2000), pp. 61–78.

14   Cruikshank, "Revolutions," p. 234.

15   Ibid., p. 89.

16   Nancy Fraser, *Justice Interruptus: Critical Reflections on the "Postsocialist" Condition* (New York: Routledge, 1997).

17   Brown, "Neoliberalism," p. 6.
18   Judy Sheindlin, *Keep it Simple, Stupid* (New York: Cliff Street Books, 2000), p. 2.
19   Nancy Fraser and Linda Gordon, "A Genealogy of 'Dependency': Tracing a Keyword of the U.S. Welfare State," in Fraser, *Justice Interruptus*.
20   Michel Foucault, *The Care of the Self: The History of Sexuality Volume 3* (New York: Vintage Books, 1988); *Technologies of the Self: A Seminar with Michel Foucault*, ed. Luther H. Martin, Huck Gutman, and Patrick H. Hutton (Amherst: University of Massachusetts Press, 1988).
21   Michel Foucault, *Michel Foucault: Ethics, Subjectivity and Truth*, ed. Paul Rabinow (New York: The New Press, 1994), p. 87.
22   Graham Burchell, "Liberal Government and Techniques of the Self," in Barry et al., *Foucault and Political Reason*, p. 20.
23   www.drphil.com; see also Phillip C. McGraw, *Life Strategies: Doing What Works, Doing What Matters* (New York: Hyperion, 1999).
24   www.drphil.com
25   Rose, *Inventing Our Selves*, p. 166.
26   www.startingovertv.com
27   Brown, "Neoliberalism," p. 6.
28   Foucault, *Care of the Self*.
29   Written Testimony of Marshall Manson, Vice President of Public Affairs, Center for Individual Freedom, House Government Reform Committee Hearing on "The Supersizing of America," June 3, 2004, http://www.cfif.org/htdocs/legislative_issues/state_issues/supersizing_america.htm
30   Rose, *Inventing Our Selves*, p. 162.
31   Quoted on George W. Bush, *Families and Children*, www.issues2000.org

Notes to Chapter 3

1   Valerie Walkerdine, "Reclassifying Upward Mobility: Femininity and the Neo-Liberal Subject," *Gender and Education*, 15:3 (2003), p. 240.
2   See, e.g., June Deery, "Trading Faces: The Makeover Show as Primetime 'Infomercial,'" *Feminist Media Studies*, 4:2 (2004), p. 211; and Helen Wood and Beverly Skeggs, "Notes on Ethical Scenarios of Self on British Reality TV," *Feminist Media Studies*, 4:2 (2004), pp. 205–8.
3   Angela McRobbie, *The Uses of Cultural Studies* (London: Sage, 2005), pp. 99–100.
4   Micki McGee, *Self-Help, Inc: Makeover Culture in American Life* (Oxford: Oxford University Press, 2005), p. 130.
5   Peter Drucker, *Management Challenges for the 21st Century* (New York: HarperBusiness, 1999), pp. 163, 194, 183.
6   Tom Peters, "The Brand Called You," *Fast Company*, 10 (Aug. 1997), p. 83.
7   Toby Miller, "A Metrosexual Eye on Queer Guy," *GLQ: A Journal of Lesbian and Gay Studies*, 11:1 (2005), p. 112.
8   Nancy Etcoff, *Survival of the Prettiest: The Science of Beauty* (New York: Anchor Books, 2000).

9 Angela McRobbie, "From Holloway to Hollywood: Happiness at Work in the New Cultural Economy?," in *Cultural Economy: Cultural Analysis and Commercial Life*, ed. Paul du Gay and Michael Pryke (London: Sage, 2002), p. 100.

10 Richard Sennett, *The New Culture of Capitalism* (New Haven, CT: Yale University Press, 2006), pp. 9–10, 93.

11 Drucker, *Management*, p. 163.

12 Nikolas Rose, *Inventing Ourselves: Psychology, Power, and Personhood* (Cambridge: Cambridge University Press, 1996), p. 159; McGee, *Self-Help*, p. 166.

13 Trinny Woodall and Susannah Constantine, *What You Wear Can Change Your Life* (New York: Riverhead Books, 2005), p. 11.

14 Laurel Graham, "Beyond Manipulation: Lillian Gilbreth's Industrial Psychology and the Governmentality of Women Consumers," *Sociological Quarterly*, 38:4 (1997), pp. 539–65; Don Slater, *Consumer Culture and Modernity* (Cambridge: Polity Press, 1997), p. 28.

15 Wendy Brown, "Neoliberalism and the End of Liberal Democracy," *Theory & Event*, 7:1 (2003), p. 3.

16 Cronin quoted in David Gauntlett, *Media, Gender and Identity* (London: Routledge, 2002), p. 129.

17 Christopher Lasch, *The Culture of Narcissism: American Life in an Age of Diminishing Expectations* (New York: W. W. Norton, 1979), pp. 53, 61.

18 Kathy Peiss, *Hope in a Jar: The Making of America's Beauty Culture* (New York: Metropolitan Books, 1998), p. 144; see also Laurie Ouellette, "Inventing the Cosmo Girl: Class Identity and Girl-Style American Dreams," *Media, Culture & Society*, 21:3 (1999), pp. 359–83.

19 Valerie Walkerdine, Helen Lucey, and June Melody, *Growing Up Girl: Psychosocial Explorations of Gender and Class* (New York: New York University Press, 2001), p. 10.

20 Walkerdine, "Reclassifying," p. 238.

21 Gavin Kendall and Gary Wickham, *Understanding Culture: Cultural Studies, Order, Ordering* (London: Sage, 2001).

22 John Saade and Joe Borgenicht, *The Reality TV Handbook: An Insider's Guide: How to Ace a Casting Interview, Form an Alliance, Swallow a Live Bug, and Capitalize on Your 15 Minutes of Fame* (New York: Quirk Books, 2004).

23 Lasch, *Culture of Narcisissm*, p. 65.

24 Sennett, *New Culture*, p. 99.

25 Paul du Gay, *Consumption and Identity at Work* (London: Sage, 1996).

26 Sennett, *New Culture*, p. 140.

27 McGee, *Self-Help*, pp. 128, 130.

28 McRobbie, "Holloway to Hollywood," p. 102.

29 Paul Smith, "Tommy Hilfiger in the age of Mass Customization," in *No Sweat: Fashion, Free Trade and the Rights of Garment Workers*, ed. Andrew Ross (London: Verso, 1997), pp. 252–69.

30 McGee, *Self-Help*, p. 131.

31 Kiri Blakeley, "Tyra Banks On it," *Forbes*, July 3, 2006, pp. 120–6.

32 Margena A. Christian, "Tyra Banks: Says 'It's a Lot More than Just Looks' to Become 'America's Next Top Model'," *Jet*, May 26, 2003.

Notes to Chapter 4

1 Ulrich Beck, *Risk Society: Towards a New Modernity* (London: Sage, 1992) and *Ecological Politics in the Age of Risk* (Cambridge: Polity Press, 1995).

2 An essay that discusses some of early programs that tied "public health" to social management is Michel Foucault, "The Politics of Health in the Eighteenth Century," in *Power*, ed. James O. Faubion (New York: New Press, 1994), pp. 90–105.

3 This is a subject throughout Foucault's writing. See for instance, Michel Foucault, *Madness and Civilization: A History of Insanity in the Age of Reason* (New York: Vintage, 1988), *Birth of the Clinic: The Archaeology of Medical Perception* (New York: Vintage, 1994), "The Birth of Social Medicine," in *Power*, and "Psychiatric Power," in *Ethics*, ed. Paul Rabinow (New York: New Press, 1994).

4 As Rose has noted about the current stage of liberalism, "the social logics of welfare bureaucracies and service management have been replaced by a new configuration of control agencies – police, social workers, doctors, psychiatrists, mental health professionals – [that] become connected up with one another in circuits of surveillance and communication designed to minimize the riskiness of the most risky." Nikolas Rose, *Powers of Freedom* (Cambridge: Cambridge University Press, 1999), p. 260.

5 Mark Andrejevic, *Reality TV: The Work of Being Watched* (Lanham, MD: Rowman & Littlefield, 2004).

6 Randy Martin, *The Financialization of Daily Life* (Philadelphia, PA: Temple University Press, 2002).

7 The WorldCom bankruptcy was estimated to involve roughly $107 billion, as stock shares plummeted from $62 in 2000 to 9c in early 2002. The Global Crossing bankruptcy was estimated to involve roughly $25.5 billion, as stock shares fell from $64 in 2000 to less than $1 in early 2002.

8 Martin, *Financialization*, pp. 93–4.

9 Ibid., particularly "In the New Economy's Embrace," pp. 45–54.

10 Since the early 1980s, CNN has been the oldest all-news network in the United States and globally that developed programs exclusively for financial news.

11 CNBC developed out of a merger during the early 1990s between the Consumer News and Business Channel and the Financial News Network (FNN). While CNBC/FNN became affiliated with NBC during the mid-1990s, the CNBC acronym (unlike MSNBC's) does not refer to its current parent-company except as a matter of public perception. CNBC became a global network in 1998 when it took over the European Business Network (EBN).

12 Martin, *Financialization,* p. 106.

13 Ibid., p. 101.

14 Ibid., p. 43.

15 Michel Foucault, *The Order of Things: The Archaeology of the Human Sciences* (New York: Vintage, 1970/3).

16 Andrejevic, *Reality TV.*

17 Self-reflection, as a strategy for risk management, does not always involve reviewing the past. As we also have seen in *Honey, We're Killing the Kids* (Chapter 2),

weighing the future risks of bad health-care is accomplished not just by replaying actions but by digitally *projecting* one's future life. Whether by watching video replays of one's past self or by digitally producing forecasts of a future self, contemporary TV programs such as these operate as a technology for self-objectification – for putting one's self in the palm of one's hand in order to observe and reflect upon, and thus to rationalize, personalize, and customize techniques for self-care.

18 Raymond Williams, *Television: Technology and Cultural Form* (Middletown., CT: Wesleyan University Press, 1992). Mobile privatization refers to the interdependence and mutually constitutive dynamic between how societies shape spheres and technologies of privacy (establishing a place removed from but with a specific relation to an outside or public sphere) and how their world is made to move. In this sense, TV could be said to have developed and mattered not only within a particular conception and design of house and home but within a home life that assumed and required particular forms of transport. Hence, one might consider how TV, privacy, and mobility each shaped the other two – how, for instance, "living at a distance" (to use Williams's phrase) in a post-World War II suburban house required particular technologies such as TV or telephones as well as automobiles and freeways as a private, personal system of transportation.

19 For theorizing the historical link between regimes of safety and communication, Hay's essay recommends the work of the Dutch philosopher, Lieven de Cauter, who has argued that media, as extensions of man, enhance speed and increase flow/networks, which in turn have hastened the development of forms of protection – or what de Cauter refers to as "capsularization" (Lieven de Cauter, "The Capsule and the Network: Notes toward a General Theory," in *The Cybercities Reader,* ed. Stephen Graham, London and New York: Routledge, 2004). De Cauter's perspective is particularly useful because it underscores that mass suburbanization – the regime of mobility and privacy within which TV developed – has been a program of capsularization. For de Cauter, network-theory, which emphasizes the "space of flows" and an environment organized to maximize *speed*, too often fails to recognize (indeed obscures) the *capsule* – membranes designed to insulate the body and to minimize the risk of flow, speed, and networks. Individuals inhabit capsules rather than networks, and one's access to the network is via a capsule. The capsule is thus a requirement and effect of network formation: "No network without capsules. The more networking, the more capsules. In other words, the degree of capsularization is directly proportional to the growth of network."

Because de Cauter sees capsularization as a condition of speed (of freedom enacted by a hypermobile self and the modern technology of transport), he considers suburbanization as having supported both a form of securitization that is "hyperindividualist" and a form of self-governance that is "neoliberal" in its expectation that the risk-taker avail her/himself of available forms of capsularization (the "technology of the self" as a technology of safety, of watching out for and over oneself).

20 James Hay, "Unaided Virtues: The (Neo-)Liberalization of the Domestic Sphere and the New Architecture of Community," in *Foucault, Cultural Studies, Govern-*

mentality, ed. Jack Bratich, Jeremy Packer, and Cameron McCarthy (Albany: State University of New York Press, 2003).

21   The number of companies providing home-security services and technologies proliferated over the 1980s. Two of the oldest US security services, the Brinks Co. and Advance Detection Technologies, formed home-security divisions in the early 1980s.

22   Fears of privacy violation, for instance of personal, everyday exposure through one's trashcan, also have contributed to the proliferation of the domestic paper-shredder. Since the 1980s, paper-shredding devices generally became a component of house-holds reorganized and managed around "personal computing." The console for home computing increasingly has become comprised of fax and copy devices and thus has become a command-center for managing various home-computing risks (e.g., viruses, worms, hackers, spammers, fishing-schemes). This array of program-mable safety devices, part of the paradigm of suburban living in the United States since the 1980s, is worth recognizing because some of it preceded and then extended the safety regime surrounding personal computing, which developed as a central (but certainly not the only) way of enacting the smart household.

23   The makeover of one family's house installed a security system by Safeguard; the makeover of another family's house installed security systems by Silent Knight and Home Control Systems.

24   See, for instance, *Surveillance, Closed-circuit Television, and Social Control*, ed. Clive Norris, Jade Moran, and Gary Armstrong (Aldershot, England: Ashgate, 1998).

25   James Hay and Jeremy Packer, "Crossing the Media(-n): Auto-mobility, the Transported Self, and Technologies of Freedom," in *Media Space*, ed. Nick Couldry and Anna McCarthy (New York and London: Routledge, 2004).

26   Much has been made of the contradiction between the Bush administration's emphasis upon "limiting government" and its institution of an ambitious federal agency such as the Department of Homeland Security, an agency that serves as a ridgepole for all its other policies and programs. The department is unlike many other and previous federal agencies, however, in that its role has, from the start, been mostly about facilitating and coordinating "do-it-yourself" security – pro-viding informational resources and links for citizens to learn for themselves how to apply themselves as managers of their own welfare and security. The current federalism that conceives of the solution to centralized and "big" government as the localization, privatization, and personalization of welfare's administration, requires a network such as the TV–Web nexus through which the population most engaged with this network can maximize their self-sufficiency. In this respect, there is nothing particularly paradoxical about the enormity of the scope of a Homeland Security – about the reinvention of government through a new federal bureau and bureaucracy – and the survival (indeed the deepening) of the requirement that government be a "public–private partnership" and that citizens look after their own welfare and security. The stridency of the libertarian opposi-tion to a nanny state (and nanny culture), i.e., of a state-government that is constantly surveilling, correcting, and limiting personal conduct and freedoms, is more uneasy about a federal "bailout" of Hurricane Katrina victims, which has yet to materialize, than it is about the do-it-yourself plans for securing a "home-

land." See James Hay and Mark Andrejevic, *Homeland Insecurities*, special issues of *Cultural Studies*, July–Sept., 2006.

27 As Hay has noted, the formation of a Homeland Defense continues a long-standing practice in the United States of a primarily privatized and personalized "civil defense," even though the Department of Homeland Defense developed through a different governmental rationality about self-defense, and through a different regime of privatized and personalized security programs, than before the 1980s. See James Hay, "Designing Homes to be the First Line of Defense," *Cultural Studies*, 20:4–5 (2006), pp. 349–77.

Notes to Chapter 5

1 The household or neighborhood that TV enacts is a fiction (a representation on TV), but one that has a relation to physical places where TV's fictional neighborhoods are watched and circulate. And this *formation* (constitution) of TV neighborhoods occurs through a *mode of production*. The most common critical perspective about media (by TV criticism and political economists) has been about how media *make* meaning and/or money through a "mode of production." *Supernanny* or the other programs considered in this chapter are different from older TV series where neighborhoods and households were constructed on Hollywood sets. That these recent households and neighborhoods are not produced on a Hollywood set and are not populated by professional actors situates them within a different mode of production than earlier TV in the United States.

2 The drafters of the US Constitution used the constitutions of regional territories and "states" as templates for a national constitution, and *federalism* (a governmental arrangement emphasizing the sovereignty/rights of regional and local constitutions under government by the nation-state) has been an ongoing dimension of liberalism. The legislative and judicial activism supporting federalism in the United States since the late 1970s has been particularly integral to projects for "reinventing government" and thus is of interest in this book.

3 Just as state government is rationalized through and administers formal laws for citizens, governmentalities also are *constituted* around formal and informal rules and guidelines that are intended not only to authorize and sanction, but also to make rational and fair, specific forms of association, participation, and membership. These various, localized, private and personal, formal and informal ways that liberal government is constituted (and reconstituted or reinvented through daily life) comprise a *field of government* – the many reasons/rationalities of its administration in daily life.

4 As noted in the Introduction, this is a term recently developed by Tony Bennett, "Civic Laboratories: Museums, Cultural Objecthood and the Governance of the Social," *Cultural Studies*, 19:5 (2005).

Also, as explained in the Introduction, a "civil society" is not only an aggregate of private, "nongovernmental" institutions and associations administering to different social and life needs; civil society is also an array of private and self-directed rules and techniques through which we enter into our own government – the resources of self-regulation that operate through society and that collectively become the means to individual empowerment and civility. A civil society (in both senses) is thus the primary objective, resource, and terrain of liberal government.

5   Consider, for instance, how the formation of TV's domestic comedy during the 1950s offered sets of instructions about the suburban household and neighborhood.

6   The history of TV programs on PBS, such as *Mister Rogers' Neighborhood* and *Sesame Street*, are examples of how TV program development as citizen education (as constituting the rules of neighborliness) was driven and supported as an initiative of state government (see Laurie Ouellette, *Viewers Like You? How Public TV Failed the People*, New York: Columbia University Press, 2002), though the history of commercial TV programming has itself been a response to government policy and to reasonings about the role of government and about the role of TV within public and private techniques of citizen education (see Introduction). The current stage of TV examined in this book has developed out of prior public and commercial TV practices of citizen education.

7   They included the Crenshaws (whom the series' publicity described as a devout Christian and African-American couple), the Eckhardts (a Native American and Caucasian couple whose spirituality was described as "pagan"), the Gonzalezes (a loud and "boisterous" Hispanic family), the Lees (a Korean-American family that runs a sushi restaurant), the Morgans (a Caucasian family whose mother has a "secret," which the series reveals is "stripping"), the Sheets (a Caucasian family whose bodies are covered in tattoos and piercings), and the Wrights (a Caucasian lesbian couple who have adopted an African-American boy).

8   The legal action threatened by GLAAD differed from the action threatened by the NFHA in that it pertained mostly to *televisual representations* of discriminatory practices (and, according to this rationale, TV's discriminatory practices). GLAAD's web site proudly lists various actions that it successfully brought against various instances of media/companies' gender and sexual discrimination (e.g., convincing the *New York Times* to adopt the term "gay" in their editorial section and to include same-sex marriage notices in its wedding announcement section, mobilizing viewers of the TV series *Ellen* to "Let Ellen Out," and campaigning against Eminem's and other recording artists' "anti-gay" lyrics). When GLAAD announced its concern about *Welcome to the Neighborhood* (soon after the program's production was announced by ABC), the series' producers agreed to allow Damon Romline, the media director for GLAAD, to view several episodes in order to decide whether the series' representation of a transformation by the homeowners satisfied GLAAD's misgivings about the game's rules and about the sentiments expressed in the first episode by certain homeowners about the alternative lifestyles and families cast as contestants.

9   The Better Community "brand" (as ABC/Disney calls it) promotes the corporation's role in "partnerships," which include Habitat for Humanity, the Points of Light Foundation's Volunteer Center National Network, the National Center for Healthy Housing, and the Council for Better Business Bureaus. For more on this see Chapter 1.

10   See, for instance, Stephanie McCrummen, "Redefining Property Values," *Washington Post*, Apr. 16, 2006, p. A1, which discusses marketing research and strategies for the Ladera Ranch subdivision. Brooke Warrick, from Ladera's marketing firm,

"American Lives," notes that "Neighboring is one of the biggest concepts in America. People want connections. And as good developers, we should recognize what it means to create community." The article identifies Warrick as one of many marketers of residential developments who has turned the strategies of media market research (used to identify the taste cultures, lifestyle clusters, and "values subcultures") into strategies for identifying values that might design a more neighborly neighborhood.

11 See Anna McCarthy, "Stanley Milgram, Allen Funt, and Me: Postwar Social Science and the First Wave of Reality TV," in *Reality TV: Remaking Television Culture*, ed. Susan Murray and Laurie Ouellette (New York: New York University Press, 2004).

While acknowledging that the social-scientific aspiration of commercial TV programs has not figured prominently in histories of US TV (arguably because of TV criticism's bias toward understanding TV culture through fictional, narrative TV – an analysis that has emphasized questions of style, identity, and meaning rather than technical knowledge and self-formation), TV's design of programs as social-scientific experiments are part of an equally long history of social-scientific research about TV's effects on audiences.

12 In the finale of the spring, 2005 season of *Survivor*, contestants were rewarded with toothpaste and mouthwash – as product placement – for having completed certain tasks successfully.

13 Chantal Mouffe discusses a similar paradox which she attributes to German political theorist Carl Schmitt's writing about democracy: "No doubt there is an opposition between the liberal 'grammar' of equality, which postulates universality and reference to 'humanity', and the practice of democratic equality, which requires the political moment of discrimination between 'us' and 'them'." Mouffe contends that Schmitt was wrong to have presented this conflict as a contradiction "that is bound to lead liberal democracy to self-destruction" (Mouffe, *The Democratic Paradox*, London and New York: Verso, 1999, p. 44). We would add that the vein of reality TV discussed in this section in fact involves ritual demonstrations of this paradox's importance to a current reasoning about liberal government.

14 For an explanation of "communities of practice," see Etienne Wenger, Richard McDermott, & William Snyder, *Cultivating Communities of Practice: A Guide to Managing Knowledge* (Cambridge, MA: Harvard University Press, 2002).

15 This dynamic also was foregrounded when Trump appeared with current and former contestants on the QVC network to sell a DVD from the first season along with his latest advice book. Contestants repeatedly stated how much they had learned from their participation on the show as a way of supporting the premise of a link between Trump's books and the series DVD.

16 *The Apprentice* became one of the most widely watched TV programs in 2004–5, the height of the Bush–Cheney administration's campaign to privatize and personalize Social Security. For more on the connection between reality TV and the push to "overhaul" Social Security, see James Hay, "'Overhaulin' TV and Government: Thoughts on the Political Campaign to Pimp Your Ride," *Flow*, 1:9 (2005).

17 Currently, *The Contender*'s future is in doubt. It is being rerun on ESPN (a sports network). As much as the series is an experiment and game in upward social mobility (like *The Apprentice*), its lack of traction in the current governmental

rationality may be its emphasis on alliances and group governance among contestants who represent a population that is entirely male and predominantly an
economic underclass and/or racial minority.

18   Observations are based upon the manuals and rights posted on ABC's web site
for *Wife Swap* for broadcasts during the spring of 2006.

19   The series was the highest rated reality TV series on a basic cable network (F/X)
since MTV's *The Osbornes*.

20   Much of the program's première episode in 2006 interspersed scenes of the subjects' physical transformation by professional makeup technicians and scenes of
the subjects' confessions to one another about how they felt to embody racial
difference and hybridity (as bodies that were alternately black/white) and to play
by the rules for black and white.

21   While the two families were differentiated racially by the program's title, and
while the two families described themselves as "average" black and white families,
blogs, newspapers, and magazines revealed that Bruno Marcotulli was the boy-
friend/partner of Carmen Wurgel and not the biological father of her daughter,
Rose, in the family identified as the Marcotullis.

22   This retro-trend is most formalized in the community of professional architects
and city planners who describe themselves as New Urbanists. For more on the
New Urbanism's rationale about the destructive effects of suburbanization, see
The Charter for New Urbanism (New York: McGraw-Hill, 1999).

23   See the Chamber of Commerce web sites for images of these towns and their events.

Notes to Chapter 6

1   Henry Jenkins, *Convergence Culture: Where Old and New Media Collide* (New York:
New York University Press, 2006).

2   Ibid., p. 249.

3   Ibid., p. 248.

4   John Hartley, *The Uses of Television* (London and New York: Routledge, 1999).

5   Ibid., p. 181.

6   Ibid., p. 186.

7   Ibid., p. 228.

8   Ibid., p. 178.

9   Ibid., p. 234.

10   Jeffrey Minson, *Questions of Conduct: Sexual Harassment, Citizenship, and Government* (London: Macmillan, 1993).

11   Hartley, *Uses of Television*.

12   This is potentially one implication of Williams's statement above about the need
for an analysis that does not resolve but clarifies the variety of democracies – and,
we would add, the relative interplay and interdependence among the informal
technical procedures of association, membership, and participation.

13   As noted in Chapter 5, Chantal Mouffe's *The Democratic Paradox* (by way of Carl
Schmidt) offers one way of thinking about the relation between membership and
agency.

14 Raymond Williams, *Keywords: A Vocabulary of Culture and Society* (New York: Oxford University Press, [1976] 1985).

15 Gregor McClennan, "Democracy," in *New Keywords: A Revised Vocabulary of Culture and Society*, ed. Tony Bennett, Lawrence Grossberg, and Meaghan Morris (New York and London: Blackwell, 2005).

16 The widespread use of the remote control for the TV monitor and VCR during the 1980s was part of a widespread reliance upon remote-control devices and programmable technologies in US households. James Hay, "Unaided Virtues: The (Neo-)Liberalization of the Domestic Sphere and the New Architecture of Community," in *Foucault, Cultural Studies, Governmentality*, ed. Jack Bratich, Jeremy Packer, and Cameron McCarthy (New York: State University of New York Press, 2003).

17 Center for Digital Democracy, "TV that Watches You," June, 2001.

18 Mark Andrejevic, *Reality TV: The Work of Being Watched* (Lanham, MD: Rowman & Littlefield, 2003).

19 *American Idol* is, in this respect, an example of the kind of makeover program discussed in Chapter 2, as contestants are not only judged but advised (often in very technical musical terms) about why their performance failed or how it could be improved.

20 See, for instance, *The New York Times*, May 12, 2006.

21 For instance, the organization and management of corporations as "communities of practice" (discussed in Chapter 5 in relation to *The Apprentice*) has become a model for efforts to reinvent the federal government's administrative bureaucracy. For one perspective on this convergence of private and public models of management, see James Hay, "The New Techno-Communitarianism and Residual Logics of Mediation," in *Residual Media*, ed. Charles Acland (Minneapolis: University of Minnesota Press, 2007).

22 According to the Rock-the Vote Action Center web site. The fuller rationale for Rock the Vote casts voting as a civic responsibility for youth and casts youth as empowered through this civic responsibility:

> Rock the Vote: Political power for young people.
>
> Rock the Vote is a non-profit, non-partisan organization, founded in 1990 in response to a wave of attacks on freedom of speech and artistic expression.
>
> Rock the Vote engages youth in the political process by incorporating the entertainment community and youth culture into its activities. From actors to musicians, comedians to athletes, Rock the Vote harnesses cutting-edge trends and pop culture to make political participation cool.
>
> Rock the Vote mobilizes young people to create positive social and political change in their lives and communities. The goal of Rock the Vote's media campaigns and street team activities is to increase youth voter turnout. Rock the Vote coordinates voter registration drives, get-out-the-vote events, and voter education efforts, all with the intention of ensuring that young people take advantage of their right to vote.

Rock the Vote's work doesn't end when the polls close. We empower young people to create change in their communities and take action on the issues they care about. Regardless of whether youth are signing petitions, running for office, contacting their elected officials, or taking up a sign in protest, they are all rocking the vote.

23   In Dr. Phil's interview with George and Laura Bush, he begins by stating:

> I'm really committed to putting family back in America. I think it's what you have put in the White House. I think it's what we need to put back in America, and I'm devoting so much of my third season to family first, what I call family first, and putting it back together. In preparation for a book that I've done, I've conducted a survey of 20,000 parents and asked them all the questions I could about parenting. I was shocked at one thing: Forty percent of them said, "If I knew then what I know now, I probably wouldn't have started a family."

Later in the interview, Bush discusses the "role of government" as protecting the family and household from unwanted "cultural influence" – a reference to the intrusion of the "wrong" kind of media into the home. Bush's solution is less one of intrusion by government than one of providing families the technologies to secure their own households.

24   Dr. Phil taped three specials titled "Hurricane Katrina: The Aftermath," "Hurricane Katrina: Rescuing the Rescuers," and "Hurricane Katrina: Rebuilding Lives" – all broadcast in the fall of 2005.

25   See Laurie Ouellette, "'Take Responsibility for Youself': Judge Judy and the Neoliberal Citizen," in *Reality TV: Remaking Television Culture*, ed. Susan Murray and Laurie Ouellette (New York: New York University Press, 2004).

26   Al Iraqiya was formed and financed by a CIA contractor, Science Applications International Corporation, in the first months after the US-led invasion of Iraq.

27   A bloody irony of the televisual mediation of "justice" by Iraqi citizens in the wake of Al Iraqiya's effort to export US-style reality TV to Iraq (as part of the US campaign to bring liberal government through the so-called Operation Iraqi Freedom) has been the rapidly increasing availability in the marketplaces of some Iraqi cities of home-made videos made by snipers felling US soldiers.

28   "Howard Stern Tries to Kill 'American Idol' with Kindness for a Weak Link," *New York Times*, Mar. 31, 2007.

29   The funds from this campaign were purportedly to go to the newly formed Charity Projects Entertainment Fund for distribution to groups such as America's Second Harvest: The Nation's Food Bank Network, Boys and Girls Clubs of America, and the Global Fund to Fight AIDS, TB and Malaria. Rock star-activist Bono promoted his initiative, "ONE: The Campaign to Make Poverty History," through the *American Idol* campaign.

30   Jenkins, *Convergence Culture*, p. 259.

31   Phil C. McGraw, Ph.D., "Life is Managed, It is Not Cured," in *Life Strategies: Doing What Works Well, Doing What Matters* (New York: Hyperion, 1999).

Index

ABC Television, Better Community
    initiative 40–4, 55, 56, 94, 181
addictive behavior, and life
    interventions 71–2
advanced liberalism *see*
    neo-liberalism
The Adventures of Ozzie and Harriett
    27
advertising 144–5, 210
Afghanistan 172–3
age, and makeover TV 107–10
The Age of Discontinuity (Drucker)
    19
Alias 153
All in the Family 184
Ambush Makeover 101
American Idol 127, 153, 203, 212,
    213–15, 221
    crisis of the series 222–3
America's Most Wanted 218, 219
America's Next Top Model 7, 127,
    128, 132–3
Americorp 21
Ameritrade 144–5, 147
ancient Greece, "care of the self"
    in 78, 87, 109
Andrejevic, Mark 141, 153–4,
    210–11, 221

The Apprentice 127, 129, 147, 149,
    150, 153, 175, 184, 187–91,
    193, 196
    and the political process 212,
    215, 221
Arts & Entertainment (A&E) 61–2
Average Joe 126

Bad Girls Club 155, 220
Baker, Jim and Tammy 210
bankruptcies, and financial risk
    management 142–3
Banks, Tyra 132, 133
Beauty and the Geek 126–7
Beck, Ulrich 135
Bennett, Tony 13
Berger, Joan 112
BET (Black Entertainment TV) 217
Better Business Bureau 42
The Biggest Loser 87–8
Big Love 149
Black Americans, and *Home Edition*
    52–3
Black Entertainment TV (BET)
    191, 192, 217
Black/White 194, 196–8
Blangiardi, Barbara 61
Bloomberg, Michael 219

Bloomberg Network 145, 147
Bodroghkozy, Aniko 65
Bolt Home Systems 162
branded commodities, individuals as
    104–5
Brat Camp 6, 64, 67–70, 72
Britten, Rhonda 83
broadcasting policy (US) 24–8,
    184–5
Brown, Wendy 40, 67, 86
Brundson, Charlotte 74
Burchell, Graham 78–9
Burnett, Mark 193
Bush, George W. 21–3, 24, 34, 41,
    104
    American Dream program 45
    and *American Idol* 213, 214–15,
        223
    and the collapse of the World
        Trade Center 141
    Compassion Agenda 67, 139,
        218, 219
    and Enron 142
    family policy 92, 93
    and Homeland Security 166, 167–8
    interview with Dr. Phil 217
    and the Iraq war 219
    lifelong learning policies 100
    and the Ownership Society 171,
        178
    and risk management 139–40
    Steps to a Healthier US program
        90–1
    welfare reform policies 37, 95
Bush, Laura 54–5, 217–18, 223

cable networks 30, 185, 209
    and charity TV 61–2
    and finance-TV 145–51
    and home security 161, 162–3
    and life interventions 87
    and makeover TV 101

care of the self 6, 12, 15, 17–18
    and life interventions 75–6, 78–9,
        87, 98
    and makeover TV 106, 109–10,
        121
    and risk management 151–8
Carnegie Corporation 38
Center for Science in the Public
    Interest (CSPI) 90
charity TV 5–6, 32–62, 66
    and ABC TV 40–4
    and cable networks 61–2
    proliferation of 56–62
    and public interest 34–5
    and welfare reform 33, 35–8
Chasin, Alexandra 12
Cheaters 155
Chertoff, Michael 166, 169
children
    and *Brat Camp* 6, 64, 67–70, 72
    and healthy lifestyle programs
        88–92
    and nanny programs 93–8
Chopra, Deepak 31
Citizen Corps 21, 23, 167
citizenship 7, 9, 17, 21, 23
    constitutions of 170–4
    and cultural technologies 14, 41,
        67
    democracy and viewer
        participation 203–4, 206, 211,
        218–20, 224
    and financial risk management
        147, 149, 150–1
    future of CV as citizenship
        training 224
    and group governance games
        187, 190, 192, 194, 196, 197,
        199
    and home security 159
    and life interventions 75
    and personal safety 165–9

and reinventing television 31
and survivalist TV 158
tests of 172, 174–82
and TV as a cultural technology
15–16
and US broadcasting policy 25,
26–7
viewers and DIY citizenship
203–4
civic laboratories 16, 173
civil society 9, 10, 11, 14, 137
and Iraq 219
and US broadcasting policy 25–6
Clarke, John 39, 44
class, and makeover TV 101, 123–4
Clean House 6, 93
Clinton, Bill 20–1, 22
Cold War 25
College Hill 191, 192
Community Development
Corporations 22
Compassion Capital Fund 21
computer hackers 163
computer technology 153, 160–2,
163
constitutions of citizenship 170–4
consumerism/consumption, and
makeover TV 109–10, 114–16
The Contender 193, 196
Convergence Culture (Jenkins) 203,
204–5, 223–4
Cops 160, 218
corporate citizenship 219
Corporation for National and
Community Service 21, 41, 56
Corporation for Public Broadcasting
27, 28
courtroom programs 74–7
Court TV Channel 218
Cramer, Jim 150
crime drama on TV, surveillance
and profiling in 152–3

Cronin, Ann 115
Cruikshank, Barbara 75
CSPI (Center for Science in the
Public Interest) 90
cultivation, and TV as cultural
technology 14–15
cultural technologies
and citizenship 14, 41, 67
and life interventions 72–3, 91
and makeover TV 103
popular media as 73
television as 3, 7, 13–16
The Culture of Narcissism (Lasch) 118
Current TV 213
The Cut 127, 131–2

The Daily Show 205
dating programs 2, 124–7, 154
Daughtry, Chris 214
Deal or No Deal 150
decluttering programs 93
Decorating on a Dime 92
democracy 1–2, 203–24
and group governance games
186, 187, 193
and media education 203–5
reality TV and the political
process 213–23
and self-government 205, 206–7
TV as a spectacle of 205–8
TV and the technology of
counting 208–13
and US broadcasting policy 25
Democracy Player 213
depression (1930s), and federal
welfare programs 35–6
deregulation, and charity TV 33, 34
Diebold, Inc. 214
digital television, US government
funding of 73
Direct TV 210
Discovery Channel 87, 158

Dish Network 210
Disney Corporation 27, 34, 41, 42
diversity in programming 27
docu-soaps (reality-based soaps) 2,
    6, 81
domestic management programs
    92–3
Dr. Phil 63, 64, 77–8, 79–81, 85,
    217
Dr. Phil Foundation 63
Drucker, Peter 19, 104, 105, 108,
    130
drug addicts, and life interventions
    71–2
du Gay, Paul 23–4, 103, 127, 130
Duggan, Lisa 36

East Side/West Side 65
education
    and finance-TV 146–51
    lifelong learning 7, 24, 100, 119
    media education and the politics
        of participation 203, 204–5,
        223–4
    televised liberal arts education
        28
Educational Television Network
    (ETV) 26
Eisner, Michael 34
Enron 142–3, 149
entrepreneurialism
    and charity TV 44
    government and TV 23–4, 219
    and life interventions 69, 82–4,
        86–7
    and makeover TV 100, 110, 131,
        132
    and "reinventing" television 24
    of social work 91
    and talent/job searches 127
"entrepreneurs of the self" 103
Etcoff, Nancy 107

ETV (Educational Television
    Network) 26
excellence management philosophy,
    and makeover TV 130
Extreme Makeover 3, 7, 40, 64, 101,
    104, 105–8, 109
    see also Home Edition

failure, reality TV's celebration of
    220
Faith-Based and Community
    Initiative (FBCI) 21–2, 23
families
    and charity TV 60
    and life interventions 92–8
Family Channel 207
Family Safe Media 163–4
fashion designers 131–2
fashion modelling 121–2, 132–3
FBCI (Faith-Based and Community
    Initiative) 21–2, 23
Fear Factor 155
Federal Emergency Management
    Agency 139, 218
federalism, and risk management
    139
femininity, and makeover TV
    118–27
feminism
    and life interventions 75, 76
    and makeover TV 119–20
    and social work 65
The Financial Freedom Hour 147–8
financial risk management 141–51,
    145
    and global and US financial crises
        141–3
    and personal finance 143–51
flexible economy, and makeover
    TV 100, 101–8, 110, 119,
        127–8, 129–31, 133
Ford Foundation 26

Forman, Tom 48
Foucault, Michel 15, 18, 67, 84, 87, 109
  on liberalism 9–12, 114–15, 171
  on security and risk management 135–6, 137, 138–9
  and "techniques of the self" 75, 78–9
Fowler, Mark 34
Fraser, Nancy 76, 77
Freedom Corps Volunteer Network 21, 37, 41
Frost, Jo 95–7, 170

Gaebler, Ted 20
games *see* group governance games
gender
  and *The Apprentice* 188–90
  and makeover TV 101, 106–7, 118–27
  see also men; women
Gilens, Martin 52
Gilliom, John 51
Global Crossings 142
Goodwin, Andrew 30
Gorder, Genevieve 199
Gordon, Linda 51, 77
Gore, Al 20, 213
government
  liberalism as a rationality of 9–12
  of the self 205, 206–7, 211
  see also reinvention of government
Gramsci, Antonio 11
Grant, Amy 57, 60
Great Society 28, 29, 36, 59
Greenspan, Alan 100, 119
group governance games 8, 184–202, 204
  and democracy 209, 211–12, 215–16, 220

Habitat for Humanity 42, 55, 139
Hackers 163
Hansen, Mark Victor 41
Hark, Dr. Lisa 88
Hartley, John 203–4, 204–5, 224
Hatch, Richard 187
Hayek, Friedrich von 19
Heads-up Poker 150
healthcare, and charity TV 32, 40, 58
healthy lifestyle programs 87–92
Help Me Rhonda 83
Hicks, Taylor 213
Hilton, Kathy 129, 130
Home Edition 42–56, 62, 178, 199
  casting needy individuals 47–54
  and Hurricane Katrina 54–5, 56, 140
  and Laura Bush 217–18
  and the Ownership Society 44–7
Homeland Security 21, 22–3, 134, 138, 218
  and Hurricane Katrina 166, 168, 169
  and personal safety 165, 166–7, 169
  Ready.gov campaign 168
  and risk management 140
Homeland Security (made-for-TV movie) 168
home ownership, and charity TV 44–7
home security makeovers 134, 158–65
Honey We're Killing the Kids 3, 6, 64, 88–92
household constitutions 170–1, 194–6
housing, and charity TV 32, 33, 40
How Clean is Your House 64, 92–3
How Do I Look 101

How to Tell Your Children about Terrorism 165–6
Hurricane Katrina 23
  and Dr. Phil 63, 140, 217–18, 219
  and *Home Edition* 54–5, 56
  and Homeland Security 166, 168, 169
  and risk management 139–41
  and the Weather Channel 157

industrial capitalism 35, 65
In Praise of Bureaucracy (du Gay) 23–4
Insight Communication 162
interactive television 85, 203–4, 205, 221
  technologies of 210–13
Intervention 6, 70–2
Iraq 62, 219
It Could Happen Tomorrow 157–8
It Takes a Thief 134, 160, 161, 162, 163
I Want to Be a Hilton 127, 129–30

Jackass 155–6, 220
Jenkins, Henry 203, 204–5, 223–4
job searches 127–33
Joe Millionaire 124–5
Johnson, Lyndon B. 28
Judge Judy 74–7, 81
judicial trials, reality TV programs as 173–4

Kemp, Jack 20
Kennedy, John F. 28
Kerry, John 217
King, Larry 210
King, Samantha 55

Labor and Materials 62
Lasch, Christopher 118, 119
leadership, and group governance games 190, 193
Leavitt, Mike 41
liberalism
  and citizenship 171, 172–3, 183
  Foucaultian view of 9–12, 114–15
  and life interventions 72
  and makeover TV 114–15
  and "reinventing" government 18–19
  and "reinventing" television 30
  and security and risk management 135–41
  and TV as a cultural technology 15–16
  and welfare reform 35–8
  see also neo-liberalism
library funding, and charity TV 59
life interventions 40, 63–98
  daytime TV 73–86
  empowering "unruly" individuals 66–73
  primetime TV 86–98
  and risk management 140–1
  and surveillance 154–5
  and TV viewers 65–6
  types of 63–4
lifelong learning 7, 24, 100, 119
lifestyle audit 81, 103
lifestyle management 208
lifestyle maximization 69, 72, 86–7

MacDonald, Dwight 26
McGee, Micki 104, 110, 130–1, 132
McGraw, Dr. Phillip 63, 64, 77–8, 79–81, 85, 104, 140, 217, 219, 224
McLennan, Gregor 208

McMurria, John 43
McPherson, Stephen 34, 35, 41
McRobbie, Angela 103, 107, 131, 132
Made 101
Mad Money 150
A Makeover Story 101
makeover TV 2, 7, 64, 99–133
  dating shows 2, 124–7
  and the flexible economy 100, 101–8, 110, 119
  makeovers as instructional games 108–18
  talent/job searches 127–33
Malakar, Sanjaya 222
Management Challenges for the 21st Century 104
Manson, Marshall 90, 91
marriage, and life interventions 76–7
Martin, Randy 141, 143–4, 145–6, 151
Matthews, Chris 221
Mayer, Vicki 106
media education, and the politics of participation 203, 204–5, 223–4
men
  and makeover TV 106–7, 120–7
  and risk-taking programs 155–6
Miller, Toby 105
Minow, Newton 27–8
Minson, Jeffrey 205
Miracle Workers 32, 34, 35, 38
Mission: Organization 6, 64, 93
mobile privatization 159
Mr Personality 126
Mr Roger's Neighborhood 173, 175
MSNCB 220–1
MTV 29, 30, 61–2, 81, 101
  Rock the Vote campaign 216–17, 221
Murrow, Edward 205

Nanny 911 6, 64, 93, 95, 97, 98
nanny programs 93–8
National Fair Housing Association (NFHA) 179–80
National Partnership for Reinventing Government (NPRG) 20–1
natural disasters, and the Weather Channel 157–8
Nazi Germany 19, 25
neighborhoods
  and citizenship tests 174–84
  and group governance games 198–202
  neighborhood constitutions 171
neo-liberalism 4, 12, 18, 19, 38
  and charity TV 40, 52–3
  and life interventions 70, 76–7, 79–81, 89–92
  and makeover TV 100
  and security and risk management 137–41
network society 31
networks of government 172
New Deal reforms 36
NFHA (National Fair Housing Association) 179–80
NPRG (National Partnership for Reinventing Government) 20–1

older workers, and the flexible economy 107–8
Omnibus (Ford Foundation) 26
The Oprah Winfrey Show 77
Orman, Suze 147–8
Osborne, David 20
Ownership Society 171, 178
  and *Home Edition* 44–7

parenting skills, and nanny programs
    93–8
participation, technologies of
    208–13
pastoralism 10–11
Peiss, Kathy 119
penal policies 67
Pennington, Ty 55
Perfect Disasters 158
personal responsibility 2, 21, 24
    and *The Apprentice* 191
    and charity TV 48, 58, 60, 62
    and life interventions 68–9, 74
    and nanny programs 94, 97
    and the Sears American Dream
        campaign 46
Peters, Tom 104–5
Pimp My Ride 61
Points of Light Foundation 41, 42,
    55
poker, TV 150
policing
    and public safety 136–7
    and TV programs 218
political economy, and liberalism
    11–12
political process, democracy and
    reality TV 213–23
political rationality, and charity TV
    44
postfeminism, and makeover TV
    112, 119–20
power, Foucaultian view of 9, 10
presidential elections (US) 213,
    216–17, 220–1
Presidential Program on Physical
    Fitness and Sport 91
President's Challenge 91
privatization 2, 19, 24, 67
    and charity TV 32
    and life interventions 74, 91
    mobile 159

and the Sears American Dream
    campaign 46
of welfare 12, 36–8
profiling, and risk management 153
Project Runway 127, 131
public broadcasting 184–5
public health and safety 135–7
public interest
    and charity TV 34–5, 41
    and US broadcasting policy 25
public–private partnerships 19, 20,
    22, 28, 41
    democracy and viewer
        participation 204, 215, 221
    and security issues and risk
        management 138, 139–40, 157,
        166
public safety 136–7
public sector 6, 59, 103
public service
    and life interventions 76–7
    and US broadcasting policy 26, 27

Queen for a Day 33
Queer Eye for the Straight Guy 121–3
QVC (shopping channel) 147

race, *Black/White* and group
    governance games 194, 196–8
Random One 61–2
Reagan, Ronald 19–20, 34, 92, 216
Real Housewives of Orange County
    198, 202
The Real World 184, 191–3, 194
Red Cross 139
reinvention of government 2, 4, 6,
    12, 18–24
    and constitutions of citizenship
        172–3
    democracy and viewer
        participation 209, 211, 215,
        223

and group governance games
190, 199, 201
and life interventions 88
and security and risk management
134–5, 140–1
reinvention of television 2, 24–31
remote-control devices 209, 210
Ridge, Tom 168
risk management
and care of the self 151–8
financial risk 141–51
and liberalism 135–41
risk society 135
risk-taking, programs on the
pleasures of 155–6
Road Rules 169, 184, 191, 192–3
Robertson, Pat 185, 207, 210
Rock the Vote campaign 216–17,
221
Rose, Nikolas 11, 13, 18, 19, 41,
138
on control and risk management
138, 140
on cultural technologies 67
on healthy lifestyles 91
on home ownership 46
on "lifestyle maximization" 69,
72
on the paradox of liberalism 72
on welfare reform 35, 36, 44
Ross, Andrew 131

Safer America 165
satellite television 28–30, 161,
162–3, 210
school funding, and charity TV
58–9
Schramm, Wilbur 26
Schumer, Charles 219
Seacrest, Ryan 213
Sears American Dream Campaign
45–7, 54, 55

security issues 7–8, 134–69
home security make-overs 134,
158–65
and liberalism 135–41
private and personal security
165–9
see also risk management
self-actualization 3, 29–30, 31, 213,
224
and group governance games
191, 196
self-care *see* care of the self
self-empowerment 7, 21, 39
empowering "unruly" individuals
66–73
and life interventions 73–86
and makeover TV 104, 106, 110
and nanny programs 98
women and risk management 156
self-esteem
and life interventions 75–6, 83
and makeover TV 103
self-fashioning 101–18
self-help 3, 6, 30–1, 85
self-management 31, 78
Sennett, Richard 107–8, 127–9
service sector work, and makeover
TV 107, 120
Sesame Street 184–5
Sheindlin, Judith, and *Judge Judy*
74–7
Slater, Don 114
"smart" technology, and home
security 160–2, 164–5
Smith, Paul 131
Smith, Shanna 179–80
social welfare, and "reinventing"
government 19, 22–3
social work
and life interventions 64–6, 71,
72, 89–90, 91–2
and nanny programs 94

Soviet Union 19, 25
Spying on Myself 154–5
Stallone, Sylvester 193
Starting Over 6, 81–6, 103
the State, and life interventions
      66–7, 86–7
Stern, Howard 222
stock market 141, 144
Storm Stories 157
Streeter, Thomas 38
Strike it Rich 33
Supernanny 3, 6, 64, 93–8, 170,
      171, 174
surveillance 39, 138
   and care of the self 152–5
   and home security 164–5
   and makeover TV 111–12
Survival of the Prettiest (Etcoff) 107
survival programs 158, 169, 185–7
Survivor 158, 169, 185–7, 188, 189,
      190, 196
Survivorman 158, 169
The Suze Orman Show 147–8
The Swan 101, 120, 123–4

talent searches 127–33
teamwork skills
   and survival programs 185–7
   and talent/job searches 129, 131
techne, TV as 14
"techniques of the self" 75, 78–81,
      82, 84
"technology of the self" 15, 115,
      173
telephones, and TV viewer
      participation 210
Ten Years Younger 101, 108–10
terrorism 8, 135, 165–6, 168
Terrorism in the Hands of Justice 219
Three Wishes 33, 56–61
Todd TV 1–2, 4–5, 16, 211–12,
      221

Too Posh to Wash 93
Top Chef 193, 196
Total Request Live 217
Town Haul 198–202
Trading Spaces 199
Truman, Harry 23
Trump, Donald 129, 130, 147, 149,
      150, 187–90, 215
TV Guide 212

Vanzant, Iyanla 83
viewer participation
   citizenship and democracy 203–4,
      208–13
   and life interventions 65–6
   and makeover TV 116–17
   and the political process 213–23
Viva la Bam 155, 220
volunteerism 21, 24, 37
   and charity TV 44, 48, 55–6
Volunteers for Prosperity 21

Walkerdine, Valerie 100, 120, 123,
      124, 126
War on Poverty 36
Waterson, Sam 144–5
Watson, Mary Ann 65
Weather Channel 156–8, 165, 218
Web-based technologies 31
   and viewer participation 210–11,
      212–13
Welcome to the Neighborhood 8,
      175–84, 185, 188, 198, 201,
      202
welfare reform
   and charity TV 33, 35–8, 44
   and *Home Edition* 50–3, 54–5
   and life interventions 64, 67, 73,
      74, 75, 79, 91
   and nanny programs 95
Welfare State 6, 11, 12, 35–6, 50
   and life interventions 64–5, 77

welfare-to-work policies 6, 20–1,
  67
  and life interventions 76–7
  and makeover TV 103, 110
What Not to Wear 7, 99–101,
  110–18
What Should You Do? 156
Who Wants to be a Millionaire? 150
Wife Swap 92, 149, 175, 194–6,
  197
Williams, Raymond 158–9, 207
women
  and the feminization of work
    118–20
  and finance-TV 147–9
  and household constitutions
    195–6
  and life interventions 75, 76, 77,
    92–3

and makeover TV 99, 101, 106,
  115–16, 123–4
and nanny programs 96
and risk management programs
  156
and US presidential elections 217
work
  feminization of 118–27
  and makeover TV 99–100,
    103–5, 107–8, 113–14
  talent/job searches 127–33
work ethic 77, 97, 118
Worlds Apart 169
World Trade Center collapse 141

X-Files 153

Your Home: Make it Safe 159
YouTube 212–13, 223